SPACE, TIME
AND SELF

SPACE, TIME AND SELF

Three Mysteries of the Universe

E. Norman Pearson

This publication is made possible with
the assistance of the Kern Foundation

The Theosophical Publishing House
Wheaton, Ill. U.S.A.
Madras, India/London, England

For permission to reproduce any portion of this book please write to:

The Theosophical Publishing House
306 West Geneva Road
Wheaton, IL 60187

Library of Congress Cataloging in Publication Data

Pearson, E. Norman
    Space, time, and self : three mysteries of the universe / E.
      Norman Pearson — 2nd Quest ed.
      p. cm. — (Quest books)
    ISBN 0-8356-0658-9 : $9.95
    1. Theosophy. I. Title.
  BP565.P335 1990
  299'.934—dc20   89-40623
                                    CIP

Be humble if thou wouldst attain to Wisdom. Be humbler still, when Wisdom thou hast mastered. Be like the Ocean which receives all streams and rivers. The Ocean's mighty calm remains unmoved; it feels them not. . . . The way to final freedom is within the SELF.

The Voice of the Silence
H. P. Blavatsky

Contents

Publisher's Preface to
the Revised Edition

This revised edition of a popular introductory book presents the essential ideas of the Ancient Wisdom called Theosophy in a clear and contemporary way, often in the context of modern science. The text has been brought up to date in several ways. Sexist language, used uncritically in the time when the book was written, has been changed to inclusive language. A few scientific facts and concepts have been brought in line with contemporary thought. A few illustrations thought to be extraneous have been omitted. Some out-of-date expressions have been changed, and there has been very light editing for smoothness of expression. To the best of their ability, the editors have retained the concepts, style and meaning of the original.

Introduction

It has often been said that truth is stranger than fiction, and few people would challenge the veracity of that statement. But in no case has it been demonstrated more clearly and dramatically than in the story of the earth, as gathered from the multitude of sources which are now available.

If we look back, in our imagination, over the kaleidoscope of world events as they have emerged from the mysterious darkness of prehistoric times, we may feel almost overwhelmed by the picture that appears before our eyes. Ceaseless time! Tremendous change! Age succeeds age and events follow upon events. A world bare and lifeless gradually becomes a world teeming with living things. They come, in seemingly endless succession, out of the sea. They cover the land. They fly in the air.

Primitive peoples appear upon the scene; but they do not remain primitive. They begin the conquest of the environment. They make tools, gradually improving their usefulness to extend the power and range of their craftsmanship. They make clothes, produce fire, build houses, and grow their own food. Thus they gain release from many of the restrictions that nature placed upon them. Time marches ever onward and their conquests continue unabated, for their minds can never rest content with things as they are but must forever probe into the unknown. With restless energy and almost fantastic dreaming, humans envision the future and then set into action every power and faculty at their command to bring to pass the things that they have dreamed.

Humankind has penetrated the depths of forest and jungle. We have sailed the seven seas. We have scaled the highest mountains. With amazing instruments, cunningly devised products of our fertile imagination, we are pursuing the unknown and mysterious in realms of chemical affinities and atomic structures. Our minds have now encompassed the earth and have dared to challenge the mysteries of the sky. We have photographed the stars, probed the planets and landed on the moon. Our insistent searching has led us onward to the limits of the solar system. Even there we have found no resting place, but have pressed on and on through the mighty expanse of our island universe and still further to the galaxies of outer space and even, dimly, though still daringly and persistently, to those unmeasured depths which would seem to touch the very borders of the infinite.

Now, from the great melting pot of the past, there has suddenly appeared, in a blaze of material triumphs, the fabulous world of today. New materials, new tools, new methods and instruments for gaining knowledge, new powers beyond anything ever known before, are now within our grasp. Living conditions have been entirely revolutionized. Old landmarks have been destroyed. Old standards have been discarded and an entirely new age is with us, in which it seems certain that we will be confronted with almost unlimited opportunities for rising to hitherto undreamed-of heights of progress and enlightenment.

Humankind has come far since the days when our remote ancestors lived in caves and hunted the wild boar or woolly elephant, and foraged the land for such edibles as could be found. Yet we still have far to go. We have accomplished much for the welfare of our bodies but, spiritually, let us admit, our conquests have been few and our errors have been many. Because of this we have suffered and our knowledge has not assuaged our wounds. So, as this newer epoch dawns, deeply fraught with potency and promise, it is not surprising to find that many anxious eyes are scanning the far horizons, earnestly looking for signs that light, perchance, may come to scatter the spiritual darkness of the world. Fervently they hope that we may turn, at last, to look *within* ourselves to learn the secrets of the human soul. Why are we born? Why must we die? And why must we tread this span of "three score years and ten" only to vanish at its close into the silence of apparent oblivion? Is there a God who created all things? Must we be forever beset by doubts; be satisfied with mere belief? Or *can we know*?

It is the purpose of this book to try to show that we *can* know. For so far have our penetrations into nature's secrets now been carried out that they have brought us to the very borderland of other "worlds" that lie beyond the things of earth and gradually there is being revealed, for those who have eyes to see, evidence, clear and convincing, of a God—an intelligence: mathematician, architect and master-builder—who is developing a mighty plan which is unfolding all around us. The general principles of scientific knowledge are well known to the majority of people today. Articles about scientific matters and popular expositions of its major advances appear in newspapers and magazines, and are carried immediately into millions of homes via satellite. In problems moral and spiritual the religions of the world can offer help and guidance. Were they studied and their teachings applied, the world would be a better place in which to live. Yet few would deny that, in many respects, these sources do not satisfy the intellectual hunger of an inquiring mind and, often, it is not possible to justify their dogmas at the bar of reason.

But it is not so widely known that there is another source of knowledge which can be so justified and is consistent also with the findings of science. It has existed for centuries. Originally in the sole possession of initiates of mystery schools and transmitted only to worthy pupils after adequate preparation, this knowledge was called "Theosophy" (divine wisdom) by Ammonius Saccas in his "Eclectic Theosophical School" at Alexandria in the third century. The word has persisted up to the present day. Other thinkers such as Plato, Plotinus, Simon Magus, Paracelsus, and Bruno have promulgated many of its tenets. But the most complete exposition was given by H. P. Blavatsky, a Russian noblewoman, in her monumental work *The Secret Doctrine*, first published in 1888. Theosophy embraces much of the finest teachings of the world's great religions. It combines the wisdom of the East with the logic and clear thinking of the West, and it weaves these into a living philosophy that offers spiritual illumination and intellectual satisfaction.

Many modern scientific discoveries and ever-widening fields of research have added support to the theosophical outlook. For example, many areas of science point to a holistic view of nature and the universe, with everything interconnected and mutually dependent. Theosophy offers its esoteric knowledge to suggest purpose and plan and to illuminate facts with an understanding of their place in the scheme of life. Scientific research into the nature and structure of the atom has shown that theosophical statements regarding the permeability of matter are basically sound and that the apparent solidity of any substance is only a product of the mind. Such a phenomenon, therefore, can be reproduced on any plane of nature. Many of the ancient teachings illuminate knowledge only recently gained and can point to the directions in which future discoveries may be made. The existence of subtler bodies and of superphysical worlds which interpenetrate the solid earth throw much light upon obscure regions of the subconscious and superconscious minds, and the problems of sleep and death. In fact they open up an entirely new avenue in which future research can be carried out. The theory of reincarnation, claimed by many to be known as fact, which shows us coming into physical birth bearing the fruits of many earth lives of the past, yet having to mature a physical body to fit newer needs, forms a notable contribution to the problem of child education. It can offer as a basic premise the thought that a really effective educational system must use methods which will draw out from the reincarnating soul the powers and qualities it already has developed and will not surround the child with crystallized thought patterns that only interfere with its own endeavors toward creative expression.

Because of the fundamental nature of the concepts that Theosophy offers, it is applicable, in some measure, to every branch of science and every form of art. It offers an idealized religious philosophy which is free from dogma or creed. It presents a reasonable explanation of immortality and proclaims universal brotherhood to be a fact in nature.

It is from a background of knowledge of some of the simpler concepts of Theosophy and modern science, and with a deep appreciation of the many sublime teachings of the founders of the great religions of the world, that the author has presumed to offer this modest contribution to what he feels to be the paramount need of today—that humanity, with utopia within our grasp, yet having control of powers which could bring about our own destruction, shall now begin to explore, deeply and sincerely, into our inner worlds, the worlds of spiritual experience, there to learn the plan of life and to use our growing powers and understanding for our emancipation.

Let us ever remember: science is not a great genie, which can perform miracles, causing the blind to see and the lame to walk and voices to circle around the earth. Science is the observation and classification of the ways in which nature works, *as these ways affect human consciousness.* Scientists have observed the ways in which nature responds to environments and stimuli. They provide the environments and stimuli. Nature performs the wonders! And nature is an expression of God. Theosophy is not a system of thought that will ensure a safe and easy passage through the mazes of life. It is an ever-increasing revelation of an inner truth, in response to a seeking mind. An occult commentary states: "Thou canst not travel on the Path until thou hast become that Path itself." A study of religion will never bring union with the Supreme. Religion must become an inner vision and experience before that goal can be achieved.

In this book an endeavor has been made to explain some of the priceless teachings of the Ancient Wisdom in a manner that will be acceptable to present-day readers, and to show that it is not inconsistent with many of the newer findings of science, insofar as they may be understood by the layman. Many of the interpretations of Theosophy presented are my own. This is inevitable and I accept full responsibility for them. But for the fundamental concepts of its teachings I am indebted to many great thinkers who have dedicated their lives to study and research along these lines of thought. Some aspects of Theosophy have been given a greater prominence than is generally accorded to them, because I am convinced of their outstanding importance to an understanding of life. Those who have studied the subject may note the absence of many well-established words and phrases which have been omitted because it is felt that they may cause some confusion in the minds of those who have no background of theosophical knowledge.

It has been said that "one picture is worth a thousand words." Recognized leaders in the world of education agree that this is true. A picture will leave a deeper and more lasting impression on the mind than any spoken or written words. So illustrations have been used freely throughout the book. The reader is urged to study them carefully, for they will help to clarify and amplify the text.

Those to whom these thoughts are new should be prepared to stretch their minds to encompass greatness. The plan of evolution, which covers the whole vast field of the cosmos, is of tremendous proportions, extending far beyond the limits of our imagination. And yet we may gain glimpses of its greatness; but it is surely to be expected that, in approaching Truth, our minds will need to range far beyond the simple areas of mundane existence. Perhaps some of the thoughts presented in these pages may seem to approach the sensational. Such an effect is entirely foreign to the purposes for which this book is written, and yet it is conceded that, at times, some statements may seem to approach the incredible. They should not be rejected on that ground alone. It is hard to believe that an atom may send out vibrations which have a frequency of thousands of millions *every second*. Yet science tells us that it is true. So, if to state what the author feels to be a truth, it becomes necessary to write those things that seem to pass beyond the bounds of credibility, they will be written; but in each case the reason for such statements will be given and an effort will be made to show the place that they occupy in the total theosophical concept, as it is understood by one who asks no greater honor in life than to be counted among those who sincerely aspire to a knowledge of Truth.

As these few words are written, I sit in the lengthening shadows of an Indian summer's eve. The sun, once more, has hewn its fiery path across the heavens. Now a great refulgent glow lights up the western sky, splashing upon that wide expanse huge flames of living gold. Silent and magnificent the great orb speeds on its way leaving, for a brief spell, this its most glorious gift. Soon it will be gone. Before me a broad, winding river flows lazily into the sea. I can hear the music of the waves rhythmically beating upon the shore. Birds are coming home to roost within the shelter of the spreading trees that line the river banks. With song and chatter, they throw themselves upon the evening breeze in one last ecstasy of joyful flight before they go to rest. The night is coming now—and with the night will come the stars.

How wonderful life is. No sooner does darkness fall and hide the world from view than, displayed up there before our eyes, are other worlds and other suns and mightier wonders still. We are not bound when darkness comes. From the tyranny of earthly things we are released to feast our eyes upon the glories of the sky; the only limit is our puny power to see and understand.

It is my sincere hope that, in these pages, some may find a measure of release from things of earth, the stress and strain of life and, as the mundane things recede from view, may learn thereby that consciousness can soar to higher realms, the worlds of Truth and Beauty, of intellectual achievement and spiritual perception.

E. Norman Pearson

Adyar, Madras,
   India

I

Reality and Illusion

Behold how, like the moon reflected in the tranquil waves, Alaya is reflected by the small and by the great, is mirrored in the tiniest atoms, yet fails to reach the heart of all. Alas, that so few men should profit by the gift, the priceless boon of learning truth, the right perception of existing things, the Knowledge of the non-existent!

The Voice of the Silence
H. P. Blavatsky

1

Consciousness

It has been pointed out by historians that the idea of progress is a rather recent addition to human thinking. Especially before the light of evolution threw its revealing rays upon the manifold activities of nature, the world was considered by the mass of humanity to be a fairly static institution in which humans, together with all the lower forms of life, lived and suffered and died. But more recently the fact of change and progress has become so increasingly evident that it has thrust itself forward as an ingredient of living which demands consideration and explanation. For, since progress is now so clearly evident in the changing pattern of events, there must be some great driving force behind it all.

Unfortunately, in spite of these facts, scientists still persist in excluding the idea of deity from the area of their investigations and continue their futile attempts to explain the marvels of nature without postulating the existence of a creative and directive intelligence behind them all. Thus they deny in the larger field of the universe that which they know full well applies in every human creative effort in our smaller field—that all the productions of our hands have originated in, and been directed by, the creative and directive activities of our minds. Because of this attitude, consciousness itself remains to them a mystery, and will so remain while that attitude is maintained. It is interesting to note, however, that their position is becoming less tenable with almost every new discovery that is made, and scientific writers, in increasing numbers, are recording their belief that the deeper problems now being faced by physicists will never be answered without recourse to a belief in God.

Turning to Theosophy we find a very different story.

In the theosophical concept there is postulated a First Great Cause, an Infinite REALITY, in which all manifestation has its source. From this Root Cause of all there arise two fundamental and opposite polarities, spirit and matter. Between these two a relationship springs up. This is the "field" of future manifestation, a tension between the two polar opposites which, having been divided tend always to reunite. *As that reunion takes place, it gives rise to the phenomenon we call consciousness.* Therefore, consciousness partakes of the nature of Reality itself, in fact, it *is* the partial expression or reflection of Reality in manifestation.

It will be seen that consciousness, on any plane or world, is the "reality" of that plane. It is as though a white light were shining through a number of differently colored glasses. Through each piece of glass the one

Fig. 1

white light would seem to be colored. That color would represent just that portion of the real light which could penetrate any particular glass, or the particular wavelength which that glass could transmit. It would, of course, also depend upon the measure of the ability of the viewer to respond to the color. Abstractly, therefore, it should be obvious that as the reunion of the previously separated spirit and matter takes place in increasing measure, consciousness will expand and we can predicate, though not actually comprehend, that "conditioned consciousness" will develop and expand, through the continually growing union of the polar opposites, until it becomes one with "Universal Consciousness." (Fig. 1.)

H. P. Blavatsky wrote, in *The Secret Doctrine*,

> On whatever plane our consciousness may be acting on, both we and the things belonging to that place are, for the time being, our only Reality.

The words "for the time being" should be noted carefully, for it is a temporary condition only. "We," that is the Self, acting on that plane, may seem to be the real Self, since there are many people who think that they are nothing more than their physical bodies; but that is not true, and she goes on to say:

> But as we rise in the scale of development, we perceive that in the stages through which we have passed, we mistook shadows for realities and that the upward progress of the ego is a series of progressive awakenings, each advance bringing with it the idea that now, at last, we have reached "reality" but only when we shall have reached absolute consciousness and blended our own with it shall we be free from the delusions produced by Maya.

In pondering over such statements as those just presented, it must be recognized that we are endeavoring to encompass the infinite with that which is finite—obviously an impossible task. Yet there are ways in which we can gain help toward stimulating our intuitive faculties to some degree of comprehension by observing the operations of nature that we can understand. The laws of nature are one and apply at all levels from the seemingly insignificant to the great cosmic regions. The emergence of manifestation from that which is "non-existent" cannot be grasped by the reasoning mind, and yet parallels to this may be seen in operation within the range of everyday experience. No one knows what electricity really is. It exists everywhere, and yet it is itself known only through effects it produces upon those things which can be observed. Like the unmanifest Reality, it must be considered as existing, unmanifest, behind all phases of electrical energy. In Fig. 2A this fact is shown diagrammatically, and in Fig. 2B the same principle is shown, but here it is applied to cosmic processes. In Fig. 2C an electric lamp has been introduced between the two polar opposites, permitting them to partially reunite. Immediately, in place of darkness we have light. The electrical wiring in our homes is hidden from view and the electricity carried on the wires cannot be seen. The switches, themselves, can give no light; but when a pathway of reunion (a lamp) is provided and that which was separated can come together again, the unmanifest comes into manifesta-

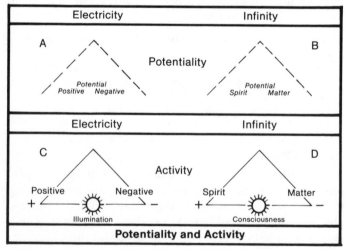

Fig. 2

tion. Though we do not know the nature of electricity itself, through the observable effects it has upon other things, we can learn a great deal about it. So also in the larger field of nature, spirit and matter are both hidden (Fig. 2D). We do not know them as they really are. We cannot fully comprehend the infinite; but when vehicles of consciousness are formed (and every living thing is such a vehicle to some degree) then, through them in varying measure, spirit and matter can come together again and, through the many states of consciousness that arise, we can catch faint glimpses of the real.

2

The World of Consciousness

We shall now attempt to reduce these abstractions to their practical application within ourselves and in relation to our daily life. Here we can discover a fact which, when really understood, can revolutionize our whole outlook upon life and unravel many a tightly tangled skein of puzzles which have defied solution. It is this: *The world in which we live is not a world of things and places at all—it is a world of consciousness: our consciousness!* We do not *create* that world. It arises within our consciousness in response to impacts received from spirit and matter. Therefore, since consciousness, as we have seen, is a reflection of reality, this world partakes of the nature of that reality. The physical world arises within us in response to sense impressions. For example: sound results when waves, of a certain frequency carried by the air or other media, impinge upon the ear drum, are transformed into lymph waves, then into tiny electrical impulses and finally are transmitted to the brain and, through it, to the consciousness. *It is within the consciousness that the various physical impulses are transformed into sound.* Electromagnetic waves of other frequencies affect the eye and finally reach the consciousness. There they become light. The same fact applies to all our sense impressions, and it is from these sense impressions that our physical world arises. But the world we know is within us, not outside us. (See Fig. 3.)

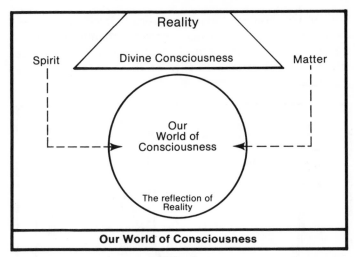

Fig. 3

An almost exact analogy may be seen in our television receiving sets. Invisible, intangible waves of different frequencies are broadcast through the electromagnetic field. They pass by us, even through us, yet we are not conscious of them in any manner whatsoever; but when they are "picked up" by a receiving set, which is properly attuned to the right channel, they will be transformed into the shorter wave lengths of light, variations of which give rise to the picture which appears upon the screen. Other frequencies are similarly transformed into the longer waves of sound, which are heard as the music, voice and other effects coming from the loud-speaker. So, in the activities of nature, as they are taking place around us, we can find analogies of activities in higher realms. The television set produces a simulation—a copy, imperfect, yet recognizable—of a scene which in reality is taking place elsewhere. In the space between the "real" and the "apparent" there are only waves, silent, invisible, and mysterious. But in the receiving set those mysterious waves become light and sound. So, from the reality behind all, there come "waves," shrouded in mystery, to which we give the names "spirit" and "matter."

Within the body—a living, vitalized "receiving set"—
there arises consciousness in response thereto. It, too, is
a simulation, a copy, imperfect yet recognizable by the
intuitive mind, of the Reality of the Unmanifest. (See
Fig. 4.)

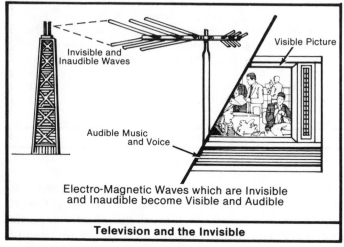

Television and the Invisible

Fig. 4

For hundreds of years, the leading thinkers of the
world believed that matter was indestructible. Being
indestructible it was, therefore, eternal: the one reality
of existence. Consciousness and thought they looked upon
as mere accidental or incidental appearances in the
scheme of things. But toward the close of the nineteenth
century drastic changes began to take place in the scientific
outlook. Through the work of such men as Bohr, Planck,
Millikan, Michelson, Jeans, Einstein, and many others,
it became apparent that the ideas of the older thinkers
were not true and should be eliminated from our outlook
upon life. Sir James Jeans expressed the opinion that the
universe is the thought of a mathematical thinker, created
at a time not infinitely remote and moving toward an
end that cannot be seen. Four hundred years ago, Giordano
Bruno said "The act of Divine Thinking is the substance

of the Universe." About four centuries before Christ, the great philosopher Democritus wrote: "Sweet and bitter, cold and warm, as well as all the colors, all these exist in opinion and not in reality." And the great Irish philosopher George Berkeley, wrote in his colorful and convincing style:

> All the choir of heaven and furniture of earth, in a word all those bodies which compose the mighty frame of the world, have not any substance without the mind. . . . So long as they are not actually perceived by me, or do not exist in my mind, or that of any other created spirit, they must have no existence at all, or else subsist in the mind of some Eternal Spirit.

So, in the light of today's wider knowledge, this tremendous concept is now coming into more general recognition and looming ever more convincingly before us as a major step toward a real understanding of the worlds around and within us. The mechanical universe of the older thinkers has gone, and a greater and more wonderful universe is rapidly taking its place. These facts will assume a still wider significance when we come to consider the superphysical orders of matter in a later chapter, for they offer an entirely new basis for the study of such problems as sleep and dreams, and the existence of the spiritual person after the death of the physical body. We shall see that worlds unknown to us now can, and will, become real and tangible under other circumstances.

3

The Human Trinity

The Christian scriptures tell us that we are made "in the image and likeness of God." In the Hindu *Bhagavad Gita* we read the words of Shri Krishna, "I am the Self, seated in the heart of all beings." Similarly, there is an almost universal agreement among the great religions that we are spiritual beings, partaking of the nature of the divine creator. So we should now begin to realize the very close bond of union between humanity and God. We see how intimately "in Him we live and move and have our being." For the human monad (which is the true Self—the divine seed) is rooted within and proceeds from the consciousness of God. Therefore, since God is a trinity, the human too must be a trinity.

In Fig. 5 this relationship of humanity to God is illustrated. The human monad is seen to derive its being from the divine consciousness and the human trinity is shown as a reflection of the divine trinity. We can also approach this question from the point of view of actual everyday experience, using the method of the introspective psychologist and endeavoring to analyze the content and functioning of our own consciousness. Let us then sit quietly for a few moments, avoiding, so far as possible, all distracting sounds and sights—anything that might draw our attention away from the purpose we have in mind. Try to maintain an emotional and mental balance, with the mind poised and alert. Now, gradually try to

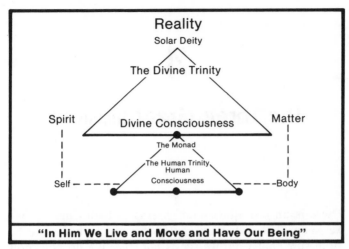

Fig. 5

awaken an awareness of the workings of your consciousness. You will find that you can classify the results under three basic divisions. You are aware:

1. OF THINGS	Of a material world, which is around you.
2. OF BEING CONSCIOUS	Of changing states of consciousness arising from, or independent of, current stimuli.
3. OF SELF	Of that within you which makes you YOU, a being separate from other beings.

It should not be difficult to discern this triple nature of your consciousness and note that it agrees with the ideas just presented when we approached this question from "above" rather than, as now, from "below." So are we "Gods in the making."

4

The Three Great Illusions

There is an old adage that "seeing is believing." Today we know that statement is not true. In fact, we can be quite sure that what we see is *not* true. We do not know the whole truth about anything. With physical things as well as spiritual, we only "see through a glass darkly." The world looks flat, but we know it is not. The sun seems to move across the sky. That is an illusion caused by the earth turning on its axis. We seem to see many stars in the heavens, but they are not where they appear to be, but are millions of miles away. We think our body is a fairly solid object, but science tells us that all the really solid matter it contains could be put into an ordinary thimble. Put a stick into water and it seems to bend, but it does not change.

In the National Academy of Science, Washington, D.C., hanging from the dome of the building, there is a Foucault pendulum. It consists of a long steel wire, suspended on a frictionless point, and to its lower end a heavy metal ball is attached. The ball swings slowly and steadily over a dial, placed horizontally below it, which is marked like the face of a clock with the twenty-four hours of the day. As time passes, the ball marks off the passing hours, appearing to change the direction of its swing as they go by. That is only what it appears to do. Actually the ball does not change the original direction of its swing at all. Instead, the dial, the building, the whole world,

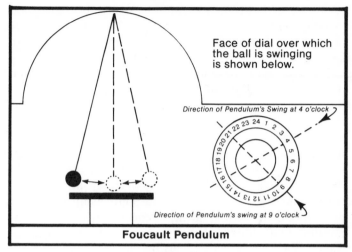

Face of dial over which the ball is swinging is shown below.

Direction of Pendulum's Swing at 4 o'clock

Direction of Pendulum's swing at 9 o'clock

Foucault Pendulum

Fig. 6

move underneath it, while the ball keeps on swinging in the same direction as before. (See Fig. 6.) The illustration on the face of the dial in Fig. 6 is simplified to clarify the drawing. As shown, the dial would be correct only when placed at the true north or south poles. At Washington, D.C., the period would cover more than thirty-eight hours. Period of apparent rotation =

$$\frac{24 \text{ hours}}{\text{Sine (degrees of latitude)}} = \frac{24}{.6285} = 38.4.$$

The air, which sometimes seems so still on a summer's evening, presents another illusion. It is not still. In every cubic inch of invisible air, science tells us, there are more than 500,000,000,000,000,000,000 molecules each of which is in rapid motion, colliding with another molecule about 1/42,000th of an inch of its journey and being turned from its path 5,000,000,000 times every second. Small though molecules are, atoms are smaller. And now, as we all know, scientists have revealed the fact that the atom, once thought to be the ultimate and indivisible unit of matter, is not solid at all but is made up of a central nucleus with one or more units, known as "electrons," revolving around it, and at comparatively very great distances from it. So the "solidity" of the matter we see around us, seemingly the most real thing that we can know, is only apparent. It is an illusion.

The list could be continued almost indefinitely, but repetition would be of little value. The inadequacy of the sense organs is now fully recognized. Touch, taste and smell do little more than give us certain information which is of value for our physical welfare. Our sense of hearing covers eleven octaves of vibration from sixteen to thirty-two thousand per second. But many animals, birds, and insects can hear sounds far beyond the point where the human ear fails to respond. Nature may be providing them with great experiences of which we know nothing. Out of sixty or more known octaves of radiant waves, the human eye is sensitive to only one. Yet our knowledge of our environment depends upon the faculty of sight more than upon any other. In spite of our fragmentary knowledge, however, the world as we know it is a wonderful world. Its beauties and marvels should indicate to all, except those who stubbornly refuse to see, that a magnificent plan is unfolding, one which becomes more entrancing with every new discovery that is made. And yet, *it is a world of illusion.* That does not mean that it does not exist, but that we do not know it as it really is. *The world as it exists in human consciousness is not identical with the world as it exists in the consciousness of God.* In other words, reality lies in the infinite and unmanifest. The world of limitation and manifestation is a world of illusion. But we should not fall into the error of thinking that the unmanifest is an indefinable "nothingness"; rather it is an indefinable "allness." All manifestation is dependent upon limitation. A "thing" can exist only by virtue of a limitation which separates it from other "things." Even such vastness as a solar system or a cosmos is limitation in space. *The infinite or unmanifest is that in which all opposites exist and yet are dissolved into the reality which lies behind and gives rise to those opposites.*

We now come to the climax of the train of thought we have been following step by step, and to another major key to an understanding of life. Reference to Fig. 7 will show a similarity to Fig. 5, but more has been added. When the human consciousness functions through its three aspects, each one of them presents a different illusion. When consciousness is turned outward and is dealing with material things, it becomes snared in the illusion of *things*, which exist in *space*. As we have already seen, things are not what they seem to be. All objects,

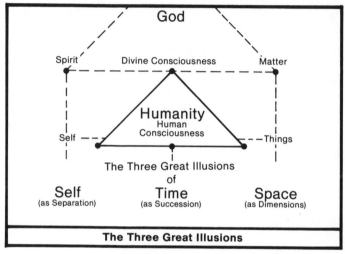

Fig. 7

we say, have extensions and dimensions. They have what we call size and shape. We think of them as large or small, as occupying much or little space. And yet size is only relative and can be expressed only in terms of comparison with some other object. To humans, a marble is small; to an ant it must seem large. The earth is immense—or so it appears to us. But one million earths could be put inside the sun and there would still be room for more. So, compared with the sun, it is small. No object, in itself, is either large or small. The measure of largeness or smallness that it possesses is dependent upon the observer, or another object with which it is being compared.

When the consciousness is turned to a study of consciousness itself, it becomes snared in the illusion of *time*. It sees a steady growth of unfolding awareness taking place, and is conscious of events succeeding events. Varying circumstances can produce a wide difference in our mental reactions to equal measurements of time. A simple illustration—which must have been experienced by every one of us—may be drawn from the old saying, "A watched pot never boils." That is almost true.

When consciousness turns to things of the *spirit*, it becomes snared in the illusion of *self*. It sees self as separate from other selves. In the beginning it thinks of the physical body as the self. To overcome the illusion of the separated self is perhaps the most difficult task which lies before us, and there are many stages of illusion to be mastered before the true self is found.

So, as shown in Fig. 7, there are three great illusions in life which we must face and conquer: the illusion of *space* (as dimensions), the illusion of *time* (as succession), and the illusion of *self* (as separation).

5

The Plan of Life

In the light of the ideas just presented, the whole plan of life can now be seen as the mastery of the three basic illusions—*space, time* and *self*—and, looking back over the past, we can see how that conquest has gradually been developing step by step.

To overcome the illusion of *space* (as dimensions), we must pursue our studies of the many manifestations of matter. Science has been doing this for many centuries, and is making great strides toward the conquest of material illusions. This is the pathway of *knowledge*. We must learn to know things as they are and not be content with belief based upon appearances. In this way we shall learn to know the world—in fact the whole of nature—as it really is and, finally overcoming the illusion of size and dimensions, realize *space as infinity*. To master the illusion of *time* (as succession) we must follow the pathway of *reason* and gain an understanding of the plan of life. Philosophers through the ages have been doing this and, through their efforts, the tyranny of time is being banished and glimpses of the real are coming to light. Finally, we shall unveil the mystery of the Eternal Now, and realize *time as eternity*. To overcome the illusion of the self (as separation) we must follow the pathway of *devotion*. Great teachers of the past have revealed the laws of the spiritual life and founded religions to guide us along the way, from our earliest years on earth. As we

The Three Aspects (Limitations) of God	Spirit	Consciousness	Matter
	Reality		
Give Rise to the Three Great Illusions	Self as Separation	Time as Succession	Space as Dimensions
To master them we must learn about	God	The Plan	The World
Through a study of ...	Religion	Philosophy	Science
Which lead to the three pathways of	Devotion	Reason	Knowledge
These will bring us mastery over illusion and we shall attain to illumination of	Self as Unity	Time as Eternity	Space as Infinity
	Reality		
The Three Great Illuminations			

Fig. 8

develop the things of the spirit and cultivate the inner
voice divine, we shall come to the place of illumination
where *Self* is realized as *unity* and we shall know that all
life is one. (See Fig. 8.)

Thus, understanding space as infinity, time as eternity,
Self as unity, and each of them as a facet of the One
Reality, human consciousness will merge with the consciousness of God, and the evolution of the human monad
will be complete.

II

The Illusion of Space
(As Dimensions)

Help Nature and work on with her; and Nature will regard thee as one of her creators and make obeisance. And she will open wide before thee the portals of her secret chambers, lay bare before thy gaze the treasures hidden in the very depths of her pure virgin bosom.

The Voice of the Silence
H. P. Blavatsky

6

The Field of Manifestation

All things occupy space. This applies to ourselves while we are in physical existence, as well as to all other objects that we find around us. To understand the plan of life we should have some idea of where we are. We should try to see in true perspective the relationship that we bear to our environment of space and things and what that environment really is, insofar as the human mind has been able to discover it.

For hundreds of years, as we have seen, the horizons of human knowledge have been slowly, though steadily, pushed back, and the known universe has been growing larger, until today there stands revealed an expanse of creation that is truly inspiring to those who can catch even a glimpse of its magnificence. We must expand our minds to take in the fullest measure we can of that magnificence. Francis Bacon wrote:

> The universe is not to be narrowed down to the limits of our own understanding, which has been the practice up to now, but our understanding must be stretched and enlarged to take in the image of the universe as it is discovered.

We should do well to ponder deeply over these words of wisdom, for when we come to study the earth upon which we live, we find that it is part of a vaster scheme the limits of which, like the far horizons, continually

33

recede beyond our reach, silently goading us to further and greater effort. We cannot expect the great wonders of the plan of life to reveal themselves in the pettiness of an everyday world of trivialities. We cannot hope to perceive the vastnesses of space and understand its mysterious depths within the limitations of an imprisoned and fettered imagination. Our minds must be "stretched and enlarged to take in the image of the universe as it is discovered." We must dare to break through the comfortable security of the commonplace and permit our minds to soar into the heights, free, determined, and unafraid.

In pursuing this brief study, we shall have to deal with sizes that stagger the imagination and with distances that pass far beyond any possibility of full comprehension. Yet the effort to understand, though it may not meet with complete success, will be of definite value in preparing the mind to grasp the vastness of the plan of life itself.

Though the efforts of our ancient forefathers laid the foundations upon which the astounding developments of later years were built, they held many strange beliefs.

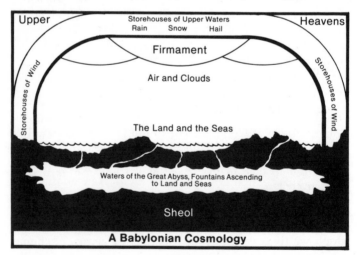

Fig. 9

In Fig. 9 we have represented a Babylonian conception of the world. It was flat, hollow, and filled with awesome things. Under its surface were strange rivers of darkness flowing from the waters of the Great Abyss. Fountains hurled the waters upward to the land and seas. Below all was "Sheol," the abode of departed spirits and perpetual torment. Looking upward to brighter scenes we find the storehouses of the winds located at the four corners of the Earth. The air and clouds are seen above, and the storehouses of rain and snow and hail are placed in appropriate positions to discharge their contents upon the Earth below. Then for those who qualified for such empyrean delights were the upper heavens of everlasting bliss. The Sun, of course, was transported across the sky by day and during the night returned to its proper starting point once more to bring daylight to the Earth. But greater knowledge soon dawned.

The "flat Earth" was discarded. Thales of Miletus first taught that the Earth was a globe, standing rigidly in space. Then the few "wandering stars" were recognized as planets, like the Earth. Ptolemy endeavored to explain the movements of the heavenly bodies by suggesting that they revolved around the Earth on a series of invisible crystal spheres in cyclic motion, with the postulation of "epicycles" to correct certain obvious errors of the simpler theory (Fig. 10A). This became known as the "Ptolemaic System." For no less than fourteen centuries this idea persisted with little change, although Pythagoras, in the sixth century B.C., had declared that the Earth moved around the Sun. In the sixteenth century, Nickolaus Copernicus gave well nigh indisputable evidence that the Sun remained stationary while the planets, including the Earth, moved around it. But so far was this idea removed from the overwhelming evidence of the senses that the Sun *did* make its daily journey from east to west across the sky, that it was not until fifty years later, when Galileo constructed his first crude telescope and, peering through it into the sky, saw visible evidence of the truth of the arguments advanced by Copernicus, that the old ideas collapsed and the new ones found a general acceptance (Fig. 10B). It will be noted from this diagram that the stars were now considered to be revolving around the sun, for it was not until the true nature of the stars (as suns themselves) was discovered that the universe suddenly expanded to an extent never even dreamed of before.

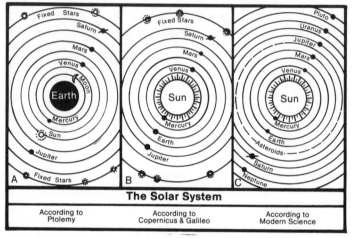

Fig. 10

Now the solar system (Fig. 10C) is known to include nine planets with their satellites and several thousand asteroids—small planetary objects of from four to four hundred miles in diameter, considered by some to be the remains of a world which broke into fragments in the far-distant past.

The Sun is 865,380 miles in diameter and is by far the largest, and of course the ruling, member of his system, producing heat and light for all the worlds. The Earth is almost 8,000 miles from pole to pole and yet so great is the volume of the sun that more than 1,000,000 globes the size of the Earth could be placed within it. Not less surprising is the smallness of the planets compared with the Sun and the immensity of the distances from it at which they are placed. The Earth is some 93,000,000 miles from the Sun. Pluto, the farthest planet is nearly

4,000,000,000 miles away. Such figures, however, are so large they fail to register in the mind. So, let us reduce the scale to figures that we can understand.

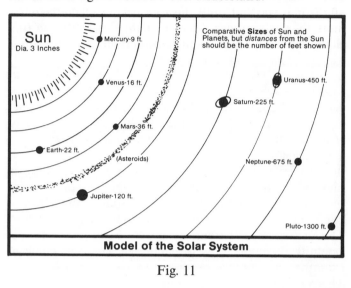

Model of the Solar System

Fig. 11

Suppose the sun is represented by a ball three inches in diameter, as shown in Fig. 11. Then, drawn to the same scale, the planets would be no larger than the dots to which their names are attached. In fact, for the sake of clarity, the dots have been shown larger than they should be. The asteroids would be invisible. The correct distances from the sun cannot be represented on the same scale as we should need a straight line which would extend through more than 650 of these pages. But let us imagine that our three-inch ball is poised in "empty" space. Nine feet away we place a pin head; that is Mercury. Sixteen feet away we put a small seed; it is Venus. Still further, at twenty-two feet we put a slightly larger seed. That is our Earth. At thirty-six feet we put another small seed to represent Mars. Now we go to a point 120 feet from the ball and place a pea. That is the "giant" Jupiter. A smaller pea at 225 feet is Saturn. Then two more seeds are placed, one at 450 feet, the other at 675 feet. They represent Uranus and Neptune. Now we place another pin head, this time at no less than 1,300 feet from the ball. This indicates the position of the most remote of all the planets, Pluto. And now we have reached the outer limits of our miniature solar system. Now, with the ball as the center and Pluto as the terminal point of the radius, we will draw an imaginary circle. It will be about a half mile across. *The only "solid" matter within that circle will be a three-inch ball, two peas, five small seeds, and two pin heads.* Perhaps we should add about as much fine dust as could be picked up between the thumb and finger to represent the satellites, some comets and the asteroids.

It seems incredible that objects so tiny compared with the distances and space involves, as are our Sun and its planets, should form a complete system, with precise and regular motions, controlled by forces emanating from a common center. It is not only incredible; *it is not true*. The picture we see from the purely material outlook is woefully incomplete, as we shall see when we come to examine the subject in the light of the teachings of Theosophy.

But, although in actuality the solar family occupies a slightly elliptical space 7,000,000,000 miles between its opposite borders, that space must sink into utter insignificance as we compare it with the distances now to be considered.

Let us examine Fig. 12. There we see illustrated (left to right) the planet Earth and the solar system. It is now known that our Sun is a star amid countless other stars which, also, are suns. The step we must now take is to learn that, together, these stars form what is called an "island universe" or "galaxy." Like the planets, they, too, revolve around a common center. In our galaxy there are no less than 100,000,000,000 stars. Furthermore—and here we take one more step—thousands of such galaxies have been observed through modern high-power telescopes. Those galaxies are not stationary nor do they drift aimlessly in space. On the contrary, astronomers have evidence that they, too, revolve around a common center and form what we may call a "supergalaxy."

What sizes and distances are involved in such vast-nesses? We have gone far past the stage where measure-ments in miles can be used, for they would involve too many figures. In such matters, the astronomer uses a "light year" as the unit of measurement. This is a distance equal to that covered by a ray of light in one year, and a ray of light travels at the rate of 186,000 miles every second. The distance to remote stellar objects—the quasars—is around 8 to 9,000,000,000 light years!

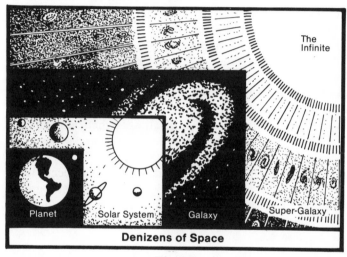

Denizens of Space

Fig. 12

In the midst of all this we are avidly pressing forward in our quest for more and greater fields to conquer. From the inconceivable minuteness of the atom's nucleus—1/1,000,000,000,000th part of a centimeter—up and up to the farthest galaxy of space which has so far been observed, the ever-active human mind has penetrated, observing and classifying. *Yet, within that five to six feet of living machinery that we call our body, there are mysteries that we have over-looked which hold the key to the very purpose of our existence.* And while, from the smallest to the largest objects which form our environment, immediate or remote, we find everywhere that there is natural law, only very few have yet realized that natural law must also apply to the things of the spirit, to the slowly awakening divinity that lies within. But it does!

7

From Infinity to Humanity

We have rapidly surveyed the vast amphitheater of the heavens, have caught faint glimpses of its boundless expanse and have seen order and law everywhere in evidence. In attempting to visualize the immensities of structure and distance that we have explored, it must have become apparent that the whole mighty and magnificent plan of existence is of proportions that are far beyond anything we could imagine were it not for the revelations of modern astronomers, who with keen observation and consummate skill have pressed their researches ever onward into the endless depths of space, disclosing for all a knowledge of the cosmos greater by far than anything ever envisioned before by the human mind. Furthermore, it is known that the stars—suns, like our Sun—pass through definite life cycles. They are "born"; they mature and they "die." There is strong evidence to indicate that space is not empty, but is filled with great masses of cosmic dust and gases, the residue from suns which perished in the far-off past and from which new suns will eventually come into being.

But, going a little beyond the limits of direct observation, resorting to extrapolation and using what would seem to be valid reasoning: since our Sun has a family of planets circulating around it, we can surely assume that the other suns in space—at least vast numbers of them—at some time during their career, must have planets also. Furthermore, since this world—the Earth—has given birth to all the teeming forms of life we know, should not the other planets, at some time, produce results at least approximately similar? Our Sun is an ordinary sun—there are larger and smaller suns, younger and older ones. The Earth is just an ordinary planet, average in size compared with the others. The same chemical elements, with possible minor exceptions, occur in all known celestial objects. The same gravitational laws apply everywhere, so far as is known. Light is a universal phenomenon. There seem to be no special conditions which would single out our little planet on which to produce unusual results. In fact, it would be surprising, in many ways, if on other planets other living creatures were *not* produced. Looked at from that point of view, the whole cosmos becomes instinct with pulsating life in every phase of its being, and evolution is seen to pass outward and upward, surpassing by far the limits that the more mundane mind, tied to the limits of Earth, would place upon it.

Great as these things are, when we come to study them in the light of Theosophy, all limitations begin to fall away, for we have offered to us a concept which not only binds all the parts into one coherent whole, but the greatness of the plan is suddenly transformed into something of immeasurably greater satisfaction as, to the knowledge we have gained, we add a revelation of the sublime *purpose* for which it was established and the methods by which that purpose will be achieved. We find ourselves going beyond the mere husks of outer phenomena and penetrating into the realities that lie within. As we study it, we begin to sense the existence of an infinite cosmos with life, life everywhere, and intelligent beings rising upward in an ever-ascending scale, until because our puny powers of comprehension fail, they are lost to view, as the highest musical note fades into silence because it passes beyond the range of our auditory responses. We see law, order, and purposeful activity. We see gods and greater gods, in an ascending order of glory and power and somehow we know that all is well. Though here, in our first faltering efforts to awaken the god-like powers that lie slumbering within, we abuse those powers as they awaken, not knowing the values which they possess. There, in the infinite spaces, seemingly empty but actually so full of life, there is, to quote the words of the Lord Gautama Buddha, "a power which moves to righteousness; only its laws endure."

We have already discussed, at some length, the great Being whom we call "God"—frequently "the Logos" in theosophical writings—the creating and guiding Intelligence of our solar system, and our relationship to that Being. As we then had to expand our consciousness past the limits of God's system to take in, as well as we could, the totality of the celestial bodies, the galaxy, the super-galaxy and the things that lie beyond, so we must now take a further step, one which ties together all known material manifestations and their indwelling life into an ordered scheme of ever-increasing inclusiveness with an identity of purpose which animates every portion of it. In Fig. 1 we saw portrayed the emanation of the "trinity in manifestation" from the unmanifest reality. The trinity there shown, it must be realized, includes the whole of the cosmos. In Fig. 5 we saw, in diagram, the threefold nature of our Solar Deity. The latter trinity is a replica at a much lower level, of the former. Between these two, however, there are many stages; how many no one can say.

Theosophy has taught for ages that the Deity of our solar system bears the same relationship to a greater Being that we do to the solar Deity (Fig. 13). In the light of modern knowledge we can, with reasonable certainty, identify that greater Being as the Galaxial Deity, in whose charge lies the evolution of all the Solar Deities in that island universe. And so on; in ascending stages the same principles apply. We must realize that, through the whole gamut of creation, there is intelligent direction every step of the way.

In our lowly state of unfoldment, we cannot fully

apprehend such lofty concepts. But the more we study, the more shall we find that the laws of nature are one and that the simple facts which confront us in everyday experience are actually reflections of the greatest cosmic laws. Size is an illusion. Its apparent reality and the comparisons we make between one thing and another are dependent entirely upon the degree of limitation in which our consciousness is functioning. To another being the values would be entirely different. In *The Secret Doctrine*, H. P. Blavatsky wrote:

> From Gods to men, from worlds to atoms, from stars to a rushlight, from the sun to the vital heat of the meanest organic being, the world of form and existence is an immense chain, the links of which are all connected. The law of analogy is the first key to the world problem, and these links have to be studied co-ordinately in their occult relations to each other. (Vol. 1, p. 662)

Many of the difficulties we meet in trying to understand the relationships that exist between us and God arise from an incomplete appreciation of the nature of both. We struggle on and are urged forward by forces within us that we do not understand. The ways of God are often

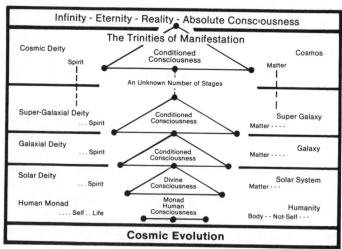

Fig. 13

obscure and the very things that we feel are so unjust, the pains we think are so uncalled for and the endless frustrations with which we are so frequently confronted, though we do not understand, may be the very steps by which we scale the heights toward the vision splendid on the mountain top. And God—the Solar Logos—though immeasurably greater than anything we can imagine even in the moments of our greatest exaltation, is still going onward and upward, expanding into still more sublime heights. C. W. Leadbeater in *The Christian Creed* has written:

> Though at levels so exalted as these, differences in glory and power can mean but little to us, we may yet to some extent realize how vast is the distance between the three Great Logoi and the Logos of a single system, and so avoid a mistake into which careless students are constantly falling. Yet, though it is true that the distance between the Absolute and the Logos of our solar system is greater than our minds can grasp, it is nevertheless also certain that all the greatest of the qualities which we have ever attributed to the Deity—His love, wisdom and power. His patience and compassion, His omniscience, omnipotence and omnipresence—all these and many more are possessed to the fullest extent by the Solar Logos, in whom in very truth we live and move and have our being.

8

The Nature of Matter

We are surrounded by material things. In all directions there is an almost infinite variety of objects of various kinds, from the dust beneath our feet to the sun, moon, and stars in the sky. For centuries we have wondered how such a vast variety of things arose. Is there some basic element from which all substances, whatever their kind, derive their existence? More than a thousand years ago the Greeks said there was. A great Greek philosopher-scientist, Democritus, said that if one took any substance and kept up a process of division, there would finally be reached an ultimate particle which could not be broken up any further. He gave it the name *Atomos* which means "uncuttable." Democritus and his contemporary thinkers considered the atom, as we now call it, to be so small that it was invisible. It was also incompressible and immortal. It could not be destroyed. There were, he surmised, three special types, as shown in Fig. 14.

Solid matter, he thought, and most of his contemporary thinkers agreed with him, was the result of a combination of atoms that were rough and heavy. Some suggested that they had hooks on them. So, when they touched similar atoms the hooks locked and they could be separated only by the use of sufficient force. Other atoms were smooth and heavy and they would slide freely over each other. They produced the liquids, like water. Still a third type

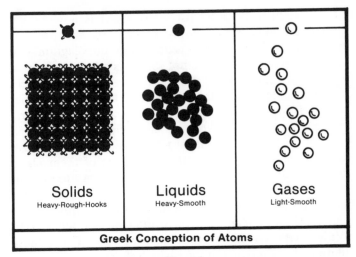

Solids	Liquids	Gases
Heavy-Rough-Hooks	Heavy-Smooth	Light-Smooth

Greek Conception of Atoms

Fig. 14

were smooth and light. They would float easily in space and so they made up the air and other gases.

The Greeks were right about the existence of an ultimate particle, but wrong in their idea of the nature of that particle. Nuclear physicists are still searching for the ultimate particle as they contemplate quarks and string theory. Earlier in this book, mention was made of the great revolution that occurred in scientific thinking as the twentieth century dawned. One eminent scientist, in the last decade of the nineteenth century, declared it was likely that all important laws in the field of physics had now been discovered and little remained to do but to repeat previously made experiments and possibly to add a few refinements to the well-established facts. How wrong he was became evident with dramatic suddenness for, even before the century closed, new discoveries on the nature of matter had brought about an almost total destruction of the old mechanistic concepts and a new era dawned, in which the human mind quickly soared into entirely new heights of achievement.

The atom is still considered to be the raw material out of which all substances are built. But the idea of a solid atom has been entirely discarded, for it is now known to consist mostly of "empty space." So abstruse has knowledge of the atom become that no diagram can correctly portray its structure. Scientists fall back upon mathematical equations. In Fig. 15 we see what may help to form some idea of the structure of two of the simpler atoms. Basically, all atoms are said to consist of a central nucleus around which one or more electrons revolve in circular or eliptical orbits, at terrific speeds. The illustration shows the hydrogen atom, simplest of them all; it has only one electron. Others have up to a hundred or slightly more. The more complicated atoms have various electron orbits and upon the number of electrons in the outer orbits depends the possibility of any atom combining with another to form a compound. Fig. 15 also shows an atom of oxygen, which has eight electrons, two in the inner orbit and six in the outer. Since the full complement of electrons for the second orbit of any atom is eight, and every atom seems to endeavor to fill its outermost orbit by adding electrons, or to discard it by losing them, the oxygen atom will easily unite with two

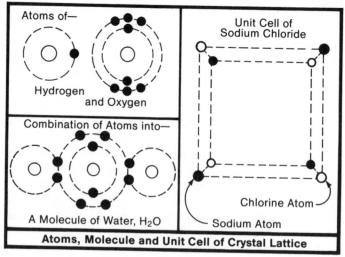

Atoms, Molecule and Unit Cell of Crystal Lattice

Fig. 15

hydrogen atoms, as shown in Fig. 15. When this occurs, both atoms lose their original characteristics and take on new life—in this case, they become a molecule of water. And sextillions of such molecules will make one little drop of that precious fluid. And a sextillion is a unit followed by twenty-one zeros!

Atoms are tied together in definite structural arrangements when they form molecules. This same fact applies in the case of crystals and in Fig. 15 we also have illustrated the arrangement of atoms in a crystal of rock salt.

A fascinating glimpse into the way in which nature, through sound waves, will build geometrical forms can be demonstrated by a Chladni "sound plate," which is shown in Fig. 16A. This is a hard brass plate, mounted on an appropriate support to give it rigidity. Onto this plate some sand is scattered (Fig. 16A). When a violin bow is drawn across the edge of the plate, a musical note is produced. At the same time, the sand will arrange itself into a definite geometrical pattern, often quite complex (Fig. 16B). Changing the pitch of the sound will destroy the old pattern and will build a new one (Fig. 16C).

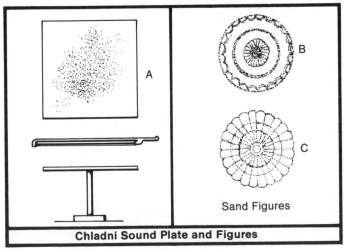

Chladni Sound Plate and Figures

Fig. 16

These few illustrations, simple though they are, will serve to show that the ordinary things we use in daily life are not ordinary at all. Some time, when you have an opportunity, stoop down and pick up a handful of earth—plain, common earth—and look at it carefully. Look at it even reverently. For you will never hold in your hand anything more amazingly wonderful. All the gold and silver and copper, the precious stones, the architectural wonders of the world, the mechanical wonders—all have emerged from the depths of Mother Earth in a bewildering succession of miracles. Could we penetrate fully into the structure of a grain of dust, we might become lost in wonder that such mighty things could be. Not only do we find order and arrangement, but within the nucleus, the inner core, of every atom, there has been found to exist a force which has changed the course of world history, which, if not controlled, could destroy humankind.

So we see that every object can be reduced to crystal or molecule and atom. The drawings here used are but a few lines and curves. They can no more truly represent the realities of matter than a few written symbols on a sheet of paper can convey the feeling of a majestic symphony. But there is more. The electron, we have seen, is of such a nature that it can with equal truth be described as a particle or a system of waves. Actually, it is something that includes them both. And electrons, whole atoms and molecules produce wave patterns or, as one writer has put it, "matter can best be described as a ceaseless rhythm."

We see, then, that scientists, digging down deeply into the nature of matter, have found that it is in essence *a system of waves*, thus supporting the idea, previously suggested, that the world as we know it—with all its endless variations of sound and color, of forests, rivers and mountains, the fragrance of the flowers and all the things we see and touch "the choir of heaven and the furniture of the earth"—is the response within our consciousness to these many waves. The clarity, the tangibility, the "reality" of the images we build are reflections of the true

Reality within the consciousness of God. All this is made possible because we are "made in God's image and likeness" and, from afar off, we are learning to create.

As we realize this tremendous fact, we understand that every new glimpse of natural law, every new fact we gain about the world, is leading us nearer to the Real. We no longer live in a world of inanimate matter; it becomes living, vital, pulsating, instinct with the life of God, from the vast mass of the mighty planet as it hurtles along through space down and down into the inconceivable and imperceptible minutiae of each molecule and atom of which it is built. Though still illusion—for it is so incomplete—a mere shadow of the world we shall someday come to know, each tiny penetration into the as yet unknown brings us one step nearer to the days of ultimate attainment.

9

Physical and Superphysical

We must now prepare to expand our world once more; this time to go beyond the borders of normal sense perception. Our bodies, we know, have areas in which are located specialized receptor cells, which are grouped into five main categories. These are:

1. Visual   The sense of sight
2. Auditory   The sense of hearing
3. Olfactory   The sense of smell
4. Gustatory   The sense of taste
5. Cutaneous   The sense of touch
   and Kinesthetic

These have been referred to as the "windows of the soul," for each one of them is an opening through which the spiritual person may become aware of the material world. Through these specialized areas—sense organs—as they respond to stimuli which beat upon them from outside, consciousness is aroused and visual images, or other impressions, are awakened in the mind. But only a very minor part of the knowledge we have amassed has come through our sense organs unaided by any supplementary device. Sensorially, we are in many ways inferior to the lower animals. There are insects, birds, and animals that can see farther, hear more, and have a keener sense of smell than we. Our sensory response to environment is far from complete.

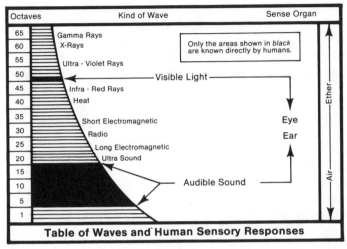

Octaves	Kind of Wave	Sense Organ

Table of Waves and Human Sensory Responses

Fig. 17

In Fig. 17 we see this fact graphically illustrated. Approximately seventy "octaves" of vibrations or waves are shown. If a reed or other object is caused to vibrate at a rate of two oscillations a second, the first octave is produced. Each time the rate is doubled—four, eight, sixteen, etc.—we have an additional octave. When the fifth octave is reached, with a frequency of thirty-two vibrations a second and a wave length of thirty-five feet, a low sound will be heard. As the frequency is increased, and the wave length grows smaller, the pitch of the sound will rise. When the sixteenth octave, with a vibration rate of 65,536 a second and a wave length of about one-third of an inch, is passed, the sound will die away. But it has not ceased. The waves will continue to beat upon the ear drums as before, only that organ can no longer carry the messages inward to the consciousness, for the waves have passed beyond the limit to which it can respond. This is the region of "ultrasound." How very real these waves are may be judged from the fact that not only do some animals hear them, but they are used for many purposes. By their use we can boil water, drill glass, clean small machined parts, drill teeth, cut diamonds, and kill bacteria. As shown in Fig. 17, passing through these regions of ultrasound which are waves produced in the air or denser medium, we come to fifty octaves of electromagnetic radiations, known only indirectly, the waves becoming progressively shorter until we reach the forty-ninth octave. Here we find that our eyes respond and we can "see." This is the region of visible light. Wave lengths of visible light decrease in length from one thirty-six thousandth of an inch to one seventy-two thousandth of an inch in length as we pass from the red rays, through the orange, yellow, green, blue, and indigo to the violet, which is the limit of human vision. Beyond that our eyes will not respond. But the camera can see where we are blind.

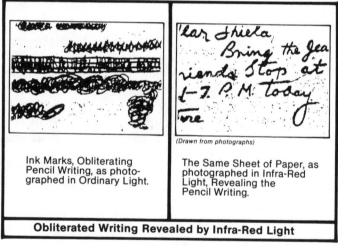

(Drawn from photographs)

Ink Marks, Obliterating Pencil Writing, as photographed in Ordinary Light.

The Same Sheet of Paper, as photographed in Infra-Red Light, Revealing the Pencil Writing.

Obliterated Writing Revealed by Infra-Red Light

Fig. 18

In Fig. 18 two drawings are shown. They are copied from two photographs of the same sheet of paper. In Fig. 18 (left) many ink marks entirely obliterate some pencil writing beneath them. The photograph shows the paper as we should see it in ordinary light. Fig. 18 (right) was taken with a special film in infrared light which, to us, would be in darkness. It shows the writing clearly, while the disfiguring marks do not register at all. Similarly, pictures taken by ultraviolet rays make many things visible which, in ordinary light, cannot be seen by the human eye.

Reviewing these facts, it is startling to note that, while out of some twenty octaves of waves which have air for their normal medium of transmission, about eleven are registered by our sense of hearing, out of fifty or more known octaves of electromagnetic waves *only one octave— visible light—is known directly by us.* The others are known only by the use of indirect methods, such as their effects upon objects that can be observed. Knowing the large part that the sense of sight plays in the mental pictures that we build of our world, we can scarcely refrain from speculating upon the wonders that might be revealed were our sensory perceptions extended to cover the whole gamut of electromagnetic radiations, known and unknown.

A study of the sense organs reveals a number of very interesting facts, as shown in Fig. 19. Our sense of touch is primarily concerned with matter in a solid condition. It requires actual contact. The sense of taste can function only in contact with matter in a liquid state. For us to become aware of anything through the sense of smell, it must be in a gaseous state. Actual contact is not required if the object itself gives off a gaseous emanation of sufficient intensity. These three senses, functioning in the solid, liquid, and gaseous states of physical matter, are of the greatest importance to the body. Through them, our primitive state, we could know if food were edible or the air were free from noxious gases which might endanger our life. We learned of temperatures and something about the nature of the various substances which were necessary for our physical needs. Today, they are still highly important for our welfare, though we are not so dependent upon them as we were.

When we come to examine the sense of hearing, we are introduced to something entirely new and of profound importance to more than our material welfare. Our ability to hear has been developed in close coordination with the power to produce controlled sound, and controlled sound has been elaborated into the amazingly complex systems of articulate speech that we now enjoy in communicating with each other. By this means, we have broken down some of the seemingly insuperable barriers that must have existed before the advent of our power to speak. Now we find it possible to exchange with each other even our deepest thoughts and feelings, which otherwise would have remained forever hidden behind impenetrable walls of silent isolation. Here neither contact nor close proximity is needed; we can become conscious of sound which arises at great distances from us.

		The Sense Organs Are Particularly Linked to—
Atomic	Media of Extra-Sensory Perception	The Soul (Ego)
Sub-Atomic		
Super-Etheric		
Etheric	Sight	
Gaseous	Hearing Smell	The Mind
Liquid	Taste	The Physical Body
Solid	Sight	
The Seven States of Physical Matter		

Fig. 19

While the first three senses, we found, operated primarily for the benefit of the body and the next one contributed to the development of the mind, the sense of sight, which we now come to consider, extends its reaches still higher to contribute to our spiritual welfare. Who has not reveled in the ever-changing enchantments of nature, the exquisite beauties it exhibits day by day? Through the sense of sight we can even break through the boundaries of earth and soar unhampered to lose ourselves in the sublimities of the vast empyrean.

It can be seen, therefore, that as we move through the denser and heavier states of physical matter into those of finer and more delicate structure, through use of the soul windows that nature has so cleverly fashioned for us, we gradually transcend the limitations of the physical world and find ourselves making contact with greater things that lie beyond. We should see clearly that the functions of the physical body are not confined to its own particular needs, for hearing and sight can, and normally do, lead us to experiences which are elevating both to mind and soul.

Light, according to science, is either a wave undulating in a nonmaterial medium or a succession of particles of energy known as "photons." According to theosophical concepts, light is a wave motion within what is called the "ether"—a state of physical matter more rarefied than the gases. It is a substance the nature of which makes it the normal carrier of the rapid oscillations of light waves. However, such a view of light is not consistent with the experiments which have been carried out by scientists like Michelson and Morley, nor the theory of relativity created by Einstein, and it is possible that further research must be carried out by both parties before a complete understanding will be reached. But finer than the ether are three still more attenuated states of physical substance known as "superetheric," "sub-atomic" and "atomic." As we go forward into the future, still climbing the path of physical, mental, and spiritual evolution, the higher forces naturally associated with those subtler states of matter will become more and more actively in evidence and we will develop more sense organs—windows—which will bring us consciously into contact with them, thus enormously developing our knowledge and understanding of the physical world.

Summing up: Theosophy declares that there are seven states of physical matter, to contact which we have so far developed five sense organs or areas of perception, with others yet to be developed during the course of our future evolution, which will bring us "extrasensory perception."

In this study, so far, we have considered only what are really seven *sub-states* of one kind of matter, which we call the physical. It should have become clear by now that we must never place a limit on the extent of any subject which is studied, for the unknown in nature is so vast that we shall have to expand our knowledge into the infinite before we reach the "end"—if such there be. In the seven subdivisions of physical matter we learn of the media through which the many kinds of physical forces are expressed. But there are forces around us which extend far beyond the limits of physical expression. We are more than vitalized material bodies expressing the forces of emotion and feeling of many kinds. We can create them within ourselves and are affected by these forces as they are expressed by other people. This does not come only through the medium of words. Love and anger, for example, can be *felt*, not merely apprehended as mental concepts because somebody tells us of their love or anger. So emotion is a *force*, and as such it needs— and has—a specialized substance for its transmission. This substance is known as astral matter, as shown in Fig. 20.

There is a still higher power—the power of thought. Here, too, the same principles apply. A strong, clear thinker stimulates us mentally and when in close proximity to such a person we all know that we can think more clearly. This is true because there is a mental substance, which carries the waves of thought, sensitivity to which is much more common than we may realize. Love and will are forces too. They are strong, powerful forces, which are continuously playing a part in the conditions under which we live day by day. Fig. 20 shows all these states of matter. However, although for clarity they are shown one above the other in degrees of density, it must always be clearly kept in mind that they all interpenetrate. Also, each one has its seven sub-states which correspond to the conditions we saw existing in the physical world. Since we have seen that all matter is really a wave motion affecting—or not affecting—the consciousness, these various states of matter do not mutually interfere with each other any more than do the many radio and television waves of different lengths. So we can see the possibility of our being surrounded by many worlds which are visible or invisible according to the nature of the vehicle or vehicles of consciousness that we are using.

Divine	Divine Manifestation		They All Interpenetrate
Monadic	Monadic Manifestation		
Atmic	Will	Spirituality	
Buddhic	Love	Intuition	
Mental	Knowledge Thought	Synthesis Analysis	
Astral	Emotion	Feeling	
Physical	Action	Sensation	
The Seven Fundamental States of Matter			

Fig. 20

The actual process by which the unmanifest comes forth into manifestation in these seven basic orders or states of matter is beyond the power of the human intellect to comprehend fully in its present state of development. But once more, from the workings of natural law in the simple things around us, we may find hints which will help toward that goal. Everyone today knows of the famous experiment performed by Sir Isaac Newton in 1672, when he separated white light into its seven component colors (Fig. 21A) by using a glass prism. When a beam of white light is passed through a three-sided piece of glass, as shown, it emerges from the opposite side split up into a band of colors: red, orange, yellow, green, blue, indigo, and violet. All things that we know through the sense of sight are cognized because of the fact that objects absorb or reflect certain of these rays of light in various ways, producing a world of color. Were there nothing but pure white light we should live in a ghost world or no world at all. At all levels there must be limitation for manifestation. Similarly, at the loftiest levels the same principles apply. The One unmanifest Reality, acting through the divine Trinity, gives rise to the seven basic states of matter, through a combination of which all things inanimate, animate, human, and divine are produced (Fig. 21B).

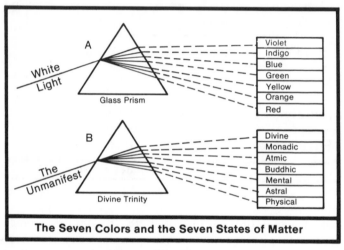

The Seven Colors and the Seven States of Matter

Fig. 21

Another illustration may be of value. Matter exists in many and varied states, but basically all of them proceed from one ultimate atom type with its parts assembled in different combinations. Life expresses itself in many ways, but however varied its expressions, basically it is the One Life behind them all.

On the left side of Fig. 22, the five states of matter with which our life is particularly concerned are shown. And here we must interpolate—though it will be dealt with at length in another chapter—that we have bodies of all these substances, which interpenetrate the physical

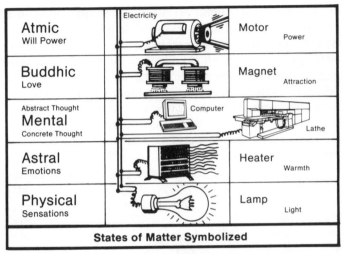

Atmic Will Power	Electricity	Motor Power
Buddhic Love		Magnet Attraction
Abstract Thought Mental Concrete Thought	Computer	Lathe
Astral Emotions		Heater Warmth
Physical Sensations		Lamp Light
States of Matter Symbolized		

Fig. 22

vehicle and by means of which we can express the powers appropriate to them. So, in atmic matter the force of will finds its expression; in buddhic matter, the force of love. There is mental substance in which thought power, abstract and concrete, finds its avenue of transmission. The emotions are expressed in astral matter, as all forces of vitality are specialized within and used by the physical vehicle. These different orders of matter are arranged in different ways so that they can oscillate at the needed frequencies for each phase of the One Life they are to express.

Once again, we will resort to a simple illustration. The force of electricity can be used to produce many different results. If we take various material components and arrange them into the proper shape and internal structure that we call an "electric motor," we can connect the electric supply to it and produce power, which we may say symbolizes the world of "will," the dominating note of which is *power*. If we take similar material and arrange it in such a manner that it becomes what we call an "electromagnet," we can produce a strong force of *attraction*, which is the dominating note of the buddhic world, the world of love. Or if we vary our construction and produce what is known as an "electronic computer," electricity is then instrumental in solving our mathematical problems for us, which may well symbolize the world of *abstract thinking*. Connecting the current to an electrically driven lathe, we are able to use the mind to *create material things*, the keynote of the lower mental world, the world of concrete thought. An electric heater *produces warmth* and gives rise to comfort and pleasing emotions, an astral world effect, while an electric lamp produces *light*, so necessary for the important sense perception of seeing. As the same electric current operating through differently fashioned instruments can produce widely different results, *the One Life, showing itself through the different material structures of the various states of matter, does so in widely different manifestations.*

We can now go on to consider the application of these principles to the Earth.

We are all well aware, at least in a general way, of the physical appearance of the Earth and of its place among the other planets of the solar system. We shall examine the Earth in the light of the other states of matter that we have been discussing. In Fig. 23 the dark area in the center represents the physical planet. We know that around it and extending for some miles into space there are various spheres of rarefied substances, the most important of which are the gaseous envelope we call the "atmosphere," the more rarefied "stratosphere" and a specially conditioned region known as the "ionosphere." Extending still further into space, in fact reaching almost to the orbit of the moon, Theosophy tells us, is the astral region connected with our globe. It is a sphere of astral matter with the physical Earth, which it interpenetrates, at its center. Still larger is the mental sphere, which extends far beyond the astral regions, interpenetrating them and the Earth.

When we come to consider the still finer regions, the buddhic, atmic, monadic and divine, new considerations enter and we find ourselves facing a new and surprising situation. *For in these regions there is no separation of structure, and the solar system is seen as one complete and internally organized mass, from its center to its periphery, which lies at an immense distance beyond the orbit of its outermost planet.*

We shall now take a number of steps which will build up an increasingly impressive concept of the solar system, and we may come to realize that there is no "empty space" at any point within it, nor any place where life, purposeful and vital, does not exist. The life of God is everywhere, and in the regions of the subtler substances, where the dull response of physical sense organs cannot respond, divine life is more potent and glorious by many times than it is on the physical Earth.

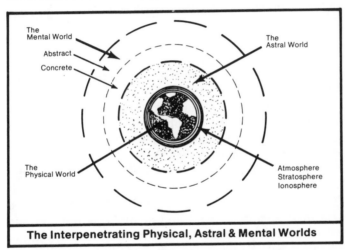

The Interpenetrating Physical, Astral & Mental Worlds

Fig. 23

In Fig. 24, we see a representation of the physical planets of the solar system. Each black area represents the planet which is named. In addition to the nine planets which are known to us, two more are shown: Vulcan, which has its orbit within that of Mercury and, therefore, is nearer to the Sun than that body, and an unnamed planet, "X," the orbit of which lies outside that of Pluto. According to occult research, these worlds actually

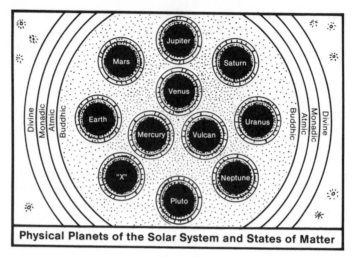

Physical Planets of the Solar System and States of Matter

Fig. 24

exist, and it is expected that they will be discovered by telescopic observation some day. All the planets have their own astral and mental counterparts surrounding and interpenetrating them, but they are all immersed within the total mass of subtler materials which form the higher states of matter and stretch out beyond the orbit of the farthermost planet, "X," in increasing measure, until the borders of the divine world mark the limits, the "ring-pass-not," of the solar system. Within this continuous mass of subtle material, the physical planets, with their attendant astral and mental atmospheres, are seen as centers into which force from the Sun is constantly being poured. We must remember, too, that these planets are in constant motion, turning on their axes and making their circuits around the Sun, thus contributing to the intense activity pervading the whole.

Fig. 25 is purely symbolical. In drawing the interpenetrating worlds in this way, the fact is emphasized that the greatest degree of separation occurs in the physical globes, which are shown as black triangles. Extending below the base are seen the astral and mental regions, closer to their counterparts on other worlds but not

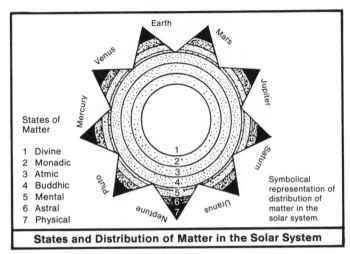

States and Distribution of Matter in the Solar System

Fig. 25

united. But the four higher regions, the subtler worlds of the buddhic, atmic, monadic and divine, are common to the whole system. In these few drawings, the density of the shading is intended to portray a corresponding state of matter and is an endeavor to place an emphasis on the fact that, though to our normal way of thinking these states of matter may seem to be highly unsubstantial, yet in reality they are regions of much greater life and potency than the physical. The forces released by chemical reactions and the electrical effects which arise from electrons in the atom are far less powerful than those lying in the almost infinite smallness of the atom's nucleus. Correspondingly, the forces which are generated by the still subtler matter of the higher worlds are much greater than any arising within the physical regions. In these diagrams there has been no attempt to show that on each of the seven basic types of matter in the solar system, the subtypes or subplanes, extend much farther than the more solid subplanes, until the atomic subplane is cosmic in extent.

Also in Figs. 24 and 25 the sun is not shown, for it would be impossible to show in such diagrams the actual relationship of the Sun to the solar system itself. So great is the Sun that we can never describe its greatness. Perhaps we might come near to the truth by saying that it is the heart of God, for from it flow divine forces into all the worlds.

So far, we have considered only the *physical* planets; but there are *nonphysical* planets too. They possess only various degrees of superphysical matter and form, by far the greater part of the planetary population of the system. To consider this part of the subject, it will be well to look at it from "above," i.e., to begin with the Solar Deity who commences creative activities through what is often called the "third aspect." Referring back to Fig. 21B, we see a representation, in symbol, of the emanation of the seven basic orders of matter through the action of the divine Trinity in a manner comparable with the dispersion of white light into the seven colors of the spectrum when it is passed through a prism.

The same symbolical representation can be applied to another of the divine activities; the projection from the one consciousness of seven mighty intelligences, who are to be its representatives in the coming evolutionary activities. They are referred to in many of the world scriptures and other sacred writings. The Hindus speak of them as the "Seven Prajapatis" (Lords of Creation); the Zoroastrians, as the "Seven Amesha Spentas" (Immortal Holy Ones). In Egypt they were termed the "Seven Mystery Gods." The Jews call them the "Seven Sephiroth." In the Christian Bible they are referred to as the "Seven Spirits before the Throne of God" (Fig. 26). In the theosophical concept the term "Seven Planetary Chain Logoi" is generally used. Frequently the word "Logos" is used to denote the supreme ruler of the solar system. However, in these pages, the word "God" has been freely used because of the many spiritual and inspirational associations connected with it. It is recognized that this word has all too often been associated, in some minds, with ideas utterly incompatible with the attributes of a divine Being—hate, jealousy, anger, injustice—but it is hoped

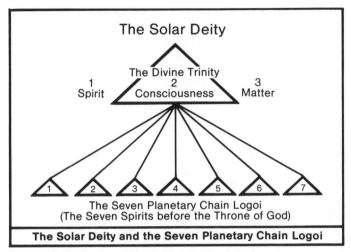

Fig. 26

that, at least among the readers of this book, such in-
congruities will find no acceptance; rather that they may
find herein some thoughts which may help toward a
deepening and widening of all the beautiful conceptions
of God, for none can possibly approach the greatness
and glory of that Being.

We must learn that such a stupendous project as that
which is taking place, and in which we are participating,
calls for a commensurate organization, so that at many
levels there exist orders of intelligences engaged in the
execution of many plans of action. We must learn too
that the seeming silence of "empty space" is an illusion.
Space is neither empty nor silent. It is only because our
eyes and ears are dimmed that the greatness around us
is unseen and unheard. But it is there; let us make no
mistake about that—color such as we have never seen,
enchanting, etherial and radiant; sounds such as we have
never heard, ecstatic, rapturous and pulsating with
celestial melodies. And everywhere there are unseen
workers. In the West our scriptures tell us about many
of them; angels and archangels, thrones, dominations,
principalities, virtues and powers, cherubim and seraphim.

In the East their books tell of adityas, vasus, Dhyani Buddhas, Dhyan Chohans, and many more. These are only a few of the many graded orders which work in the unseen worlds to carry out the divine plan. No army ever marched into battle without a host of unseen workers behind its operations, organizing its actions and providing its supplies. No great commercial establishment ever succeeded in its activities with only the salesmen who represented it to the purchasers of its products; there were many unseen workers in factory, warehouse, and office. So, in this great plan of evolving a universe, there are unseen workers who are vitally necessary for success. This is *not* fantastic. It is *not* imaginary. It is plain common sense. Those who wrote these things, the ancients of long ago, lived closer to nature than we do now, but the inner voice which spoke to them is scarcely heard in modern days, for the outer sounds are so insistent that the "still small voice" can seldom gain a hearing among them all.

The seven planetary chain Logoi are God's representatives, seven channels through which divine life and

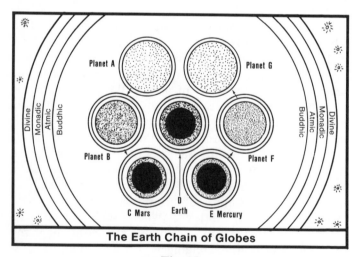

The Earth Chain of Globes

Fig. 27

forces flow into the worlds. They are agents in carrying out all the many activities of the One Life, and each one makes a specialized contribution to the work. It is not easy for us to visualize their actual relationship to the supreme Deity, for any human efforts to put such lofty thoughts as are involved into the inadequate channel of words must make it seem that they are separate from the Lord of all. This is not so. The greatest of all mysteries is the supreme fact of "the One, the Three and the Seven," seemingly separate, yet in such perfect harmony that they are truly one: seven phases, as it were, of the perfect and all-embracing Being.

Each of these Logoi is the ruler of a "chain" of worlds. In Fig. 27 we see portrayed the scheme with which our Earth is connected. Seven planets are shown, but only three of them have dense, physical globes. Planet A is composed of globes, interpenetrating each other, of the higher orders of matter: divine, monadic, atmic, buddhic and mental (abstract and concrete), but nothing of a denser kind. Planet B is of similar construction to A, but with the addition of an astral globe. Planet C we know as Mars, planet D is our Earth and planet E is Mercury. Planets F and G are of similar construction to B and A. This is a complete chain of seven planets. Later we shall probe into the fascinating story of the waves of life which circulate around these globes and, when we come to study the law of reincarnation, we shall see that, far from being something unique to humans, it is a law which applies at every level where life is known.

The next step is to know, as shown in Fig. 28, that there are seven of these chains in the solar system, and each one is in charge of a planetary chain Logos. Each Logos has a different "keynote": we might even think, symbolically, of each one being a different color, and of many shades, as in the solar spectrum (Fig. 21A). They freely intermingle their activities within the various chains and set up those differences which are so necessary for evolution to proceed. It will be noticed, in Fig. 28, that not all the chains of globes are alike in composition.

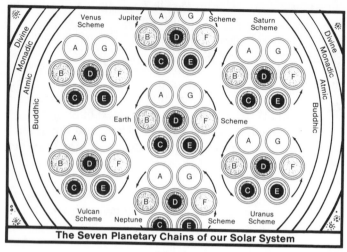

The Seven Planetary Chains of our Solar System

Fig. 28

The Earth and Neptune chains have three physical planets. The others have only one. There are other differences, which it is unnecessary for us to discuss at this time. From some sources the statement is made that there are three more chains, making a total of ten; but since there is some division of opinion on the matter and none of them is considered to have a physical planet by means of which the chain could be identified, and particularly because it does not affect the general principles which have been enunciated, these chains have not been included. The purpose of presenting this subject, in such details as have been given, is to endeavor to awaken in the reader's mind some conception of the grand picture of our solar system presented by Theosophy, drawing its information from the records of the Ancient Wisdom handed down through the ages from the far distant past, compared with the inadequate structure which is revealed by research that is necessarily confined to physical objects alone, although that information is the result of magnificent research work which can only excite our deepest admiration. The half-mile circle we drew, in which the only material objects, and therefore the only areas in which life could manifest, were a small ball and nine little objects none larger than a small pea, gives place to a vision of the whole circle, or sphere, as one vital mass of vibrant matter, thrilling with life in ever-increasing measure in every part, from its center to the circumference.

10

Cosmogenesis

Humanity, like Janus the Roman god of doors and gates, is forever looking in two directions: backward into the past and forward toward the future, endeavoring to pierce the veil which hides them both from view. Instinctively we wonder how this great drama of existence began and when, or if, it will ever cease to be. But while life is made up of a multitude of minor beginnings and endings, they have all been preceded, and will be followed by others, and to look for the ultimate in either is only to seek a will-o'-the-wisp that will bring no result. For the ultimate in anything is beyond our comprehension. However, while as yet the beginning of all things eludes us, we can go back to the beginning of our solar system and gain an idea of the manner in which it came into being. A great deal of information regarding the early history of the Earth has been gained through a study of the rocks, of changes in radioactive substances and of fossils deposited in the strata of the sedimentary rocks. Observations of stellar phenomena have provided much information regarding conditions which must have prevailed in the early periods of the formative stages of the solar family. The Ancient Wisdom, coming from revelations in the past, tells the inner side of the story of creation, for intense and prolonged activity in the subtler worlds preceded the time when combinations of the first simple chemical elements became visible and amenable to observation and analysis by scientific instruments.

The subject of superphysical states of matter has been introduced, and we have seen the much wider concept of the solar system that it presents. The existence of the superphysical planets and of the seven planetary chain Logoi has been discussed. Therefore we are now in a position to consider the beginnings of what we call "creation," with the explanation that, by this term, we do not mean the sudden emergence of something where nothing previously existed, but a change from a condition of nonmanifestation and latency into a condition of manifestation and activity. A physical atom, in its normal state, is electrically neutral, for the positive charge within its nucleus is balanced by the negative charge in its electrons. When this state is disturbed by the gain or loss of an electron, then we have set up either a positive or negative electrical condition and electrical phenomena may be produced. That which was unmanifest becomes manifest.

Let us refer to Fig. 13 once more. There we see portrayed the fact that, when the Solar Deity emerges from the condition of nonmanifestation within the consciousness of what we have termed the "Galaxial" Deity, both differentiated spirit and differentiated matter are at hand, but each of them is in such a state that it would be incognizable by our consciousness. It is, so far as we are concerned, the root-spirit and root-matter on which the Deity will act to bring a system into being. In other words, it is the root substance into which will be introduced "creative" processes by disturbing its balance, thus causing what we call "manifestation." Deity will "breathe" into it the breath of creative energies.

In the occult records it is said that this basic substance existed as "bubbles in koilon," and these so-called bubbles are the atoms of the divine world. Combinations of these atoms, in different concentrations, produce the subdivisions of the divine world and also the atoms and their molecules, of the lower, denser worlds. Reference is now made to Fig. 29 (stage 1). Acting on these bubbles, the Solar Deity saturates each one with divine energy, and they become vitalized with an indescribable power. In Fig. 22 the forces of the five worlds in which humanity is evolving were symbolized by various well-known pieces of electrical equipment, all of which were powered from the same electrical supply, coming from the same source.

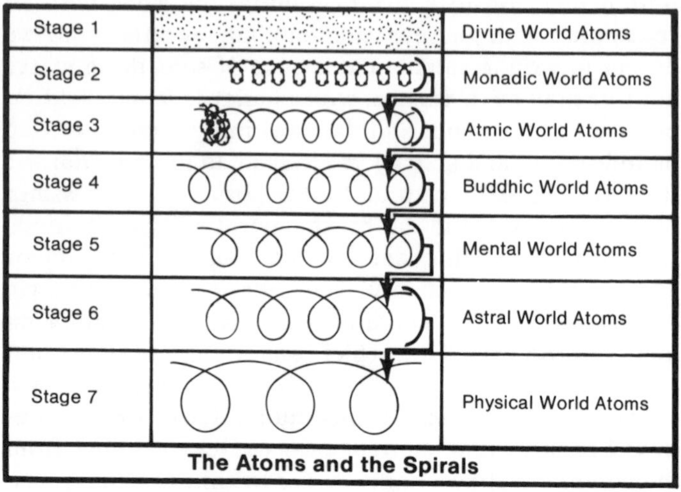

Stage 1		Divine World Atoms
Stage 2		Monadic World Atoms
Stage 3		Atmic World Atoms
Stage 4		Buddhic World Atoms
Stage 5		Mental World Atoms
Stage 6		Astral World Atoms
Stage 7		Physical World Atoms
The Atoms and the Spirals		

Fig. 29

Following this same analogy, we could place in the divine world a huge electric generator, such as is used to supply electrical energy to a city to provide light and to operate machinery. From that center the wires carry current into thousands of homes and factories to be used for many purposes. So in the divine world we find the central source of all the power of all kinds which are distributed throughout the whole system of worlds. But, as with the city electrical supply, the voltage is transformed down to various levels according to their needs, in the same way atoms of each of the worlds step down the strength, or voltage, from that of the world above, which is more subtle than itself.

In the divine world the atoms are "free." In stage 2 of

Fig. 29 we see that forty-nine of the ultimate atoms have combined together to make one atom of the monadic world. It will be noted that these are coiled together in spiral formations, each spirilla having seven of the ultimate divine atoms within it. To describe the atom of this world in such a manner is merely to quote a formula or to write down a mathematical equation. If scientists find it impossible to describe the actual conditions or configuration of the physical atom, how shall we possibly expect to gain more than a fragmentary glimpse of the actualities of these regions so far removed from our daily experience? But we can gain that glimpse and it can help us so long as we do not try to reduce it to the materialistic level of the physical world. In state 3 of Fig. 29, the atom of the atmic world is shown formed by a similar process; but each spirilla is formed of coils of monadic atoms as was shown in stage 2. One spirilla in stage 3 is shown to illustrate the process, and it should be kept in mind that this process is continued, each spirilla of one world being made up of seven spirillae of the world shown above it in the drawing. Thus the number of bubbles of divine energy in the atom of each denser world increases by powers of 49: i.e., 49; 2,401; 117,649; 5,764,801; etc.

All this is preliminary to a study of the physical atom which, perhaps more than any other thing, will show the illusion of size, that is, of space considered as dimensions. For if we can appreciate the wonder of that structure, as seen by the student of Theosophy, and actually observed by some who have developed the extrasensory powers that have been referred to, we shall have gained a truly revealing glimpse of the manner in which the whole Being of God in its manifold expressions *is actually within* —not merely symbolized by or reflected in—every atom in this great solar system. In the physical atom not only is each spirilla made up of seven spirillae of the astral world, but ten spirals are wound together side by side in a figure roughly representing a heart, as shown in Fig. 30. There are three major spirals. These are shown as dark lines in the diagram. They whirl around the atom and return to their starting point inside the core of the structure. They are energized by forces coming from the Deity directly through the three aspects, the divine Trinity. There are seven minor spirals. They are shown in lighter lines, circling around the outer portion of the atom and

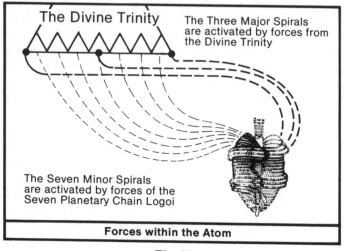

Forces within the Atom

Fig. 30

returning through the center. Each of these is animated by force coming from one of the seven planetary chain Logoi. *The number of bubbles, so charged with divine energy, in the physical atom, is more than* 138,000,000,000! No wonder, therefore, that when scientists began probing into the structure of the atom, they found it to be such a marvelous thing. And does it not fully agree with the declaration of science that the atom they study is not really matter at all, as we have thought of matter in the past, solid and indestructible? It is more correctly to be considered as a tremendously powerful center of potentiality, which can exhibit states of mass or energy under the appropriate circumstances.

The physical atom shown in Fig. 30, however, is not the atom of the physicist. In Fig. 19 we have shown the various substates of physical matter. The highest, the atomic, is the region of the atom we have been considering from the theosophical viewpoint. The atom of the physicist, from the point of view of Theosophy, is not a true atom. It is a unit of matter formed of various combinations of the true ultimate atom (sometimes called the *anu*) making up the hundred or more "elements."

The exact relationship that exists between the atom as described by the occult investigator and the atom of science has not yet been made clear. Without doubts, further investigation by both sides will eventually reveal the connecting link. However, in view of the fact that scientists have advanced the idea that the atom they study releases energy in "quanta," small packets of energy, and that light consists of "photons," similarly separate units of light of measurable amounts, the theosophical concept of the atom as being composed of individual "bubbles," or units of divine energy may become the master key to explain these and other phenomena scientists are endeavoring to understand. But that cannot be until the physicist realizes the futility of self-imposed limitations and decides to admit the existence of a deity, a creating and controlling intelligence and power behind all manifestation. True, that will not give the final answer; that lies far beyond and awaits the development of a state of consciousness that has broken through barriers which seem at present to be impregnable. Yet, since our consciousness is limited to relatives and cannot encompass the Absolute, the only logical assumption before us, as we penetrate into the wonders of nature, is that they have been caused by an intelligence commensurate with the facts that we are able to observe. Refusal to admit such an obvious deduction robs science of a secure foundation upon which its investigators could press forward with confidence into richer and more productive fields, far beyond the achievements of today.

After the formation of the atomic structures of each of the interpenetrating worlds, the molecular combinations follow in their order (see Fig. 15), and in the physical world we see that action, spread over millions of years, in the gradual evolution of the chemical elements as propounded by Sir William Crookes and developed by many scientists who followed him. Creation truly had its inception as the Solar Deity emerged from the unmanifest state within the consciousness of the Galaxial Deity, circumscribed the area of future activities and commenced the process of "breathing" divine energy into the bubbles of space. It started in the physical world, as previously stated, when physical atoms came into being and the process of combining them into chemical elements began.

From that point onward, science and Theosophy tell similar stories, though they differ in that the former, once again refusing to consider God as a factor in the situation, endeavors to find some exterior force to explain events, while Theosophy ascribes them to the same Creator who brought the atoms themselves into manifested existence. Following the lead of Dr. Fred L. Whipple of Harvard, astronomers today generally subscribe to the "dust cloud hypothesis" which is based upon a great deal of careful research. It is suggested that the rarefied dust clouds that float in space (Fig. 31A) are birthplaces of suns and worlds. Over periods of millions of years, they collect together and coagulate into denser groupings (Fig. 31B) which set up new conditions. As this process goes on, gravity causes contraction of the mass, and heat and light develop. A rotary motion arises and huge rings of matter are left in space as the central body shrinks further to become the future Sun (Fig. 31D). Meanwhile, the protoplanets have been spiralling in toward the center, and, as their speed decreases each one finds its natural orbit according to its speed and mass. Eventually (Fig. 31E) the solar system, substantially as we know it today, comes into being.

A study of Theosophy corroborates the main outlines of the statements of science; but it is asserted that the Deity sets up the rotary motion in the subtler interpenetrating worlds first and that, as it is imparted from finer to denser states of matter, it finally affects the physical substance of the nebular mass, transmitting to it the original impulse by which it was set in motion. This is

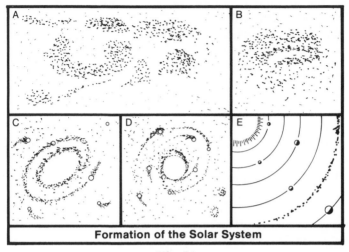

Formation of the Solar System

Fig. 31

accomplished in a manner somewhat analogous to the way in which masses of invisible air in motion can affect the denser matter of lake or sea.

We have now seen something of the magnitude of our solar system as enunciated by the Ancient Wisdom and of the manner in which it came into being, and we must surely see that, in its totality, it may well be considered to be the glorious body of God, with the Sun at its center breathing out life and power to all in every world and at every stage of expression. But when we look at the Sun, whose glory is so great that we must veil our eyes to see, let us ever remember that we are contemplating another great mystery—for such it is—in its lowest and most restricted expression. In the higher worlds, the glory of the Sun is beyond description, for it dispenses, too, the forces of the emotional, mental and spiritual worlds, drawing upward the higher forms of life toward their spiritual goal, as it draws the morning dew toward the skies.

Let us never deny the existence of the Sun because we are so completely surrounded by light, nor the existence of God because we can see on every hand the marvels of Creation.

III

The Illusion of Time
(As Succession)

Have perseverance as one who doth for ever-more endure. Thy shadows live and vanish; that which in thee shall live for ever, that which in thee knows, *for it is knowledge, is not of fleeting life; it is the man that was, that is, and will be, for whom the hour shall never strike.*

The Voice of the Silence
H. P. Blavatsky

11

The Three Outpourings

We have lifted one small corner of the veil that inscrutable nature has drawn over her vast inner domains, and we have taken a tiny glimpse into the great beyond. Small though it may be, it brings a revelation that can inspire to further effort and awakens a deep assurance that there *is* a plan. For we begin to realize more clearly that the seeming silence and emptiness of space are illusions arising from our inability to see and hear, that in fact every portion of it is filled with the manifestations of God in some form and at some stage of unfoldment.

But, so far, we have probed only into the material side of creation, the purpose of which was to produce a solar system, a sun, and its attendant planets with all the concomitant orders of superphysical substances. Now we must consider the multitudinous arrays of living beings which will appear and disappear within the many fields of operation. When we do this, we shall find that the ultimate goal of all this seeming activity is nothing less than the creation of countless divine beings, replicas of the Deity, gods who, through millennia to come, will arise from an initial condition of potentiality to a consummation of actuality. For, it may be said with all due reverence, a God could not be created a God, for such a being would be a mere automaton, acting as made to act; good because made good. So far as human intelligence can pierce into such depths, it would seem that each one must begin with the divine powers *potentially* within, as the plant and flower exist potentially within the seed. Such a one must be tested and tried in every conceivable manner, must surmount all difficulties, press on against all opposition. The future god must develop all power and knowledge and love, and become truly a God in fact by virtue of divine attainments, achieving and conquering in ever-ascending avenues of effort, until humanity is left far behind, through the acquisition of stage after stage of ever-expanding consciousness, moving upward and onward until ultimately, through choice and effort, the fullness of the stature of complete Godhood is attained.

We shall now consider the many phases of the plan of life, by means of which our spiritual powers are stimulated into the growth which will take us along that pathway to perfection.

Religion	Trinity		
Hindu	Shiva	Vishnu	Brahma
Christian	Father	Son	Holy Ghost
Hebrew	Kepher	Binah	Chochmah
Egyptian	Amun-Ra	Horus	Osiris-Isis
Zoroastrian	Asha Vahishta	Vohuman	Ahura Mazda
Scandinavian	Odin	Thor	Freya
Druidic	Taulec	Fan	Mollec
Phoenician	Anu	Ea	Bel
Trinities in the Great Religions			

Fig. 32

Mention has been made previously of the fact that most of the great religions refer to God as a trinity. As we have progressed in this study, we have seen some of the ways in which this is really fundamental to an understanding of the unfolding scenes of evolution. Some of the religions have inner teachings, still preserved, of the deep significance of the Trinity; others have lost those inner keys and have only the outer form to testify to the fact of their origin. Some of the trinities are shown in Fig. 32; many others could be listed. Misinterpretation by the leaders of the Christian Church has unfortunately debased a deep and wonderful fact into a concept of God the Father as a very personal deity in the form of a large human figure, to whom, all too often, are ascribed thoughts, passions and acts that any one of us would roundly condemn in another. How inadequate and impossible is such a being compared with the magnificent picture of the Creator which deeper knowledge reveals.

The triple nature of God's creative work is really the greatest of the mysteries which were taught in the esoteric religious schools under the symbolic names given to the Deity. The great drama of life is played in three acts, and after the play is well under way, all three of them occupy the stage at the same time. These are the three activities which are known as the "three outpourings"—three ways of creative action that emanate from the divine Trinity; one from each of its aspects. Each of these three outpourings is dual in its effects.

The first of them creates "energy-matter" (Fig. 33). This we studied in the previous section. It produces the seven basic orders of matter and gives rise to material evolution. The keynote of the second outpouring is the production of "life-form," living beings that are vehicles of consciousness of continually increasing measure. This gives rise to biological evolution, the evolution of living forms. The third brings "spirit-soul" into manifestation and also the "seven rays," a subject we shall consider later. It results in spiritual evolution. Keeping these three clearly differentiated within our minds will avoid many pitfalls. Not that they are separate streams of evolution—for the plan is one and they freely intermingle —but they have different functions to perform and often these are confused. Energy is a particular phenomenon that is always associated with matter. As matter is energy-ensouled, so no biological form can exist without "life."

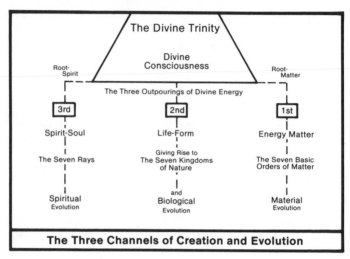

The Three Channels of Creation and Evolution

Fig. 33

When life withdraws from the form, the form disintegrates and resolves into its constituent parts. Chemically it remains the same. But actually there is a fundamental change, for it no longer has the powers of consciousness previously possessed. Theosophy states that the life has merely withdrawn to occupy a form of subtler matter. To the scientist life is a puzzle, for as yet he does not know about the subtler regions of matter, so he cannot explain what happens when life deserts a material form. Life and death, to science, are equally impenetrable mysteries for, unfortunately, it does not yet possess the one key that can open the door to understanding. But, with the rapid development of instruments which are penetrating into the unseen, it would seem that this discovery cannot be long delayed.

Spirit, too, must have its material vesture, and this, we have seen, is the soul, a subtly fashioned vehicle of the spiritual worlds, especially responsive to spiritual forces. Energy-matter, life-form, spirit-soul: these are the primary differentiations out of which all sentient existence arises.

12

The Involution of Life and Form

Speaking before a meeting of the British Association at Belfast in 1874, Professor Tyndall, the president of that organization, said, "We see in matter, hitherto covered with opprobrium, the promise and potency of every form and quality of life." Within a few decades one of his successors, Sir William Crookes, reversed that dictum and stated before the same body, "We see in life the promise and potency of all kinds of form." These two statements represent opposing viewpoints around which many a lengthy battle has raged. One school of thought points to the forces which are known to reside within the atom, to its ability to join with other atoms and hold together in the geometrically designed structures of molecule and crystal, to the manner in which molecules combine to create the living cell, and cells the many complex aggregations which build the bodies of conscious beings. Matter, they declare, has within it the power to do all these things and still greater in time to come. But the opposing school insists that life is the reality and matter is the vehicle for its power; the thing that it moves. And they advance exactly the same arguments to support their case.

It should be clear, in the light of our studies so far, that both of these viewpoints are right—and wrong. Each contains a large element of truth and yet is incomplete. Energy and matter are not two separate things; that can now be demonstrated as a fact. They are as the two sides of a sheet of paper, or the two opposite poles of electricity. This also applies to life and form. Furthermore, both viewpoints fail to differentiate between life-form and energy-matter. The latter results in motion. The former builds living bodies, vehicles of consciousness, and motion is one of the basic requirements for consciousness to function.

We will now go on to consider another pair of opposites, an understanding of which will resolve the difficulties existing between the two viewpoints just mentioned. We hear a great deal about evolution, but little about its opposite, involution. Yet it should be clear that, since powers of seemingly limitless quantitative and qualitative expansion can be observed within matter itself, those powers must have had their origin somewhere, sometime. That is, when matter began its evolutionary climb, those powers must have been there, latent within it, needing only the time and proper conditions to draw them forth.

In Fig. 29 we saw represented the successive stages of densification as the materials of the interpenetrating worlds were developed. The forces of the Deity, we saw, were being impressed stage by stage into the atomic structure of each world until the densest of all, the physical, was reached. This process was the involution of the divine powers into matter. It is little wonder, therefore, that our scientists, as they probe into the heart of the physical atom, find in it marvelous powers. But matter did not create those powers; the power and its material vesture came into existence at the same time, for neither one could exist without the other.

So also with life and form. They are not two, but one. They came into existence together and involution preceded evolution.

The interpenetrating worlds of physical, astral, and mental matter are shown in Fig. 34. Little can be said about form building activities in the spiritual worlds; they are too far removed from any of our present experiences. We can only begin as life emerges into the higher (abstract) mental world. The purpose of the initial stages of this second outpouring is to impart "qualities" to matter of each of the worlds, that is, to flood it with that phase of divine creativeness which will enable it later to be built into living, responsive forms. Matter of the mental and astral worlds, so acted upon is known as the elemental essence (Fig. 34). This is the original material created during the first outpouring, but now drawn into molecular combinations of such a nature that they can be saturated with the "life" aspect of God and become the material out of which conscious forms can be built. In these forms there will be not only "energy-matter" but also "life-form."

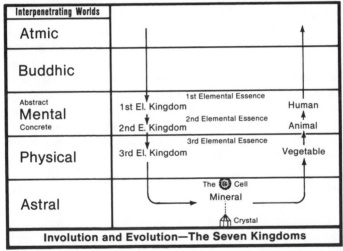

Fig. 34

Following the initial development of the elemental essence of each of the three worlds, as shown in Fig. 34, there arises a second phase of activity in which further combinations of the essences in each world are built into larger organized forms, which are called the elemental kingdoms: in the higher mental world they are known as the first elemental kingdom; in the lower mental and astral worlds as the second and third, respectively. They have only a transient existence, forming vehicles of consciousness without any individual continuity. They form and re-form in constant succession, as though the waves on the sea shore were to become living things, or the clouds that constantly shape and re-form themselves into newer contours as they drift across the sky, blown by high winds, were to come to life. In the higher regions, especially that of the higher mental world, a more apt illustration might be found in the many manifestations of fire in the physical world, as it varies in color with its temperature, sometimes glowing with friendly warmth, sometimes consuming with power and purpose, while at other times, in almost overpowering majesty, leaping upward into a thousand changing, fantastic forms of living light.

This subject may appear to be rather involved and technical and of little practical interest or value to one who feels that living a good life is the most important human need. So it is. But the facts we have just been studying are of great importance too, for they affect us intimately and continually, inasmuch as our higher bodies are built from this matter, and through a knowledge of its nature we can create responsive instruments for our use. To understand the functions of the elemental essence is of practical help in acquiring self-control and has a definite bearing upon the health of the physical body, as we shall see.

Reference to Fig. 34 once more will show that, from the astral world, the life wave passes to the physical, where it becomes involved in still denser areas of activity. Also we note that a dual stream of action is indicated, one aspect of which culminates in the cells, basic bricks out of which all living things are made, and the other in the crystals. It seems apparent that there is no precise point at which the second outpouring suddenly enters; rather it gradually overshadows the first outpouring and, by degrees, becomes the major factor.

We have previously referred to the fact that all substances are built from atoms. In Fig. 30 we have an illustration of the atoms according to occult research. The atom of the chemist, however, is more correctly described, from the occult viewpoint, as belonging to the molecular subdivisions of the physical world. In Fig. 15 a simplified diagram of the hydrogen and oxygen atoms shows the manner in which these combine to form a barely visible spot of water, many millions of which would make a raindrop.

The hydrogen atom is the simplest of them all, having only one electron. Helium has two, lithium three, nitrogen seven, oxygen eight. By adding electrons one by one (and a similar increase in the protons within the nucleus to maintain its electrical balance) all the different atoms are produced. Carbon, a normally solid substance, has six electrons, but when only one more is added, nitrogen gas is the result. About one hundred such elements are now known.

We now come to the next stage in which these two outpourings may be seen in action, and that is the process of combining atoms into molecules, producing the many compounds which we see around us in daily life. Theoretically, we might say that the second outpouring enters the physical scene at this time, although there is considerable overlapping. No doubt it has been over-shadowing activities in the atomic regions as temperature changes have given the conditions necessary for the various elements to form. Here, again, slight changes in the physical constituents cause great differences in the outer and visible characteristics of the substances produced. The problem before the Solar Deity—and we must remember that even at this great height of attainment problems must exist—was to combine these atomic creations into larger aggregations, which would become more responsive to environment and express "life" more fully.

There is a mystical saying ascribed to Jesus that "where two or three are gathered together in My Name, there am I in the midst of them." That statement is true in all phases of existence. We know it is true mentally and spiritually. Jesus is identified with the Second Person of the Christian trinity, as shown in Fig. 32. That is the aspect of love, consciousness, life. When two or three good friends meet together in a spirit of good fellowship and harmony, to exchange their thoughts on worthwhile topics, something happens. A strong bond of harmony and understanding is set up between them, and it becomes an experience of pleasure and profit. Few things can bring greater joy than such human companionship. When even a few can meet together in spiritual aspiration "in his name," it can become a truly inspiring experience, for he is there in their midst. And even in the minute recesses of the atom and the molecule, when two or three of the elements combine together with a bond between them which causes them, from that time on, to work as one, something happens—really happens. Life appears, consciousness can be observed, and the manifestation of the second outpouring becomes obvious.

Fig. 35 tells the story in simple outline. We have seen that the union of hydrogen and oxygen produces water.

	Water	H_2O
	Carbonic Acid	HCO_3
	Alcohol	C_2H_6O
	Sugar	$C_{12}H_{22}O_{11}$
	Albumen	$C_{204}H_{322}N_{52}O_{66}S_2$
	Hemoglobin	$C_{712}H_{1129}N_{214}FeS_2O_{425}$
	A Cell	All of the Above Plus RNA, DNA, Enzymes, Vitamins in a Dynamic State of Organization.
Scale of Biological Organization		

Fig. 35

If one more atom of sulphur and three of oxygen are added, we have a deadly poison—carbonic acid. With two atoms of carbon, six of hydrogen, and one of oxygen, working together as a unit (C_2H_6O), alcohol is the result. With different proportions of the same atoms in combination, we can have a very large number of different organic products. The way in which life can be observed in these lowly regions (though we think we have explained such things by calling them "chemical reactions") has been well described by Dr. Annie Besant in *A Study in Consciousness* (page 124):

> For chemical elements exhibit distinct mutual attractions, and chemical marital relationships are continually disorganized by the intrusion of couples, one or other of which has a stronger affinity for one of the partners in the earlier marriage than the original mate. Thus a hitherto mutually faithful couple, forming a silver salt, will suddenly prove faithless to each other if another couple, hydrochloric acid, enters their peaceful household; and the silver will pounce upon the chlorine and take her to wife, preferring her to his former mate, and set up a new household as silver chloride, leaving the deserted hydrogen to mate with his own forsaken partner.

Fanciful? Yes. But among these tiny lives such things are taking place with almost infinite repetition. Consciousness does exist; they are aware of each other's presence and seem to be ever seeking harmony and stability. The illustrations given in Fig. 35 could be multiplied many times; but the diagram itself clearly indicates gradual growth in complexity until we come to hemoglobin, the red coloring matter of the blood, in which 712 atoms of carbon, 1,129 of hydrogen, 214 of nitrogen, one of iron, two of sulphur, and 425 of oxygen have been combined together to act as one unit. Then, most complex of all, we find the constituents of cells from which all living things are made. The beginning of cell life marked an entirely new era in the history of the planet, and life definitely began its lengthy climb, the goal of which still lies far away in the dim and distant future. Furthermore, when we realize that in both hemoglobin and the stuff of cells thousands of minute parts in the correct proportions must work together as one, we can get some idea of the immensity of the problem of producing such creations.

Before pursuing the subject of organic substances further, we should take note of the development of the crystals. It is known now that practically all solids have a crystal structure, though in many it can only be recognized by the use of X-rays. From the elemental kingdoms, it has been said, life passes to the mineral kingdom, where rigidity finds its climax. Of all the forms of matter, metals are the most dense and heavy. And yet, even in the metals, life can be detected, and there is clear evidence of the early stages of consciousness. This was well demonstrated by an Indian scientist, Prof. Jagadish Chandra Bose of Calcutta, more than eighty years ago.

Prof. Bose made a series of brilliant experiments, which were reported to the Royal Institution in 1901. Using especially constructed apparatus, he recorded on a revolving drum electrical responses to mechanical stimuli administered to metals. He then repeated the experiment, using muscle in place of the metal. In every case, the response of tin was almost identical with that obtained from muscle. With other metals, it was similar, but there was some variation in the period needed for recovery. In Fig. 36A we see illustrated the recorded response in tin and in muscle, placed together for comparison. In Fig. 36B we see the results of repeated shocks which produced conditions analogous to incomplete and complete tetanus (prolonged contraction) in tin. This can be compared with Fig. 36C where the results of similar shock conditions on muscle are shown. In Fig. 36D we see evidence that a metal can be poisoned and then revived. Metals will also show signs of fatigue, a fact which is well known to all manufacturers of metal products which are subjected to repeated strains. Bose obtained similar results with vegetables, which he found could be fatigued, depressed, and excited.

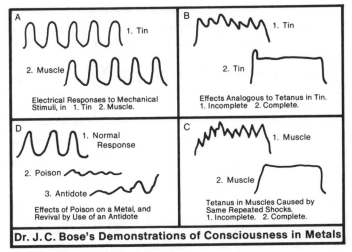

Fig. 36

So we see that, as the second outpouring, that of "life-form," appears in the physical world, scientists can use microscopes, molecular biology, and other sophisticated techniques to actually observe it in action. The details of that story, only touched upon here in fragmentary outline, are fascinating.

In the mineral kingdom (Fig. 34) we see that the nadir of progression is reached: involution and evolution are balanced. But even in the dense material of the crystal we can see evidence of the workings of the master mind of the Creator, for every crystal has a definitely patterned geometrical structure. We have seen that, according to the occultist, the physical atom has within its seven spirals the specialized forces of all the seven planetary chain Logoi. Since one of these is always predominant in each atom, there are actually seven basic types of atoms, their combinations and degrees of development producing innumerable subtypes. So it is of great interest to note that there are actually seven basic types in the densely aggregated combinations of the crystals, each again with innumerable subtypes. This septenary division

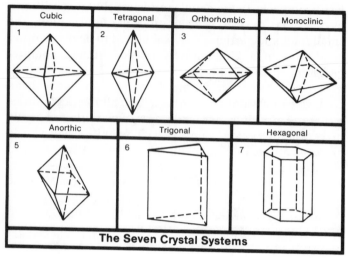

Cubic	Tetragonal	Orthorhombic	Monoclinic
1	2	3	4

Anorthic	Trigonal	Hexagonal
5	6	7

The Seven Crystal Systems

Fig. 37

arises from a classification of the crystals according to their geometrical configurations, the number of their axes, with their angular and linear relationships, as shown in Fig. 37. They are the cubic, tetragonal, ortho-rhombic, monoclinic, anorthic, trigonal, and hexagonal. The drawings merely give one illustration of the many variations which can be found of each basic structure. But, once more, it gives us a tiny glimpse of the deep inner truths of nature, working from the invisible into visible manifestation. The crystal holds its form for long periods of time, but, like all other things, it has its periods of growth, maturity and decay.

The involutionary arc of the second life wave is now complete. Life has been occupying bodies of progressively denser materials and is now within the densest substance which it will normally occupy. It is in this kingdom that physical consciousness begins. Physical atoms within the mineral forms must be awakened into responsiveness, so that they may begin to create links between spirit and matter, which will give rise to consciousness. So the material of the mineral kingdom is subjected to the most terrific impacts. In the nebular and prenebular conditions, as the solar system was in process of formation, the smaller atomic particles were submitted to heat and other conditions of a kind entirely outside human comprehension. Now, in larger masses, physical matter will experience, either in or on the earth, pressures, heat, cold, volcanic eruptions, earthquakes; all the fierce furies of nature, as well as her tenderness of warmth and gentle breezes and cooling waters. All these things will slowly awaken physical matter into a greater awareness of environment and the life within it will vaguely respond. Humanity, no doubt unwittingly, is helping too. We take the minerals from the ground. We throw them into blast furnaces. We heat them to white heat and plunge them into cold water. We cut them and drill them and hammer and rivet. We submit them to stresses and strains, so that they will hold large buildings rigidly together and keep them in the needed shapes. They must resist, in our engines, the pressures of steam and the sudden expansion of gases. In a multitude of ways we impinge upon the mineral kingdom for our own benefit and in that way help nature to provide the heavy impacts which are needed to give life, imprisoned in its densest forms, the stimuli necessary to start it on its lengthy climb upward, and to make physical matter a more responsive instrument for its use.

13

The Evolution of Life and Form

At this point our story changes. It is as though we had been sailing over the seas and now we have come in sight of land. We are to see new things and different scenery and travel by another method of locomotion. We shall cross over the plains to the foothills of the distant mountains. When we come to the mountains, the story will change again. For we now approach the second of three great events which have happened during the long history of our physical planet. The first was its birth from the black nebula of space. The second, which we are now to consider, was when *life* first appeared upon its surface.

The first known record of primitive life was the appearance of the blue-green algae, microscopic plant life which appeared on the surface of fresh water pools and along the edges of the seas and oceans. These have not only left fossil remains, but the species still exists almost unchanged after many millions of years. However, before passing on to consider the almost endless succession of living creatures as they come upon the scene in ever-increasing complexity, we should ask the biologist to tell us about that amazing little cell, which has many interesting things to reveal that will help us to gain a much clearer insight into the unfoldment of life upon the earth. If we can use our imagination in place of a microscope, we can penetrate into one more of the hidden worlds and see things that will give another inspiring insight into the Mind of the Creator.

We have seen that cells are the primary units out of which all living things are made. In the mental and astral worlds we noted that, according to the Ancient Wisdom, there were two successive surges of activity in the second outpouring, one of which gave rise to the elemental essence of each of the worlds. The other produced the forms of the elemental kingdoms from the essence especially prepared previously for that purpose. And here we come to another of those fascinating glimpses we can frequently gain of the manner in which the inner happenings carry through into physical expression, though they may not have been recognized as such. For in cells we can see an extension of the same creative activities noted in the subtler worlds. We might well look at the processes of cells as the work of the fourth elemental essence in the physical world, for they perform all the functions that are necessary to living things. It has been previously stated that in the formation of atomic and molecular combinations into the more complex units until the stuff of cells is produced (Figs. 37 and 38), we can see how the second life wave "gradually over-shadows the first outpouring and by degrees becomes a major factor." This refers to the first surge of the second life wave. When the cell is developed, the second surge of that life wave is seen, and the evolution of life upon this planet has begun.

Cells, as we know, are the "living bricks" out of which the bodies of sentient creatures are built (Fig. 38A). A cell consists of a nucleus in a mass of cytoplasm, enclosed by a semipermeable wall or membrane. It also contains two interesting little objects known as centrioles. Cells perform all the functions necessary to life, including:

(1) Metabolism: It can maintain itself by selecting proper food from its surroundings and can change that food chemically to suit its needs.

(2) Growth: It can increase its size within certain limits.

(3) Reproduction: It can reproduce itself, usually by division.

(4) Rhythmicity: It exhibits several cycles in reproduction, metabolism, etc.

(5) Irritability: It can respond to stimuli, internal and external.

(6) Adaptability: It tends to adapt itself to environmental conditions.

The cell wall or membrane protects the inner portion from harmful effects which might come to it from outside. It also regulates the absorption of food and the expulsion of waste matter.

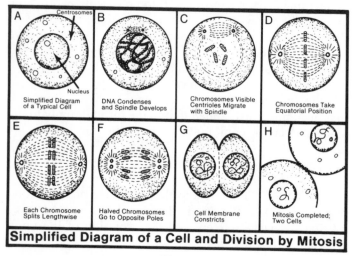

Simplified Diagram of a Cell and Division by Mitosis

Fig. 38

Most cells multiply by a process of division known as mitosis. Biologists agree that this is one of the outstanding marvels that the microscope has revealed, for a series of highly intricate events takes place in an orderly succession which at all stages is adjusted with regularity and precision. As the cell leaves the resting stage, the centrioles move apart indicating a mysterious quickening of the life forces within them. A group of fibrils appears, making what is known as the "mitotic spindle." It is evident that this is a highly magnetized area, for the main activity takes place within it and between the two centrioles, which seem to act as opposing magnetic poles. Within the nucleus, the fine network begins to thicken (Fig. 38B). The centrioles continue to move apart (Fig. 38C), and the fibrils become more pronounced. The network within the nucleus now breaks up into a definite number of parts known as "chromosomes" and the nuclear wall begins to disintegrate. The cells of every species have their own number of chromosomes and each cell, as it divides, always produces the correct number for the species. Only four chromosomes are shown in the drawings in order to illustrate the changes more clearly. However, most cells produce larger numbers: the cells in the human body, always forty-six.

In the next stage the centrioles move to opposite sides of the cell and the chromosomes assume a position midway between them (Fig. 38D). Each chromosome then splits lengthwise, producing two complete and similar sets (Fig. 38E). Then they migrate to opposite sides of the cell, and the centrioles double (Fig. 38F). When this move is completed, the cell wall begins to constrict, the chromosomes grow more diffuse (Fig. 38G) and, finally, the process is finished (Fig. 38H). Where there was only one cell there now are two, needing only a brief period of growth to become exact replicas of the original. All this action, we should realize, has taken place within a period of thirty minutes and in an area not more than a hundredth part of an inch across. There are operations within the domain of this tiny living thing that still defy penetration by even earth's greatest minds. When we ponder over such things, we should see why the higher living multicellular forms are such marvels of creation. This will be especially evident when we come to consider the way in which cells specialize their activities and all work together for the good of the whole.

So let us now take a rapid preview of the manner in which life and form have developed side by side in the physical world—the visible manifestation of the second outpouring. To help us penetrate into the record of these events, nature has given us a story book of many pages. Its leaves are of rock and the words are fossil forms which time has solidified and placed upon its pages for us to read. That story is now well known, for museums the world over exhibit a multitude of prehistoric animals, birds, fishes, trees, and other forms of life, which have been reconstructed from fossil remains and are often set up in realistic simulations of their natural surroundings. All these silently attest to the untiring devotion and clever interpretative efforts of many research students and workers everywhere, who have made such revelations possible, for in this way the progress of the vast plan is paraded visibly before our eyes that we may see. Because of this knowledge we can understand the plan of life better. Through a realization of the long, hard way along which life has come, its struggles to succeed, the efforts which seem to have been made and have failed, though doubtless they have led to the successes which followed, we can better appreciate the accomplishments which are represented in the level of life as it manifests in our time.

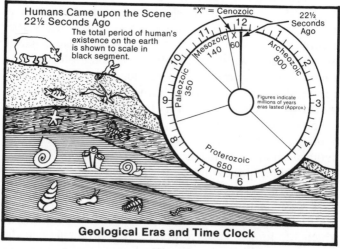

Fig. 39

Far back in the dim shadows into which we must peer to discern life's beginning, great rivers flowed down to the seas and oceans, and carried with them masses of sediment washed from the land. They also carried the remains of many living creatures and other things—leaves and branches that had fallen from nearby trees into the water, various bones, and sometimes complete individuals that perhaps had become mired in the river bank as they sought water to quench their thirst. All these, too, were deposited onto the ocean beds and were buried deeply in the masses of sediment that kept on in incessant streams age by age. As time went on, the sediment was turned into rock and the hitherto living forms were changed by chemical action into fossils. Many ages went by, the land surfaces became inundated and the ocean beds were turned into dry land. Actually, in the immense time periods that have passed, such changes may have occurred several times and a number of layers may have been deposited in the same area (Fig. 39). From a careful study of the rocks and the fossils they contain, geologists have been able to construct a fairly accurate picture of the successive stages of life's unfoldment and the periods in which the changes occurred. For such purposes earth's history has been divided into geological eras, each of which has lasted for many millions of years. These are shown on the right side of Fig. 39. But because of the millions of years involved and the difficulty of making comparisons in such large amounts, the measure of each of these eras has been shown in correct proportion superimposed upon the face of a clock. In this way comparative lengths can be seen at a glance.

In Fig. 40 we have an outline picture of the events of two thousand million years upon earth. Its purpose is to awaken within our minds some comprehension of the immense periods of time which have elapsed and the truly great changes that have taken place. As we follow through the sequence of living creatures shown in Fig. 40, let us do the same with Fig. 39 in order to keep in mind the length of time which is transpiring as we go along.

Had it been possible for an observer to have watched the earth for the whole period of the Archeozoic era of 800 million years, it is highly improbable that there would have been any sign whatever of any living thing, for no form of life, vegetable or animal, existed on land during this era. But that would not have been a true picture of events. In the seas, there was microscopic life and, all unseen, intense activity was taking place among the invisible bacteria.

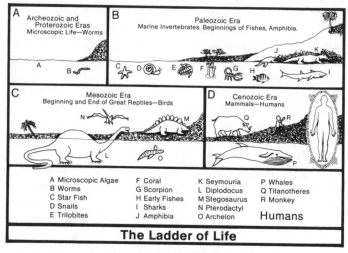

The Ladder of Life

Fig. 40

As the Proterozoic era arrived, a blue-green scum might have been seen around the coastal areas of the seas and on the beaches, and in fresh water pools that were forming among the inland rocks. These were the algae (Fig. 40A). Although each of these minute vegetable forms was microscopic in size, their large numbers would make them visible over extensive areas. At the bottom of the seas primitive plant life was developing. Some worms also might have been seen. These two eras, lasting for a total of 1,450 million years (until 8.24 hours) and therefore covering almost three-quarters of the whole of geological time, produced hardly a visible sign of life, only some primitive marine plants and a little scum. When the Paleozoic era arrived, there was some speeding up of action, and life slowly began to climb upon the land (Fig. 40B). In this era, lasting 350 million years (two hours on our clock), marine invertebrates developed. Primitive fishes appeared, land plants made their appearance, and then the amphibians. Examples of living creatures that made their appearance during this era are: starfish, snails, coral, trilobites, scorpions, sharks, and toward the end of the period the seymouria, progenitor of the reptiles which followed.

The Mesozoic era (Fig. 40C), which lasted 140 million years (one hour and twelve minutes), marked the advent of the great reptiles, creatures that began small but developed to amazing proportions. In the illustration the diplodocus is shown wallowing in the shallow water where it is believed these animals spent most of their time because of their great weight. It was a hundred feet or more over its entire length and probably weighed as many tons. The stegasaur must have looked like a walking battleship with its armored protection. It is said that this creature had two brains: one in its head, the other in its tail! This era also produced palm trees and flowering plants. These were strange years, for nature seemed determined to populate the earth with creatures of ever-increasing weight and size, and for well over a hundred million years they proliferated abundantly over nearly all the land surfaces of the earth. But that was not nature's goal. These mighty creatures, for so long lords of the earth, suddenly ceased to exist, and as the Cenozoic era (Fig. 40D) was ushered in, two minutes before 12 o'clock, a new kind of animal was seen. The mammals rapidly became the prevailing type of life. They quickly spread to all parts of the globe, showing change and progress out of all proportion to the advances made in previous eras. Weight and size gave way to cunning and agility, to superior brain power and adaptive ability. For millions of years that progress went on, and then we saw another change. Less than one half-minute ago, humans made their bow upon the stage of life, and that great drama took on a still newer and greater turn. Two minutes ago, the mammalian form of life began and already it has produced the greatest triumph of all earth's ages—the human body.

Life arose on earth in single cells, but the process did not stop there. For periods of time that stagger the imagination, life has produced an astounding array of creatures. The world has kept circling endlessly around the sun, but each cycle has found life a little higher in the evolutionary scale. Slowly, laboriously, up and up, trying, testing, failing, succeeding, through myriads of myriads of changing forms, the developments of today have come. And those who do not marvel at the miracles of life which surround and press upon them from every side, are indeed not themselves alive, though dwelling in human form, the supreme achievement of them all.

14

The Monad and the Permanent Atoms

In the preceding chapter we briefly reviewed the story of life upon earth, as it rose from a single cell until humankind was reached. But there is more than this. For again we find there is an inner story without which the outer will never be understood. Darwin believed that the evolution of living things takes place by chance mutations of parental genes, by blind reactions to environment or the survival of those individuals of any species who happen to be fitter than the rest. But nature is not blind. And there is no such thing as chance. An intelligence that could conceive of so vast a project as the evolution of a solar system and could establish laws which operate in every phase of its existence would not leave its marvelous mechanism to operate like a ship without a rudder on a stormy sea. Could the Creator possibly be less intelligent than the human being who with certainty would see that there were navigation instruments, a qualified captain and crew, and all the other requisites for a safe and successful voyage? The Creator certainly might *use* environment to call forth powers that were latent within a living form, or *use* mutating genes to raise the level of life's expressions. But these things would not be haphazard, but would be guided from beginning to end. The outer conditions might throw the switch, but the power would come from within the form itself in answer to the challenge that the need produced. And that power was involved into the form in its beginning.

We shall now consider the teachings that Theosophy has to offer and see if they will provide the background against which the outer events we have reviewed can be understood. The ideas presented may seem new, perhaps strange. But can we find any story as strange and wonderful as the autobiography that life has written in the rocks? Why has life climbed upward through all these struggles for all these many years? What is the purpose of the prehuman kingdoms? What place do they fill in the economy of nature? What is the remarkable power we call instinct, by means of which the young of every species knows, without being taught, the natural habits of its kind? These questions, and many others, should be clearly answered as we go along. We need not—*should not*—accept any statement blindly. We may intuitively recognize its truth; but we can also measure each one against the outer, visible facts and see how they put plan and purpose into what would otherwise be disorder, uncertainty and dissatisfaction. By the use of a few simple keys, applied to the locks that have barred the way, the unsatisfactory can be resolved into the satisfactory and the way be opened to further illumination.

We have seen that, the inner, the true Self of every human being is the monad. Many things will strive within the consciousness to be considered as the Self. Careful analysis will eliminate them one by one. Our feelings, our thoughts, our imaginations, our desires, the physical body itself will all try to establish their identity with the reality within. When the outer voices are stilled and the search is carried on deeply within, in silence and sincerity, the Self can be found. When it is found, all doubts will disappear.

The monad, it has been stated, is a fragment of God, a seed of divinity, and *the whole of nature is operating in every phase of its multitudinous expressions, toward the one supreme and culminating achievement that the monad, a God in latency, may become a God in fact, with all the fullness of its powers made manifest.*

The several different activities now to be described

began long before the second lifewave made its appearance in the higher mental world, and they developed concurrently with the involutionary and evolutionary processes which have already been considered.

To accomplish its purposes, the monad must have vehicles of consciousness, by means of which it may come into contact with each of the denser worlds. So, as a preliminary step, *one atom of each of those worlds is attached to it and remains with it permanently.* The atom itself is not a vehicle of consciousness, but is a center of great potency around which such vehicles will be built. Also the atoms must pass through much preparatory conditioning before their latent powers will become sufficiently developed to fit them for that function. Not many years ago, it would have been difficult to convey the idea that an atom is a center of great power. Today it is universal knowledge. We know now that we should not think of an atom in terms of size (although we can), but in terms of the forces (or energies) that lie within it. Furthermore, as we ascend the scale away from the denser worlds, its potency increases, for there is less material restriction and the divine energy can express itself more fully.

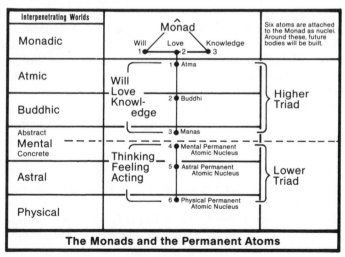

Fig. 41

In Fig. 41, we note that the triangle symbolizing the monad is shown with its three primary aspects as they show forth in outer expression. The three words "will," "love," and "knowledge" are used, though it is not possible to find a word for any one of them which will adequately convey the true qualities of that aspect. But these will become more apparent as we proceed.

With the atmic atom as a nucleus, the monad will build an "atmic body," which will become a vehicle of consciousness and expression in that world which, as we have seen, is built from aggregations of matter particularly fashioned to carry the forces of will. With the buddhic and higher mental atoms a similar process will give the monad vehicles for its use in those two worlds. These three higher links are usually known as the higher triad or atma-buddhi-manas. The units of the "lower triad," as shown in Fig. 41, are usually called the "permanent atoms." These are atomic nuclei of the three lowest or densest worlds, the lower mental, astral and physical. Actually, the lower mental nucleus is not an atom; it is a molecule, being of the fourth subdivision of that world, but for convenience the phrase "permanent atom" is generally used.

In these three densest spheres, vehicles of consciousness will develop. These are the lower mental, astral and physical bodies. By the use of these bodies, the monad will be enabled to express its powers of thinking, feeling, and acting. These, it should be noted, are reflections of the higher three. While will, love, and knowledge are qualities of the true person, thinking, feeling, and acting, it is obvious, are passing events, generally awakened by a particular need arising in the environment. But, as we shall see later in more detail, thinking (4 in Fig. 41) develops knowledge (3); feeling (5) awakens love (2); and acting (6) calls forth will(1). We may think about something, we may desire to do it, but it is when we act that will is called upon to provide the dynamic power which is necessary. In this manner, from the transitory and impermanent events of daily life we are developing the divine qualities of the monad, which once developed can never be lost; they will last forever. These events lay very far in the future from the time we are considering.

Thus the monad acquires powerful centers in each of the interpenetrating worlds; atomic nuclei around which future bodies will be built. When the existence of these nuclei is recognized and their functions are understood, it will revolutionize our existing ideas on many subjects. It enters intimately into the question of heredity and will throw a great deal of light upon many of the mysteries of the subconscious mind. It also has a direct bearing upon the subject of evolution.

15

Group Souls

The widely diversified expressions of instinct in the prehuman kingdoms of nature have always been fascinating, especially to those who feel a bond of kinship with the earlier forms of life. Modern psychologists prefer to discount the idea of instinct as a faculty and to substitute mechanical explanations claimed to be founded upon laboratory experiments. These remarkable faculties, it is said, are caused by the "maturation of inherited neural patterns." Other than substituting a rather ambiguous phrase for a single word, it is difficult for the layman to see how such a statement changes the situation in any way. Instinct is a neural pattern. It is obviously inherited, and it must await the maturation of its bodily mechanism before full expression is possible. But in many cases it does not have to wait long, for maturity in those respects is often reached at a very early period in life. Even if the mechanism by means of which the faculty of instinct expresses itself were fully understood, it would still be necessary to find out *how* instinct itself—or the "neural pattern"—was developed. To say that such a faculty was brought about by chance is merely a confession of defeat in face of a difficult problem.

There are many cases of instinct which have defied every effort to explain them away. For example, the swallows. In spite of many attempts to discount their accomplishments, it remains a proven fact that they *do* return each year to the place where they were born, after migratory flights of thousands of miles to the south. No satisfactory explanation has yet been found for this phenomenal feat except that of an instinctual knowledge born within the birds themselves. Placing rings upon the legs for identification has shown conclusively that birds from as far north as the highlands of Scotland migrate to South Africa and, making the return journey over the whole of the African continent, across the Mediterranean sea, Spain, France and England, arrive back at the exact locality which they left the year before. The instincts of salmon, which hurl themselves upstream in many rivers, even climbing waterfalls in order to reach their chosen places, is well known. Another remarkable case of instinct, in this instance occurring only occasionally, is the lemming, a small rodent inhabiting the Scandinavian mountains. At irregular and widespread intervals they become overpopulated. When this occurs they descend to the lowlands, following a straight line for many miles across country until they reach the sea. The journey may take several years to accomplish, but, as with one mind, they keep on. When they reach the sea, they walk on into the water together and all are drowned.

Then there is the spider. It is said that a spider once saved a kingdom when it gave an object lesson in perseverance to the Scottish king, Bruce. This may be denied, but it cannot be disputed that the spider is one of the cleverest engineers in existence. The spider's web has a tensile strength greater than steel. Each strand that can be seen is composed of several still finer threads. In building its web, it shows advanced structural design, and when it builds the scaffolding, preparatory to actual construction, it almost literally has to use the proverbial "sky hooks" to make a start. Often it will select a point and spin a single strand so that it will be caught by the breeze, finally making contact with a distant tree or other object. When this occurs, the thread is tightened and construction work begins, with many ingenious highlights as the project develops. It is said to incorporate a

"telephone system" into its web, so that it receives notice
of intruders who are awaiting dispatch and, if the victim
is too large for safe handling, a net will be spun around
its legs. If it still shows indications of resisting the atten-
tions of the spider, a poison may be injected into the
victim's body which effectively dispels any doubt about
the outcome of the conflict. After the preliminary inci-
dents, the spider uses clever engineering tactics once
more to haul victims to the larder. Some spiders are also
masters of camouflage, having an ability to change color
with their surroundings.

We may take another illustration: a very lowly type of
flat worm, not more than one-eighth of an inch long,
which is found in large numbers on some French beaches.
At low tide these creatures form great patches of dark
green and, though they number many millions, they all
act as one individual. They all lay their eggs at the same
time, and they mature together. When the sun is shining,
they all lie motionless on the beach; but at the slightest
disturbance they disappear as if by magic, having pre-
cipitated themselves simultaneously into the sand. In
many other ways they act as one, even when out of their
normal surroundings. These creatures have been taken
into the laboratory and their physical constitution has
been found to be of such a remarkable nature that many
of their movements and responses can be ascribed to
automatic nerve reactions to the outer stimuli. But that
still does not give a satisfactory answer to the problem,
for it does not reveal *how* and *why* such peculiar abilities
were developed. Was this little one-eighth inch of life
especially created that way? Or did it think out for itself
all these complex reactions and perform them so frequently that they became automatic? Or is there a great
Mind behind the vast number of such manifestations of
life, which is working out a plan as yet unfathomed
by the human mind?

Speaking of this mass consciousness which can be
observed in so many ways in the prehuman kingdoms,
Professor Hardy, in September 1949, suggested to the

British Association that an explanation of the mass flights of birds, operating together as one, might be because they have a "collective mind." He thought that, in this way, telepathic operations might shape herd destiny and control mass activities. More recently Rupert Sheldrake has theorized about a "morphogenetic field" for species, through which the individuals of the species share what any of them has learned. Such a statement is in harmony with the teachings that the Ancient Wisdom has to offer. And, once more, the explanation is founded upon organization in the invisible worlds, the existence of which can be substantiated by observations in the visible.

The biological processes by means of which a new individual comes to birth in the human kingdom are well known. For a long period the developing embryo is cared for, nourished and protected within the body of the mother. When this preparatory period is completed, the child comes to birth and starts its own independent existence. In a similar manner, the "lower triad" must pass through a long period of prenatal preparation as part of a "group soul" before it is launched into independent existence to begin its direct association with the monad when the human soul takes its place. The following is a quotation from *A Study in Consciousness* by Dr. Annie Besant (page 76):

> I have compared the evolution through the mineral, vegetable and animal kingdoms to an ante-natal period, and the resemblance is exact. As the child is nourished by the life-streams of the mother, so does the protective envelope of the Group Soul nourish the lives within it, receiving and distributing the experiences gathered in. The circulating life is the life of the parent; the young plants, the young animals ... are not ready for independent life as yet but must draw nourishment from the parent.

A group soul is an envelope of "monadic essence" through which specialized forces of the divine life are flowing. As a guiding and protecting envelope, it encloses innumerable lower triads, which must be submitted to various outer contacts in order to arouse the latent powers within them and prepare them to be fit nuclei around which vehicles of consciousness will be built (Fig. 42). The term "monadic essence" is applied to *atomic* matter of each of the interpenetrating worlds which has been acted upon by the second life wave. It is also applied to the highest subdivision of the lower mental world, though that is not actually atomic. Elemental essence is composed of the lower, or molecular, divisions of each of the basic types of matter finer than the physical.

Seven group souls appear in the lower mental world, one being derived from each of the seven creative centers within the Deity, the seven planetary chain Logoi (Fig. 26). In these group souls, which consist of one envelope of monadic essence of that world, countless triads are immersed and their mental permanent atoms are bathed and nourished in an especially magnetized field of divine life. In this way they become vitalized and sensitized. After a long period of time, the group soul receives a second envelope, which is of astral monadic essence and a similar conditioning of the astral nucleus takes place. The next scene of action is the physical world where

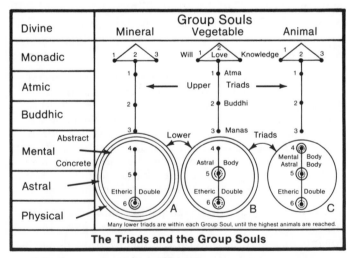

Fig. 42

there are three fundamental group soul types, the mineral, vegetable and animal, as Fig. 42 shows. The mineral group soul acquires a third envelope. It is of physical monadic essence (Fig. 42A). The vegetable group soul is dual (Fig. 42B); the physical envelope has gone. The animal group soul has only a single enveloping layer, which is of the lower mental world (Fig. 42C). In each group soul there will be many triads, especially in that of the mineral. In this (Fig. 42A), the lower mental and astral permanent atoms will remain within the protective envelope, while the physical permanent atoms, separated partially but magnetically linked with their source, will be distributed among many mineral forms, where they will share in the terrific impacts to which the mineral is submitted, as we have seen. In the group soul all the experiences of all its members are shared in common. But, gradually, differences arise and these give rise to divisions.

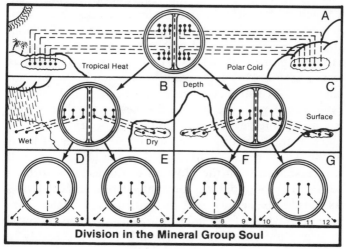

Division in the Mineral Group Soul

Fig. 43

For example, one set of atoms may be placed in the arctic regions where they will contact only constant snow, ice and frigid winds; another group may go to a mineral layer in the tropics and will experience there tremendous and incessant heat (Fig. 43A). This pronounced difference in the impacts that reach the permanent atoms will eventually cause a division, as shown in Fig. 43B and C. Then a second division might occur resulting in the conditions shown in Fig. 43 D-E-F-G. Other differences, as symbolized in Fig. 43, 1-12, will cause many other divisions to take place. In this manner the group souls increase numerically, while the number of triads within each group decreases accordingly.

When the physical permanent atoms of any group of triads have reached a point of unfoldment in which their vibratory powers can no longer be developed by remaining within the limitations of a mineral form, they are withdrawn back to the group soul. The physical envelope will then disappear, and some of its matter will be utilized in the formation of an etheric body for each triad, as shown in Fig. 42A. The permanent atoms will then be transferred into forms of the vegetable kingdom, where a much wider latitude of experience awaits them, and, in addition to physical responses, the dawn of feeling and desire will arise and will leave impressions on the astral permanent atoms, awakening them into conscious response (Fig. 42B). It is possible that, even in the mineral kingdom, the astral atom may have been stimulated into some vague response, but in the new cycle that is now beginning, the desires and feelings will occupy a definite place in the unfolding plan. So now, the center of focus of the whole group of triads within the group soul will be transferred from the physical to the astral world. As before, the group soul will constantly divide and subdivide. As a rule, experience will be gained first in the more primitive types of vegetable life. This will be followed by a gradual climbing upward, culminating possibly in an oak, with its dignity and strength, the towering majesty of a redwood, the purifying fragrance of a pine, or in the beauty of a flowering plant, depending upon which of the original seven group souls it belonged to, for all subsequent divisions still are subtypes of one of the original seven.

When all possible experiences have been gained from the vegetable kingdom, the process described in the previous step is repeated; the outer, astral, envelope disintegrates and much of the material is used for the formation of the beginnings of an astral vehicle for each of the enclosed astral permanent atoms. The triads, enclosed now only in an envelope of lower mental monadic essence, are placed in bodies of the animal kingdom, and they begin an entirely new existence, offering far wider and richer opportunities than anything experienced before (Fig. 42C). Here, however, the transfer is not to the most primitive of animal forms but a little higher up the scale; in fact it is said that there is a considerable amount of overlapping, for a fine tree might be far in advance of a primitive animal, and the point of transfer could be anywhere along a fairly extensive variation in development.

The center of focus is now upon the lower mental level, in order to awaken the latent powers within the mental permanent atom. Many new conditions now enter, and the subject, if followed in detail, would become one of great complexity. In the mineral, the physical experience was gained in masses; there were no individual forms, except possibly in a few precious stones toward the climax of the period. In the vegetable life, the physical form was semi-independent, for it had gained the powers of growth, and locomotion to a limited degree, though it was rooted in the ground. In the animal world, each form will have a separate existence. Furthermore, there will be an independent existence after the death of the physical form, for the astral body will now have developed sufficiently to function independently in the astral world, when its physical companion is separated from it. There is also a rapid cycle of reincarnation for, after a brief stay in the astral world, each triad will be withdrawn entirely into the group soul for a period of adjustment, after which it will be born once more into an animal body a little higher up the scale of evolution. Gradually, the beginnings of a mental body may be seen and, in the higher animals, it will develop to the point where its existence will show in the actions of the animal itself. The climax of animal evolution is reached when the group soul has continued its many divisions until finally there is only one triad surrounded by a protecting envelope of monadic essence of the lower mental world. This lower triad has been vitalized and sensitized to become an instrument for the higher triad, and therefore it now can be attached directly to the monad. The permanent atoms can also be used as magnetic centers around which future bodies will be built.

We will now review, briefly, the various processes which have been described and see how the inner and outer manifestations fit into a common pattern. In Fig. 40 we were reminded of the long succession of evolving forms that began with the simple scum on the seas and pools and climbed up through a seemingly endless succession of adaptations and expansions until the wonderfully complex human body was reached. All this progress was made by a series of definite changes in structure and function.

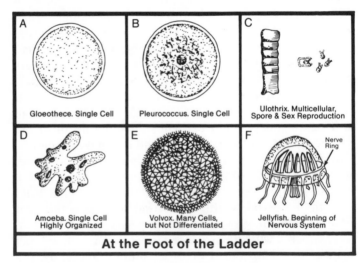

Fig. 44

These changes, of course, cannot be given in detail, but a few illustrations taken from the early stages may be of value. In Fig. 44A we see a simple one-celled microscopic plant (gloeothece). Its body is a single cell without any apparent organization. In Fig. 44B we have another one-celled plant (pleurococcus). It represents a step forward, inasmuch as there are signs of internal organization and a specialization of various parts. In Fig. 44C we have illustrated a ulothrix, a multicellular plant which is formed from a number of cells, all of which are dependent upon the others. In normal times it will reproduce by developing spores; but under special circumstances when spores would be unlikely to survive, it will produce both male and female sex cells within itself and discharge them into the water, where they will unite and produce new individuals.

Three illustrations of progressive steps in early animal life are shown in Fig. 44 D-E-F. The first is the well-known amoeba, consisting of only a single cell. The next is the volvox, a colony of many cells, but they are united only in a cluster and are not organized into a unified structure. In the third illustration, the jellyfish, we have the beginning of a major step in animal evolution to nerves. It has a single nerve ring connecting the muscles which control its tentacles. So we could go on step by step, improvement after improvement, gradually mounting the ladder of life as nature works upon her multitude of living things, urging them ever forward to fuller expression. But as they do this, the really important thing that is taking place is *the evolution of consciousness.*

In Fig. 45 we see two triangles, one turned upward, the other turned downward. The vertical line represents illusive time, the horizontal line, the unfolding of consciousness. In the mineral kingdom, consciousness is represented by a point; the vegetable, increasing a little in the degree of its consciousness, is shown as a short line. The greater consciousness of the animal is indicated by a longer line, and human consciousness by the heavy horizontal line which, it will be noted, is the median

line between lowest matter and highest spirit. Below
that line, there has been only mass consciousness, that
which the members of the group soul shared together.
Above it, self-consciousness enters, for here the link is
made between the divine within the monad, and the
lower triads, by means of which he will build many
bodies and through which he will gain those experiences
that will awaken the latent divine powers. Below, complete separation restricts consciousness to a point. Above,
complete unity (the point) expands consciousness to
its fullness.

In the light of this knowledge, many of our problems
should have disappeared. The purpose of the prehuman
kingdoms should now be clear. The group soul, with its
envelopes of monadic essence in which the specialized
forces of the Deity ever flow, directing, nourishing and
guiding the early struggles of living things toward independent existence, explains what we call instinct, which
so often can be favorably compared with a high degree
of intelligence. It explains the mass migrations of the
birds, the flight formations of the wild geese, the integrated activities of the honeybees, the marvelous organization of ant life, why young ducks take to the water and
why chickens stay away from it. It explains why the little
worms on the French beaches act as one being and why
the swallows go back to the place of their birth, which
they left the year before.

It should be clear, also, that instinct as exhibited in
the lower kingdoms comes from two distinct sources. The
first is the divine life within the protecting envelope,
which will express itself in the consciousness of the
group soul as the *idea* of the Deity concerning the lines
along which it is to evolve, thus implanting within its
members the instinctive urges that would contribute
toward such an end. The second has its source in the
experiences of the triads within the group soul, repeated
through countless generations and shared in common by
all its members. The first, for example, would implant
within the ancient eohippus the instinctive urge to choose

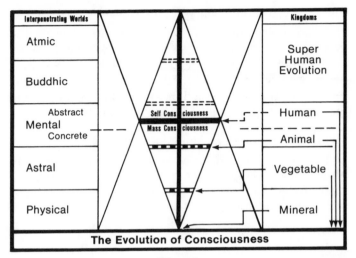

The Evolution of Consciousness

Fig. 45

such habits and circumstances as would cause mutating genes to be guided along the pattern of the divine thought, until the beauty and nobility of the present-day horse was produced. The second would establish the many lesser thought patterns which are expressed in instinctual habits from its earliest years. These, it is interesting to note, may be modified to some extent by careful and continued training.

As we study the Ancient Wisdom, its light shines ever brighter upon the dark places of life, and they become clearer step by step. We see that all the vast legions of nature—from the invisible minutiae of the microscopic world to the massive and mighty dinosaur of Mesozoic times, the smart and the stupid, the cruel and the kind, those that walk or fly or swim—all of them, yesterday, today, and in days to come, are parts of this one vast scheme which, in a seeming infinity of detail, is working toward an appointed end. The lowly forms of life, like the tiny cog in a great machine, assume their true perspectives, and we know that but for the small there would be no great. Had life not taken its first primitive steps, the hopeful signs of our days could never have come about.

We must surely see that there is one plan and one life and one perfection toward which the whole creation is moving in one magnificent sweep of unfolding consciousness. Could we but understand it all, we should gain a magnificent vision of the unity of all things. We should see that in the lower kingdoms today we are witnessing the same preparatory process which made it possible for the Self within each one of us to come into physical existence and to taste of the joys of accomplishment, and we should recognize what we see as the means by which some humanity of the future will come into being when we shall have passed onward to superhuman pathways of evolution.

16

Individualization

We now face another of those deep mysteries of life of which we may gain an intellectual grasp to some small degree, but which can only become fully understood through the intuitive mind in hours of quiet contemplation. This is the great event toward which, it has been said, the whole of nature has conspired through countless ages—*the birth of the human soul*. It is the third outstanding achievement in earth's unfolding history and it represents the provision of a proper vehicle for the Divine Self for the "journey" into the worlds of manifestation. It must be understood, of course, that such expressions are purely symbolical for the journey is in consciousness only. Within the protective life currents of the Deity the initial unfolding has taken place and now there comes the actual time of transfer when direct divine control will be withdrawn from the lower triad and the monad—the True Self—will henceforth be, or will become, the guiding power behind the tremendous increase in all kinds of activity that will now develop.

Fig. 46 is an attempt to make clear the rather involved changes which take place at this stage, which is known as individualization. In Fig. 46A we see, in diagram, the condition of the group soul just before individualization occurs. The divine forces are flowing through the envelope of lower mental monadic essence, still protecting and nourishing the one triad within it. When the triad reaches its highest possible development the envelope begins to disintegrate and some of its molecules are resolved into matter of the next subdivision, which is actually of the higher mental world. This matter is then drawn toward the permanent nucleus of that world, which is called manas, and at once, it is said, manas is vitalized into a quick response (Fig. 46B). The result is that a definite link is then formed between the higher and lower triads and therefore between the monad and its six atomic nuclei, which now become one united whole. All is now ready for the next stage in the unfolding plan of monadic growth, which is shown in Fig. 46C.

However, in connection with this stage, let us look back to Fig. 45. In the extreme right of that diagram we see three lines extending downward from the vegetable, animal, and human kingdoms. These are to indicate the fact that, on the evolving arc, each kingdom of nature, as it raises the focal point of its activities, always retains its links with the lower or denser worlds. These links joining the consciousness in the various worlds into a unified expression of consciousness are found to be increasingly remarkable as unfoldment continues. In Fig. 46C we have, in outline, the human physical and psychic mechanism, ready to start out upon the experiences of human life.

It should hardly be necessary to say again, though perhaps the warning cannot be too often repeated, that *spatial arrangements, such as shown in Fig. 46, should be entirely disregarded* so far as actual conditions are concerned. A visual aid, such as this, is intended to make its contribution at the conceptual level and not at the level of the concrete mind. The drawing, like a map, shows in *symbol* the conditions that will be met with in actuality and, like a map, it will keep one from getting lost if it is followed. So the monad is shown as a triangle because, like a triangle, it has a threefold nature. It is shown above the permanent centers because they could not be shown all together without confusion. The various orders of matter are often depicted as being one above

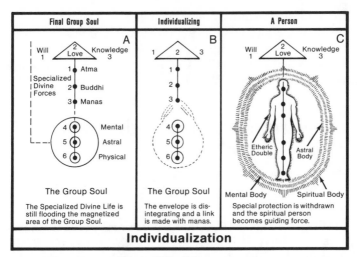

The Group Soul

The Specialized Divine Life is still flooding the magnetized area of the Group Soul.

The Group Soul

The envelope is disintegrating and a link is made with manas.

Special protection is withdrawn and the spiritual person becomes guiding force.

Individualization

Fig. 46

the other. This, of course, is done as a matter of convenience, for it would be impossible to show them interpenetrating, as they really are.

So, in order to convey the idea of subtler bodies (Fig. 46C), they are shown separately around the central area representing the etheric and dense physical bodies. But, as previously explained, although the subtler bodies extend further from the center than the dense physical body, they also interpenetrate it.

17

The Self and Its Bodies

On first contact, the idea that a person may possess more than one body is often considered to be strange, even fantastic. Nurtured in a mental atmosphere still strongly materialistic in spite of today's wider horizons of knowledge, we relegate that which is not seen or felt to a nebulous dream-world of fantasy far removed from practical considerations. However, for an introduction to the fact that we have a number of bodies, the doubter need not go beyond the physical world, nor further than the dissecting room, nor consult with any but those who have studied and know the physical body and the functioning of its many parts. For we have several bodies, right here in the physical world. More than that, these bodies are still insufficient for our needs, for as we know well, the great advances of the modern world have been brought about because we have made a host of supplementary devices which have extended the usefulness of our hands, increased the fleetness of our feet and enabled our eyes to see into space and to peer into the smaller things far beyond the limits of our normal vision. We cannot change the workings of our physical frame, but can use the inventiveness of our mind to extend our powers and break down many of the limits that nature has placed upon us. From a few simple, yet highly significant, facts we can draw deductions which will be of great assistance in this study.

First: What *is* our body? From the point of view of the chemist, it is an aggregation of chemicals which are combined together in a certain highly specialized manner. It has been taken in the laboratory and analyzed. Taken apart and reduced to its primary fragments it is found to consist of some twenty different elements, principally oxygen. This is followed by carbon, hydrogen, nitrogen, calcium and phosphorus in the proportions given. In very small quantities sulphur, sodium, chlorine, fluorine, potassium, iron, magnesium, silicon, zinc, arsenic, bromine, cobalt, copper and iodine, are also found (Fig. 47).

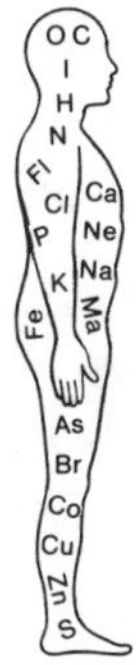

Chemically, Humans are Composed of ...

OXYGEN 72.00%
CARBON 13.40
HYDROGEN 9.10
NITROGEN 2.50
CALCIUM 1.30
PHOSPHORUS 1.25

And, in small quantities ...

Sulphur	Iron	Arsenic
Sodium	Magnesium,	Bromine
Chlorine	Silicon	Cobalt
Fluorine	Zinc	Copper
Potassium		Iodine

Are We Nothing More Than the Sum of These Elements?

The Chemical Human

Fig. 47

This same list has been expressed in a different manner, less scientific perhaps and yet essentially true:

Sugar enough to sweeten a hundred cups of coffee.
Lime enough to whitewash a small tool shed.
Iron enough for a one inch nail.
Magnesium enough for half a dozen flash bulbs.
Potassium enough to explode a toy cannon.
Sulphur enough to rid a dog of fleas.

Phosphorus enough to make twenty boxes of matches.
Fat enough to make a dozen bars of soap.
Copper enough to match a well-worn copper cent.
Water enough for a quick shower.

Suppose we take these chemicals and mix them to-gether. Trying a thousand different ways, would we find ideas growing out of them? We would not. Fashion them into the form of a person—trunk, limbs, head. Do we find that it thinks and moves and aspires to greater things? We know it would not. But we can take glass and copper and iron and assemble them into the complex structure we call a television receiving set. Does it then talk and sing and act? It does not. But, properly constructed, it will respond to invisible waves and will reproduce sound and action on the screen. In this same manner, much higher in the scale, God has assembled the human form, after millions of years of effort. It cannot give rise to the qualities of the subtler worlds, the material of which is specialized for the higher expressions of life, but it can and does respond to the invisible spiritual Self, and so shows forth our higher qualities and expressions in the physical world. How can a group of chemical elements, which in themselves hide nothing more than *energy*, suddenly develop the power to think and love when they are assembled together, unless it be that, so assembled, they become a *vehicle* through which such higher aspects can find expression?

When from the chemist we turn to the anatomist and physiologist we find that they have an entrancing story to tell. Though many ponderous tomes have been pro-duced on the subject of the human body and our knowl-edge grows richer as each day passes, yet still there are unfathomed mysteries which have defied elucidation. But amid the mass of knowledge that has been gained regarding it, there is one outstanding fact the significance of which has not been generally appreciated, but which should be self-evident to all. It is that *our physical body is not one, but several bodies.*

In Fig. 48, this fact is shown symbolically. From a maze of many parts, at least seven distinct bodies are clearly

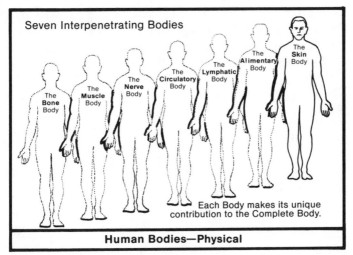

Seven Interpenetrating Bodies

The
Bone
Body

The
Muscle
Body

The
Nerve
Body

The
Circulatory
Body

The
Lymphatic
Body

The
Alimentary
Body

The
Skin
Body

Each Body makes its unique
contribution to the Complete Body.

Human Bodies—Physical

Fig. 48

seen to emerge. They are the bone body (1), the muscle body (2), the nerve body (3), the circulatory body (4), the lymphatic body (5), the alimentary body (6), and the skin body (7). Others might be shown by deeper study, but these are sufficient to show the principle involved, and to indicate clearly that the thing we call our physical body is actually a number of bodies, each one interpenetrating the others and making its own specific contribution to the welfare of the group.

The first to claim our attention is the bone body (1). This is made up of 206 parts and is a triumph of engineering design, giving rigidity combined with the essential joints and connections to permit freedom of movement. Weight for weight, the bones are stronger than the finest steel. The skull provides a strong protecting box for the brain which it encloses. The spine consists of twenty-six vertebral segments, with shock absorbing pads placed between them, and contains the vital nerve channel which is called the spinal cord. The ingeniously designed structure of the ribs protects the heart, lungs, and other organs within it with a strength that gives safety and yet permits the expansion and contraction of the lungs necessary for breathing. So strong is this body that each part could support many times the weight placed upon it. The shin bone, for example, can support a weight of 3,600 pounds, nearly thirty times the strength needed for a person of normal proportions. The marrow within the bones manufactures no less than 180,000,000 red blood cells every minute, or 260,000,000,000 every day. While the surface of the bones appears to be smooth at first glance, yet it is pierced by many tiny holes, through which arteries, veins, lymphatics, and nerves penetrate to its soft interior. This, briefly, is the bone body which gives support to all the other bodies, for without it they would be limp and useless. And into it, let it be noted, parts of the other bodies penetrate. But, by itself, it is inert and useless.

We shall now glance at the next, the muscle body (2), the main purpose of which is to give movement to the bones, but also to other parts of the corporate assembly. It is a dual body, for it has two major types of muscles—the voluntary and the involuntary. The first, as its designation would indicate, gives rise to movements which are under the direction of the mind; the other controls the internal commerce of the total body, such as the beating of the heart, the movements of the lungs, the propulsion of food substances through the avenues of digestion and a host of other duties. Just exactly *how* a finger is lifted or a foot is raised from the ground is an amazing process which still is not fully understood, though we shall gain a little insight as we proceed. Now let us assume that these two bodies, the bones and the muscles are placed together, every joint is made secure and every muscle is anchored in its appropriate place. We have now the mechanism for movement, but no movement takes place. We need telephone wires to dispatch the controlling messages to every point of the body from head to foot.

We now come to consider the nerve body (3) and again we find a twin system; in fact there are several minor divisions also. The two major nerve systems are the central (or cerebrospinal) and the sympathetic, the former controlling the conscious functions and the latter the subconscious or bodily activities. Perhaps of all the bodies this is the most important, if indeed one can be singled out for that designation. It is essentially the specialized vehicle of consciousness. Through it all sense impressions are received. We might feel awed if we were to inspect the hundreds of wires that enter a large telephone exchange and are sorted out and lead an orderly arrangement of sensitive instruments. But the telephone system within our own body is almost infinitely more complex than the largest telephone exchange ever built. A modern computer or electronic "brain" with many computer chips can attempt to emulate but never come close to the function of the human brain in which there are more than 12,000,000,000 nerve cells. The total length of nerves in the body would stretch for thousands of miles.

Let us join all these together, link them with the proper areas of action, ready to carry the messages with lightning speed to every corner of the bodies. But while we now have all the mechanism for action and the wires to carry the messages, no action takes place. Neither would there be any action in a telephone exchange until the electric current was flowing over the wires. Our man is still far from complete. Bones, muscles, nerves; but we must find the power to flood the nerves before messages can be dispatched. Before doing this, however, we should consider the fact that these bodies must at all times be carefully and effectively maintained.

Therefore we will now learn something about the circulatory body (4), which carries the blood stream throughout the entire physical body, taking food to the cells and carrying waste matter away. It consists of the arteries which carry fresh blood from the heart, and the veins which carry the impurities back into the lungs. Between these two, linking them together, are the capillaries, little tubes so astonishingly tiny that the greater part of them is not visible to the naked eye. It is said that the entire length of the whole circulatory system is not less than 60,000 miles, which is about two and a half times around the world! This system must take care of the needs of billions of cells, providing each one with its exact requirements. The central pumping station—the heart—pumps a total of 4,000 gallons of blood around the body every day. And in a normal life span it will beat two and a half thousand million times without stopping until the final beat marks the end of its activities.

But a point of outstanding interest is mentioned by Dr. E. H. Pratt, in his book, *The Composite Man*. He draws attention to the fact that, if the circulatory system could be isolated from the rest of the composite man, then since part of it would be visible and part would become gradually finer until it disappeared into the invisible, *the body would have the appearance of being surrounded by a halo*!

Another body, not so well know, but of equal importance to the others, is the lymphatic body (5). It is closely associated with the circulatory body, its larger members following the course of the arteries and veins, and the smaller ones, the capillaries. Like the circulatory body, it penetrates every portion of the collection of material shapes; however, unlike it, this body carries lymph. It might be called the "drainage system" of the body. It collects lymph, which has exuded from the capillaries in all parts of the body into the tissues, providing a cleansing action and carrying it back again into the venous blood stream near to the heart.

The next body is called, for convenience, the alimentary body (6), for it consists of the long tube that starts from the mouth, continues along to the stomach and then through the small and the large intestines. Also the breath tube should be included: the larnyx, trachea and bronchial tree. While these tubes are not as extensive as the other bodies, their ramifications and effects are felt everywhere. In the first-mentioned, food is absorbed and prepared for assimilation and in the second, of course, is the ever-active breathing device which oxygenates the blood and expels waste matter into the air.

The last of the physical bodies to be considered is the skin body (7), for we are now ready to enclose the collection in the one which will unite them and trace the outer limits of the group. Needless to say, this body is highly necessary in order to protect the others from invasion by foreign substances and also from interference with their many and varied functions. It keeps the moisture within the total body from excessive evaporation and assists in regulating its temperature. It well illustrates the instability of the physical body, for though it has many layers, they are constantly being renewed and the old material is being pushed upward to the outer layers where it appears as a microscopic scale which is dissipated into space. It is estimated that the whole of the skin body with all its layers is entirely renewed every two years.

Now we have bones and muscles and nerves. We have the arteries and veins, the lymphatics and the organs of digestion and respiration and the skin is enclosing them all. Apparently, we have a complete person. But the apparent is not true. We have the appearance of a person, that is all. For this thing is inert, it is helpless, it is dead. All we have is a collection of chemical elements assembled in a certain highly ingenious manner. But it has no power of animation. It cannot feel or think. It has no vitality, no intelligence, much less any of the really beautiful spiritual qualities which often are found in the human race. Though the brain is there it cannot think. Though the muscles are there they cannot move. Though the nervous system is there not a single message is passing over its wires. Though the heart is there it does not beat. Though there are lips and tongue, they do not speak. Is it not clear that this is a body, not a person? It is a machine, but the operator is missing.

Science tries to endow physical matter with super-physical qualities and powers. Yet there is the physical matter, every atom of it. Chemically it is complete. But all the higher attributes are missing. How can those higher things be contained within the physical substance? Such a materialistic outlook as this leads to problems which defy solution. Theosophy tells of the super-physical orders of matter, specialized for just those forces, and gives a logical, understandable answer that breaks through the impasse that science has reached.

There must be more than the purely physical. There *is* more. Science as yet has not penetrated far enough into the invisible, so we turn to Theosophy to learn of the subtler bodies that we possess, which function in cooperation with the physical body. We have seen that we have several bodies of physical matter. Each makes its own specific contribution to the family of bodies. We have also seen that they interpenetrate each other. They are not separate as shown in Fig. 48, as we well know: that is merely symbolic and expresses an idea. We have also seen that there are parts of the physical body that are visible and parts that are invisible, except that the invisible parts may be rendered visible by an extension of our powers of physical eyesight, which in this case is accomplished by the use of a microscope. All these things apply, also, to the subtler bodies which we shall now go on to consider. For convenience it will be necessary to show them separately, but they all interpenetrate. Each one has its own specific contribution to make to the family of bodies. At least one of them has been observed by purely scientific methods, and experimental evidence of others is available. Except for the next one we shall study, they are all invisible to normal eyesight. And, as it was seen that the circulatory body, if separated from the others, would appear to be surrounded by a halo, so we find the subtler bodies showing around the exterior of their denser companion in just the same manner. As the unseen parts of the physical body may be seen by using a microscope to extend physical vision, so the unseen superphysical bodies can and have been seen by those who, in the course of hastened evolutionary processes, have developed extended sense organs which penetrate the superphysical worlds.

These facts regarding our superphysical bodies are logical extensions of those which apply to the physical body. This does not mean that they rest only upon logical deductions, for they are known by many to be true. But truth can always be tested by reason, and we can take and test them in that way.

The next body we shall consider is the etheric or vital body. It interpenetrates the family of physical shapes and extends as an aura for some distance beyond its periphery (Fig. 49). An inner aura terminates an inch

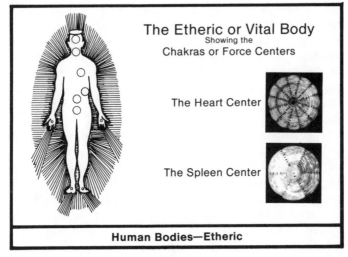

The Etheric or Vital Body
Showing the
Chakras or Force Centers

The Heart Center

The Spleen Center

Human Bodies—Etheric

Fig. 49

or so around the physical vehicle, varying a little in different parts. This body is the power supply of the system. It absorbs energy from the sun and spreads it over the nerves. It provides forces and energies related to electricity which flow through the nervous system and contribute to the overall vitality of the body, including the nervous system itself. The chemical metabolism of the body provides primarily maintenance of tissue, heat, and muscle contraction. That total response and vitality which distinguishes the animal from the vegetable requires something more, which is provided by the etheric body. It may be linked to the chemical processes through the generation and movement of electricity in tissues and nerves. Our main supply of vitality comes from the sun and is absorbed into the etheric body through a specialized etheric organ within it. In his book *Man, Visible and Invisible*, C. W. Leadbeater describes the appearance of this body. Vitality or *prana* is taken into it and, after it has completed its vitalizing activities, is projected outward in straight lines from the pores of the skin. Leadbeater describes it as "bluish-white" and as "having the appearance of being striated." This phrase is interesting in view of the fact that, about ten years later, Dr. Walter B. Kilner of St. Mary's Hospital, London, published a book entitled *The Human Aura* in which he described observations he had made of the aura—obviously the etheric body—for diagnostic purposes. Ability to see this body was induced by the use of slides made from dicyanin dyes in a solution of alcohol. Such a result is possible because, it will be realized, etheric substances are still of the physical world and, therefore, amenable to physical laws. In his book, it is interesting to note, Dr. Kilner refers to what he calls the "inner aura" (Leadbeater calls it the "health aura") and says that it is "striated." The author of this book had several opportunities of using screens made by Dr. Kilner and can vouch for the fact that they did make the etheric body plainly visible.

Within the etheric body itself, there are several force centers or etheric organs known as *chakras*. The existence of these chakras has been known for centuries, and they are described in many occult books throughout the East, particularly in Hindu sacred writings. Six of them are indicated in Fig. 49. They arise in the etheric portion of nerve centers within the spine but terminate in circular depressions, somewhat like the flower of the convolvulus or morning-glory vine. Each one is a center of intense activity. Two of them deal particularly with the physical body. The others are primarily links with the subtler bodies, bringing their forces to manifest in the dense material, as we shall shortly see. One center, not indicated, is at the back of the body over the extreme lower end of the spine. It is specialized to absorb a force known as *kundalini* that emanates from the earth and gives life to the organs of the body. This force is at present unknown to science.

The second center, situated over the spleen, is specialized to receive vitality or *prana* from the sun. In this center prana is split up and distributed to various parts of the body, vitalizing the many nerve centers and causing a flow of ethers over the physical nerves. The other centers, as we shall see, are links by means of which forces from the subtler bodies are expressed through the physical body.

So, here is the vital body. We shall place it over the others and the nerves will become "alive" and our bodily telephone system can be put into operation. We now have the physical mechanism for motion with, in addition, the vitality to produce the motion. Messages can now be sent by the brain to all parts of the denser vehicle. Action can be ordered and the multitude of subconscious operations of the body can be set in action. But there is more to us than mere vitality. We are vastly greater than an automaton moving and acting without a glimmer of understanding about it all. We can feel. We can think, hope, love, and even turn our mind to contact the sacred realm of spiritual aspirations. Action is an end product of all these greater things. An automaton moves. But we move with purpose and that makes all the difference.

We must go further. We have the physical mechanism and the vital body which gives it life and animation. But it is a heartless, senseless thing that we have produced. It has organs of sense, but it cannot use them. It does not know the fragrance of flowers or the inspiration brought by the odor of the pines. It has lips and tongue and vocal cords, but it cannot utter a word. Each of its eyes has half a million nerve fibers leading to the brain and several million rods and cones to receive light impressions from the retina which have been transformed into electrical impulses, but there is no consciousness of the glories that vision brings. The ears are ready to catch the sounds around it—ear drum, anvil, all nature's amazing devices—but only vibrations reach the awaiting mechanism, and there is nothing to turn them into the sweet cadences of melodious sound that we can contact and respond to with ecstatic joy. To supply this need Theosophy will now take us beyond the physical realms entirely and, to the collection of the vehicles of human consciousness that we have assembled, we must add three more so that the human being may stand complete.

In Plate I (Fig. 50) we are introduced to these three vehicles, the astral, mental, and spiritual bodies. These illustrations are monochrome copies of full page color plates in the book *Man, Visible and Invisible*, which has been mentioned previously. The three orders of matter corresponding to these superphysical bodies have been described and are illustrated in Fig. 20. Each body is shown in three stages of its evolution. The qualities of these higher bodies are expressed in colors, a subject which is a deep study in itself and is dealt with extensively in the book from which the illustrations are taken. In the astral body of a less evolved person, a broad band of brown red indicates the presence of sensuality. Dull scarlet tells of anger, and other colors, dull and muddy, tell of other undesirable traits. It is obviously unorganized and loosely built. In the astral body of the average person, there is evidence of improved organization and, therefore, the colors are in more orderly arrangement. In the highly developed person they are vastly improved and a great deal of yellow around the head indicates that the emotions and desires have been brought under control of the mind.

Looking at the mental body of one less evolved, we see little development. However, some yellow at the top indicates a slight amount of mental ability. Some improvement is shown in the case of the average person and, in one of high development, advanced mental powers are evident. All the colors are much more refined and delicate, and the yellow of intellect is displayed in great strength, to which is added actual beauty of appearance.

The spiritual bodies show corresponding progress. However, in the earlier stages of their evolution there

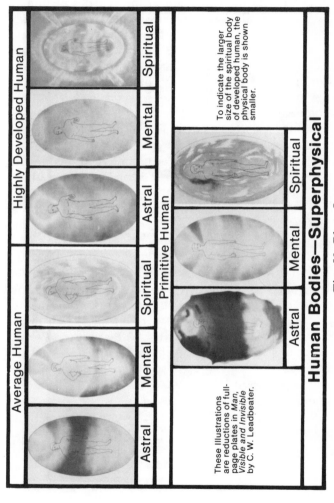

Fig. 50. Plate I

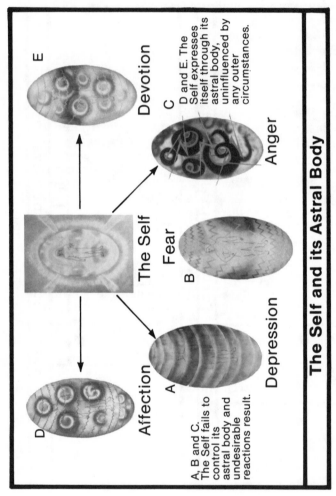

E

Devotion

C

D and E. The Self expresses itself through its astral body, uninfluenced by any outer circumstances.

Anger

The Self

Fear

B

Affection

D

A

Depression

A, B and C. The Self fails to control its astral body and undesirable reactions result.

The Self and its Astral Body

Fig. 51. Plate II

are no unpleasant colors; there is only a lack of color. *For there are no evil qualities in the spiritual vehicle; only the absence of good ones.* This lack is made up with lavish generosity as evolution proceeds, as the illustrations may show, though very inadequately. Regarding the spiritual (or causal) body of the advanced person, Leadbeater writes:

> Composed of matter inconceivably fine, delicate and etherial, intensely active and pulsating with living fire, the Causal body becomes, as its evolution proceeds, a radiant globe of flashing colours, its high vibrations sending ripples of changing hues over its surface—hues of which earth knows nothing—brilliant, soft and luminous. . . . How hopeless it seems to try to represent all this glory on paper! Yet our artist has skilfully contrived to suggest that which no brush could paint, and, however far even the cleverest image may be from that transcendent reality, it at least gives our imagination a starting point from which we may try to build a conception.

As stated in the above quotation, it is obviously impossible to give more than a feeble representation of the subtler bodies for the least attractive of them all, the astral body, is more vivid and vital and glowing with life than anything we can know in these physical realms of consciousness. They are not only beautiful but, especially in the higher stages of development, full of radiating power. They are living, vital, iridescent things, which can never be portrayed in static form. Seldom at rest, they change their appearance from moment to moment, showing new facets of their latent powers, sometimes startling in their suddenness and dramatic in their appearance, with passing emotions and thoughts, aimless or purposeful, that are constantly passing through the mind. With the spiritual body it is different. Its steady, powerful radiations sometimes glow with a greater intensity and glory than at others, but as time goes by it becomes an object of transcendental magnificence.

When colors are mentioned, it should be realized that the reference is to the color in the subtler substance which corresponds to the one we know in the physical world and is in consonance with it, but one or more "octaves" higher according to the matter in which it is being expressed.

A realization of these facts, together with the help of the illustrations, should give some idea of the reality of the human bodies, each one more charged with power and showing more strength of color than those of the world less subtle than itself.

So now we have the Self in the causal body, showing through it the spiritual powers that have been developed. This is what the Christian would call the soul. In theosophical literature it is frequently referred to as the ego. This spiritual or causal body, in our present state of evolution, expresses through appropriate channels the forces of will and love, as well as the higher reasoning powers. It also is a storehouse for the knowledge we gain throughout the normal period of human evolution. When in incarnation in the physical world, the mental body thinks, gathers information, analyzes it, and expresses creative abilities. The astral body can feel and desire, and the physical body is a vehicle for action. Through each of these we become conscious of the world to which they correspond.

Each of the bodies grows by use. The physical body grows through the exercise of its various faculties. So do the higher bodies. Use or abuse, action or neglect, will raise or lower the quality and responsiveness of the bodies. We know of this effect in the physical world. In Plate II (Fig. 52) we see illustrated the effects of certain emotions upon the astral body. Similar conditions apply to the mental body. These illustrations, are reproductions from the same source as Plate I. Plate IIA shows the effects of a deep fit of depression upon the astral body. Dull grey bands begin to form around the body, gradually transforming it into a kind of prison house of dejection if the condition is allowed to continue. In the extreme case which is shown, the other colors of the body have become almost totally obscured and the person becomes a veritable prisoner within the astral vehicle. Gradually the condition will improve as time passes and more normal circumstances claim attention. But the body will not be quite the same, for some of the grey matter which was drawn into it will remain, making it easier to repeat similar conditions. The same principle will apply to the cases shown in Plate IIB and IIC. The effects of fear are somewhat akin to those of depression. But here, rather than showing as a steady deadening effect, fear will cause grey horizontal lines to vibrate with great agitation and almost to obscure the normal colors of the body. This, too, passes and almost normal conditions will once more prevail as the fear subsides. Each such disturbance, however, will leave the body a little more prone to succumb to fear because of the kind of matter that is built into it.

Anger is another violent emotion that can cause great havoc within the astral body. Plate IIC shows the results of an intense fit of anger. Coils and vortices of blackness and vivid flashes of lurid red light almost obscure the normal coloring of the body, not only harming the body itself, but also the physical vehicle through which it will ultimately be expressed. The individual expressing such a murderous emotion as this must have given way to anger many times before, otherwise the body could not produce such violent eruptions of malice and hatred. Knowing these facts, it is well to give heed to signs of danger and to overcome the difficulty before it becomes too powerful to be surmounted and nature's drastic methods must intervene.

Note particularly that, as stated in the illustrations, *it is not the spiritual Self who gets angry, or feels depressed, or is fearful.* The person fails to control the astral body, and these conditions are allowed to occur as uncontrolled reactions to stimuli from outer conditions. Careful analysis of the conditions of our consciousness at such a time will often, probably invariably, reveal that there is an inner voice, the voice of the Self, which is vainly trying to be heard above the violent reactions of the body and desperately trying to control the body and to bring it back to a condition of balance.

Looking on the brighter side of things, we see in Plate

IID the effect produced upon the astral body by the Self expressing itself as pure affection, and in Plate IIE as intense devotion. Rose color predominates in the former, for that is the color in which affection clothes itself, while blue, the color of devotion, is more pronounced in the latter. In each of these cases the vibrating parallel lines indicate an intensely concentrated emotional condition, but the coils or vortices show a pouring out from the Self toward the object with which the emotions are identified. In contrast to the three undesirable conditions shown in A, B and C, it should be noted that D and E are examples of direct action by the Self through its astral vehicle. Such effects within the body raise its level and quality so that it will the better show forth the beauties of the Self on future occasions. In many ways the astral body is drawn upward or downward and its present degree of unfoldment in any person is a balance sheet of all his efforts of the past, for good or ill. Fortunately, an effort expended in the subtler kinds of matter, associated with the highest emotions or thoughts, produces more effect than a similar effort exerted in substances of a grosser kind, just as a given amount of energy used to walk through the air with feet upon the ground, would result in a greater distance being covered than by an equivalent amount expended in an attempt to walk on the ocean bed through the water. Gradually, by many such activities, the Self and its bodies are going forward on the pathway of life, each improving as time rolls along.

Now that the subject of subtler bodies has been introduced, we can consider some further information about the chakras, for they perform highly important functions, both in bodily health and in the evolution of the human consciousness. Each chakra performs a dual function within the body. It absorbs life and energy and also acts as a transformer by means of which vital forces generated within the body are changed in intensity so that they can be expressed through a denser vehicle, in precisely the same manner as electrical energy can be transformed from one electrical potential to another.

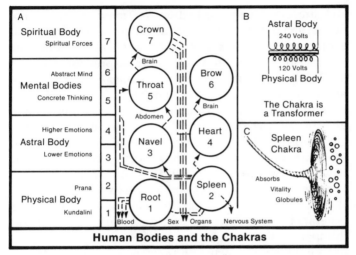

Fig. 52

In Fig. 52B we have shown a conventional symbol for such a transformer. Heavy machinery, for example, as used in a factory, would be 240 volts or higher, but for the more restricted needs of the home this might be reduced to 120 volts. To use the higher voltage directly with equipment designed for the lower, would quickly cause damage and finally destruction. Reference to Fig. 29 again will show why it is possible to reproduce emotional creations of the astral body within the physical, for it will at once be seen that the physical atom stands unique in that it has within it matter of all the other worlds and therefore it can express the life of those worlds, though in a more restricted measure. The chakra reduces the intensity of the force to the more restricted possibilities of physical matter. This same fact applies to any of the higher bodies in its relationship to the vehicles of consciousness lower or denser than itself. Once more in the physical world we find the keys that also apply to the superphysical, for the same laws exist at all levels.

In Fig. 52A these force centers are listed, as they appear in action in the etheric body. The first two are primarily concerned with the physical body, bringing it health and strength. The third and fourth transform emotional forces generated within the astral body into physical expression. Numbers five and six transform thoughts and reasoning into physical brain expression and the seventh brings into physical consciousness the spiritual forces of the person. Their appearance, as previously explained, looking at them on the surface of the etheric body, is somewhat like that of a convolvulus or morning-glory vine, though with wheel-like extensions beyond the limits of the flower, as shown in Fig. 52C. Each one, however, varies from the others in the number of "spokes" to be seen in the wheel-like extensions and in the flower-shaped hub of the wheel. In each one currents are generated which swirl around, weaving under and over the spokes in turn, giving it the appearance of the bottom of a circular basket but with the depression in the center.

In addition to the food we eat, and the water we drink, the physical body absorbs forces from the etheric atmosphere which surrounds us. One of these forces comes from the earth and has been called *kundalini*; the other comes from the sun. It is *prana* or vitality. Neither of these has yet been recognized by science, though the latter seems to be suspected by some scientists. Kundalini has a number of different levels of expression, but the one we are considering now is the lowest and densest of them all. It affects the physical construction of the dense body, giving it health and functional vigor. Those who dig in the earth, the farmers and the gardeners, know of the feeling of well-being that such an intimate contact with the soil can bring. This force is absorbed by the root chakra which is situated near to the lower end of the spine and opens out at the surface of the etheric body (Fig. 52A No. 1). After absorption and internal action, the kundalini rises up the spine and is distributed throughout the nerves of the body. It also acts upon the bloodstream and the sex organs. This chakra receives also a specialized type of prana from the spleen center which is redistributed along with the flow of kundalini and plays a highly important part when one comes to higher levels of development.

Prana comes to us directly from the sun. It is the active power in producing all vital phenomena. In physical world manifestation it clothes itself in a particularly bright little particle consisting of seven ultimate physical atoms (or *anu*). This has been called the "vitality globule." It is seen by many who do not realize what it is, for these little bright particles are present in the atmosphere on any sunny day, darting hither and thither with great speed. They are most easily seen when facing away from the sun and looking into a blue sky. Prana, in the form of the vitality globule, is absorbed by the spleen center, situated close to the physical organ so named. In this center, prana is specialized into seven different streams, arising from the seven ultimate atoms which enter into the formation of the vitality globule. These streams show themselves as different colors within the body, which closely resemble the seven colors of the spectrum. As shown in Fig. 52A, the spleen chakra sends two streams of specialized prana to the throat center. They are blue and violet in color, but before reaching their destination they join and enter the throat chakra as one stream. Two others, in color dark red and orange, go to the root center. But these also join and enter the root chakra as one. A fifth kind, yellow, goes to the heart center, a sixth to the navel center. This one is green. A seventh, rose color, is distributed throughout the entire nervous system.

The root chakra has four spokes and the spleen chakra, six. As will be noted from Fig. 52A-1,2, their main function is to bring life and vitality to the dense physical body. These forces are absorbed into the body from the atmosphere. The spleen chakra is illustrated in Fig. 52C.

The next two, it will be seen, are transformers by means of which emotional forces are reproduced in physical expression, the navel center (Fig. 52A-3), dealing with the lower and more primitive astral feelings, such as anger, fear, greed and irritability. We all know well how these things are actually felt in the pit of the stomach over the solar plexus and near to this chakra. The higher emotions, such as love, devotion, and sympathy find their expression through the transformer action of the heart center (Fig. 52A-4). Again, it is not difficult to feel that chakra in action as such emotions enter the body to find physical expression. The navel chakra has ten spokes and the heart chakra has twelve. The throat center, we note in Fig. 52A-5, brings into physical expression the activities of the mental body, linking concrete thought with the physical brain. This center vitalizes particularly the vocal organs and the thought centers of speech as a physical expression of concrete thinking. It has sixteen spokes.

It will have been observed that the number of spokes in the centers has been gradually increasing: from four in the root center to sixteen in the throat center. But when we come to consider the next (Fig. 52A-6), the brow chakra, we find something obviously different from all the others we have considered so far. For it has no less than ninety-six spokes. This becomes understandable when we realize that we have now passed from the mortal bodies to connect with the causal or spiritual body, which is immortal and remains with the person throughout many incarnations. And in the crown chakra (Fig. 52A-7) we have an even greater jump, for it has 960 spokes with an inner central hub which has twelve spokes, making a total of 972. This chakra is a center for the transforming of the highest spiritual inspirations down into physical consciousness and as a guide for spiritual action. These two are connected with the etheric portions of the pituitary body and pineal gland within the brain.

While kundalini and prana are necessary for the physical well-being and vital activities of the dense physical body, it could not function without the forces which come into it through the chakras from the astral and mental bodies. When these forces are withdrawn, the physical body, robbed of their supporting influence, dies. But to be truly a person, the spiritual forces must be there also, for these constitute the outstanding difference between the human and subhuman species. It is in the higher mental and spiritual worlds that the greatest progress will be made as evolution proceeds, and therefore these two centers will assume a widening significance as time passes. There will come a time when kundalini will unfold its higher potencies and, passing up the spine, it will stimulate all the centers into increased activity and continue on to produce far reaching effects in the brow and crown chakras, endowing the person in physical consciousness with the power to express spiritual manifestations far beyond anything hitherto accomplished.

The chakras exist in each of the bodies, the centers being coincident, but the outermost parts stretch further because of the larger size of the subtler bodies. They perform similar functions, though modified by the nature of the vehicle itself. However, each one is a transformer of force, the contiguous surfaces acting by induction to effect the transformation, exactly as the coils of an electrical transformer induce a current over space without actual contact. Thus, in the physical world the vehicles of consciousness are, as it were, welded into one and, though modified and limited by the transition, in the physical body we can express the whole range of consciousness that our several vehicles of consciousness cover.

Here, then, we find an answer to many of the deep problems of human nature. But still, to many, only the visible and tangible can possibly be true. Therefore we now turn for a while to examine some of this so-called visible and tangible evidence and see if it will stand or fall in the light of a little critical analysis.

It must be admitted that the physical body has an objective existence that appears to possess a high degree of permanence. Our senses tell us that it remains the same from day to day and only as the years go by does change creep in by slow degrees, gradually dimming the luster of its youth. These things are what the senses tell us, *but they are not true.* The body does not remain the same day after day. On the contrary, it changes with every passing moment. Perhaps many of us are aware of this fact, but have not followed it to its logical conclusion. We know that the body is made up of countless millions of cells, which are specialized for various functions and are nourished from the food we eat after it has been modified by internal chemical action to make it suitable for the needs of cell life. In this manner those tiny lives are sustained. They grow, they multiply, and they die. Far from being a stable entity, the body is changing from moment to moment (Fig. 53A), for as cells are being born, others, in equal numbers, are dying and are being eliminated from the system through the pores of the skin and the breath as it is exhaled from the lungs. Generation after generation, within the body, there is constant birthing and dying, there is coming and going, association and disassociation. And while *we* are living *our* complex lives in the world, solving *our* problems, overcoming *our* difficulties and being tested and tried mentally and spiritually, body cells are being born and are dying so that, science tells us, within a space of seven years, the old group of cells that made up the body has gone, or the material has been entirely changed, and a new group has taken their place. Actually, then, *we do not now have the same body we had seven years ago.* How could *we* possibly be the body, when it has gone *and we remain.* So, as we note in Fig. 53A, the body is a continuously changing aggregation of cells, while

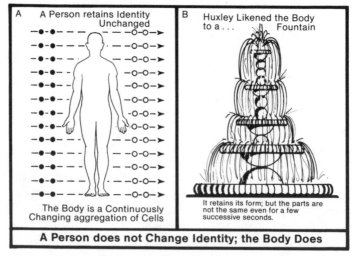

A   A Person retains Identity
      Unchanged

The Body is a Continuously
Changing aggregation of Cells

B   Huxley Likened the Body
      to a . . .   Fountain

It retains its form; but the parts are
not the same even for a few
successive seconds.

A Person does not Change Identity; the Body Does

Fig. 53

the person retains identity unchanged from birth until death.

Carrying this thought to a point which obviously is a *reductio ad absurdum* and yet can hardly be denied, if we think of ourselves as the body, then our ancestry can be traced back no further than to many packages, neatly stacked upon the shelves of a lot of grocery stores, marked "rice" and "peas" and "flour" or other similar edibles, or displayed in baskets of fruit or vegetables. We might also remind ourselves that many of the atoms we are now harboring were, in all probability, parts of the physical vehicle of some long departed ancestor; and even more of them once belonged to creatures of much humbler lineage who perished in the battle for existence before we were born. But surely the real absurdity is to believe that the body, which is not a permanent thing but only an area which harbors for a while myriads of tiny lives, transient guests of an unseen host, which entirely changes its identity several times during a normal span of earthly life, is the true reality, and that this unstable structure, evanescent, fleeting and insecure, actually called into existence the spiritual being that, in vivid contrast, will maintain a continuity of identity and consciousness throughout all these changes, from birth to death. And when death does come and the voice speaks no more, and the body ceases to function as it did, there will remain every particle of matter which was there immediately before the change. So that which has gone, not being material, must be immaterial, and since the material which is left cannot animate its own members, then that which departed most surely must have been the animating factor before the change. Years ago we did not have the wonderful knowledge about the body that we have today and such facts as we have been dwelling on were unknown. It is strange that those who did such magnificent work should persist in denying the obvious import of their own discoveries.

Not only does the spiritual Self maintain an identity amid perpetual change, but it is the presiding genius which issues orders to its mortal partner, and provides it with food.

Huxley likened the human body to a fountain (Fig. 53B) which maintains a continuity of outline, yet whose parts do not remain the same for even a few successive seconds.

Another way in which we can survey this subject is to examine the essential nature of each of these things— the one material, the other spiritual. In Fig. 54 we see placed side by side for easy comparison the powers possessed by a cell and by a person. While a cell (Fig. 54A) can absorb oxygen, built its constituents from food, select needed chemical elements from environment, and cooperate with other cells to build the wonderful structure of the body, a person can do none of these things. A person (Fig. 54B), rather than being interested in absorbing oxygen is continually gaining knowledge. Instead of metabolizing food, it is developing wisdom from knowledge gained and the many experiences through which it passes. Our environmental interests do not turn to the processes of chemical selections and rejections, but to choosing our surroundings and to controlling our mental and emotional reactions toward them. In place of physical adaptations within the body toward our outer circumstances we endeavor to condition our mind and feelings so that we can harmonize with those circumstances and live with a maximum degree of comfort and happiness. Rather than being concerned with improving details of body structure, we gradually develop social and religious institutions by means of which we may meet with others in mental and spiritual harmony with the hope, already arising in the minds of many, of ultimately gathering the whole of humankind into a spiritual unity.

The ideas which have been presented, drawn from theosophical sources, regarding the human bodies, are claimed by some to be known as facts by direct observation. However, though we may not yet be able to expand our consciousness to that level, we can take these ideas and analyze them in the light of reason, the greatest

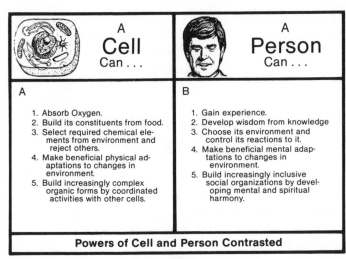

A **Cell** Can...	A **Person** Can...
A	**B**
1. Absorb Oxygen. 2. Build its constituents from food. 3. Select required chemical elements from environment and reject others. 4. Make beneficial physical adaptations to changes in environment. 5. Build increasingly complex organic forms by coordinated activities with other cells.	1. Gain experience. 2. Develop wisdom from knowledge 3. Choose its environment and control its reactions to it. 4. Make beneficial mental adaptations to changes in environment. 5. Build increasingly inclusive social organizations by developing mental and spiritual harmony.
Powers of Cell and Person Contrasted	

Fig. 54

gift that God has bestowed upon humankind, and especially compare them with the idea held by the materialists that all the human expressions of love and hate, of bravery and fear, of inspiration and depression, that all the genius which is gradually conquering the universe itself, which has developed step by step in achievement after achievement over billions of years, arose without any kind of guidance whatsoever, by an infinitude of repetitions of purest chance, out of twenty simple chemical elements from which the very people who take such an incredible attitude have never succeeded in releasing anything more than *energy* of one kind or another.

18

Elemental Essence and the Elemental Kingdoms

Elemental essence is living matter of the higher and lower mental and astral worlds. It is that part of the original substance of each of those worlds, originally created by the first outpouring of divine creative energy, which has been acted upon by the second outpouring and is, therefore, amenable to being shaped into living forms. From it, all the living things of these worlds have been made. Of this essence C. W. Leadbeater, writing in *The Inner Life* (Vol. 2, page 113), says:

> The evolution of the Elemental Essence is to learn to respond to all possible rates of undulations . . . until at last a stage will be reached when all the particles of the essence shall be ready to answer at any moment to any possible rate of vibration, and that will be the completion of its evolution.

In each of these worlds the essence is being acted upon and is producing an immense variety of living things, since it exists in each of the molecular subdivisions of the matter of each of the worlds and is further modified by the seven basic atomic types previously referred to and also by innumerable further subdivisions. Outstanding in each of these worlds are two types or groups of living forms which have been mentioned previously, but which, it can now be shown, react upon each other in a manner which is of very great importance to everyone. Without this knowledge, basic urges which arise within our bodies can go unchecked, but with it we can understand what is taking place and can act accordingly, to our great advantage.

The first group is composed of the many forms of the elemental kingdoms, or elementals. These have been referred to before. They are involving into denser matter, ever seeking lower and coarser and more enduring substances with which to build their forms. From the third elemental kingdom, as we have seen, that life goes on into the mineral, where it finds its nadir of expression (Fig. 34). From that point onward the life is *evolving* and, as shown in Fig. 34, it climbs "upward" through the subtler worlds. That leads to the second group or type, which is that of the astral, mental, and causal human bodies, and to a lesser degree the subtler bodies of the vegetable and animal creations. These human bodies are formed of the various kinds of elemental essence, as are the members of the elemental kingdoms. But, unlike them, the human body is *evolving* (Plate 1), while the elemental forms are *involving*. It should be realized that the various colors we see in the bodies are of the different types of elemental essence, which have been drawn into them from time to time (Plate II), in response to the various emotions or thoughts which have arisen within them, whether good or ill. As explained before, each emotion or thought leaves the body a little higher or lower as the case may be and so, generally, the bodies improve as time goes on, for the life within them is on the evolving arc.

The relationship that exists between these two groups which exist in the mental and astral worlds leads us to the problem of self-control, though this phrase we shall see is not well chosen, for how can we—the Self—control the Self? We really mean "body control." One of the most important duties before us is to develop control of our bodies, for they are living things and they can get out of hand. We should train our bodies so that they respond to our commands at all times. We saw illustrated in Plate II the fact that depression, fear and anger were produced by the failure of the Self to control the reactions of the astral body to the stimuli of outer circumstances. It was pointed out, too, that each such condition, while of a temporary nature, would leave the body a little changed, because the violence of the emotion would draw into it elemental essence of a correspondingly low quality to express that emotion and, while normal conditions would finally be restored, some of that material would remain.

But the question arises, why should we be the victims of such outbursts as these, in spite of the fact that we so often fight with real determination against them? The answer to that puzzling question lies in an understanding of the elemental activities. If *we* do not control our body it can, and possibly will, be taken over by some elemental form in the vicinity (Fig. 55). *Elementals are seeking always to prolong their existence as separate living things by taking lodging in a human shape, which can be vitalized into a violence or to a depth not to be matched by any other living forms.* An outburst of anger or a fit of depression in the astral body as a reaction to some outer circumstance, a blow returned for a blow, hatred aroused by

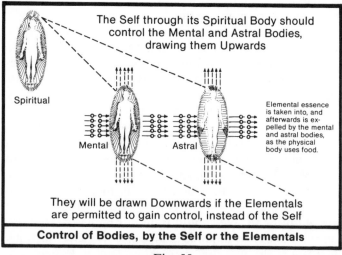

Control of Bodies, by the Self or the Elementals

Fig. 55

injury, all take place because the Self does not control the actions of its vehicle. This leaves the body wide open for the entrance of an elemental, drawn by magnetic attraction, which will magnify the original outburst many times, to the fierce delight of the elemental itself which glories in the vibrations of such primitive passions. No doubt each one of us has had some experience of such an event. We know how we fought against it, clearly indicating that it was not of our creation, and we have felt, as a foreign element within us, the excited satisfaction of the elemental life with the very thing that we have been striving against.

Another fact to remember is that all our so-called lower bodies are unstable insofar as their material constituents are concerned. This fact is shown in Fig. 53 with reference to the physical body. But as indicated in Fig. 55, this fact applies to the astral and mental bodies too. And therein lies the possibility of improvement, for by selection and purification we can make them healthy and strong and of ever-increasing value to us as instruments of consciousness and activity. As the physical body takes in food and water to renew what it lost as waste, so the astral and mental bodies are continually taking in elemental essence (which we can think of as the organic substances of the appropriate worlds), for the same purpose. Thus with beauty of character, purity of emotions and mental alertness will come a corresponding improvement in the bodies, which will draw from the higher types of matter to permit their expression. As this takes place, the lower material is expelled, and the bodies are continually changing for better or worse.

This is a vast subject, and one which is still far from being fully understood, but by knowing the underlying principles we can work out methods of application for ourselves. Many of the abnormal conditions of our mental and emotional nature, the psychoses and neuroses with which we are afflicted, can be explained when the relationship between the elemental and human kingdoms is realized. Another revealing phase of this subject will be considered when we come to a study of reincarnation.

In Fig. 56 these thoughts are extended into another channel. Many of our bodily movements are automatic. A sensory neuron is stimulated and there is an immediate response, as for example when the hand unknowingly touches fire it is withdrawn quickly by muscular contractions which were not ordered by the conscious mind. Fig. 56A shows the pathway of such a series of events along the nerve channels of the body. Three kinds of neurons (nerve cells) are involved. A sensory neuron carries the nerve impulses from the skin to the association neuron and from that directly to the motor neuron, which activates the needed muscular movements. No conscious control intervenes. Though the neurons do not touch each other, these nerve impulses jump the gaps between them, and the response is almost instantaneous.

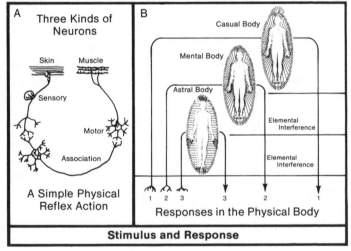

Fig. 56

Other stimuli are of a different kind (Fig. 56-3). Through the sensory neurons and nerve centers of the body they penetrate into the astral body and awaken an emotional response. The resulting emotional state will then, in a reverse process, activate the physical motor neurons, finding its final expression in physical action. If this action and reaction take place within a sphere in which the feelings are rightly employed, all may be well; but if the reaction results from lack of emotional control, then elemental interference may take place, with undesirable results.

Still other stimuli will penetrate through the astral to the mental body (Fig. 56-2) and produce response from that source, with a similar variation in results, for good or ill. But the only complete and effective circuit of action and reaction takes place when the sensory stimulation penetrates through the astral and mental bodies to the Self within its causal body in the higher mental world, and the Self initiates a considered response through the instrumentality of the appropriate vehicle to implement its decision (Fig. 56-1). When we learn to move always in the center of our circle, as the motivating power behind all action and the master of the bodies which work in our service, then we will move swiftly forward on the pathway of our evolution.

In Section Two we surveyed the field of evolution from the small to the great and followed the story of earth's becoming and its preparation for the great events which were to follow. We saw the minute and the massive, almost from infinite to infinite. And we gained some glimpse of the illusion of space as limited by dimensions or measured in terms of size. For there can be no small or large except within the consciousness that perceives them.

In this section we have traced the origin of the human body, back over aeons of time, to the first primitive cells that floated as a scum upon the surface of the water spaces of a barren earth, millions of years ago. We saw also that there are physical phenomena that repeat billions of times a second. Again, we passed almost from the infinite to the infinite, but in what we call time. Here, too, we must have glimpsed the fact that to limit

time to the measurements of humanly devised instruments creates another illusion, for long or short, too,
depends upon the perceiving consciousness.

We have followed the sequence of earth's stirring
events up to the advent of human beings. The divine Self
has made its contacts with the bodies, and spiritual
evolution now takes the center of the stage upon which
the drama of life is being played. We have crossed the
plains and have reached the foothills.

IV

The Illusion of Self

(As Separation)

The unwary Soul that fails to grapple with the mocking demon of illusion will return to earth the slave of Māra. . . . If through the Hall of Wisdom, thou would'st reach the Vale of Bliss, Disciple, close fast thy senses against the great dire heresy of separateness that weans thee from the rest.

The Voice of the Silence
H. P. Blavatsky

19

Psychogenesis

The coming of the monads into their lower vehicles is known as the third outpouring, and is the third outstanding event in the world's history. The first of the outpourings prepared the raw materials out of which all things were made. The second built those raw materials into living forms of surpassing wonder and beauty. The third brought the immortal divine Selves to inhabit mortal bodies, when the human form with its inner psychic links had been produced. We should now be in a position clearly to perceive that the ultimate consciousness within each one of us is and will forever remain, the Self, by whatever name we may call it. To find our way successfully through the many difficulties and illusions of life, we should always be aware of this one fundamental fact. To quote the words of an ancient scripture, "I AM THAT SELF; THAT SELF AM I."

In Fig. 57 this fact is graphically illustrated, for there we see the Self, represented as the central Being, within the bodies which surround it. Each one of the bodies is an instrument by which the Self will become conscious of the various worlds and also a vehicle for the expression of its powers. The Self is represented with the words, "I AM," for that expression is the essence of its existence, and is surrounded by the bodies, each of which, let it always be remembered, is a living thing, with a consciousness of its own. The collective consciousness of all the bodies operates within the consciousness of the Self, and for the Self to realize itself as Self, it must be able to review the consciousness and activities of each one objectively and know them all for what they are. The Self has—or will have during the course of its higher evolution—an atmic, buddhic, and causal body by means of which it will express its powers of will, love, and knowledge, though at the present normal level of humanity these all find their expression mainly through the causal body. The Self has a mental, astral, and physical body, by the use of which it can think, feel, and act. The latter three are mortal: they are born and they die many times. The higher bodies are immortal, but it is through the passing experiences of the mortal bodies that the three basic qualities or powers of the Self are being awakened. Following the broken lines on the lower right of Fig. 57, we see that thinking results in the acquisition of knowledge. Feelings gradually awaken love and the experiences

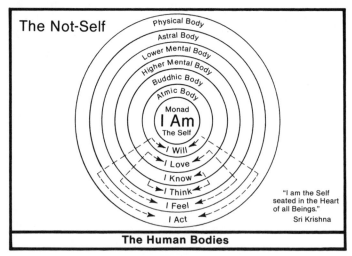

The Not-Self

Physical Body
Astral Body
Lower Mental Body
Higher Mental Body
Buddhic Body
Atmic Body
Monad
I Am
The Self
I Will
I Love
I Know
I Think
I Feel
I Act

"I am the Self seated in the Heart of all Beings."
Sri Krishna

The Human Bodies

Fig. 57

and activities of the physical vehicle, difficult as they are, call forth the power of will to overcome the difficulties and to express the powers of the Self in physical action.

So we see that fleeting thoughts, passing emotions and many physical activities, all of which come and go without permanence, give rise to the divine powers of knowledge, love, and will, which once acquired can never be lost. For the Self is divine and these powers are not conveyed to it. No outer activity adds any powers to the Self; they are called forth from the potential divinity which lies within him. In the words of Sri Krishna, "I am the Self, seated in the heart of all Beings."

But let us beware. The bodies, in turn, will endeavor to assert themselves as the Self. And in that fact lies one of the greatest difficulties which lie before us in our attempts to understand what seems to be our own nature. We mistake body urges for our own, but we must learn to differentiate between them and to know the true from the false. To many people, as we know, the physical body is the Self. They think that birth was their beginning and that death will be the ending of all for them. How strange that, knowing the wonders of creation as we do today, we can think that the originator of such marvels could at the same time be so devoid of reason as to thus destroy its greatest achievement. To others, the feelings represent the Self; their desires and emotions are the center around which they live. There are still others who live in the mind. It is to them the ultimate reality. There are subtler illusions, too. Reason, love, and the power of will can become the apparent reality around which all revolves. They are powers of the Self, to be used. But they are not the Self. Each one of these creates a self that derives its existence from some aspect of separation, though sometimes it is clothed in amazing subtleties and even of seeming wisdom and beauty. But when the Self realizes itself as Self, that realization brings an understanding that it is in essence and actuality part of the One Self, which is the Reality within every human being.

Looking at Fig. 57 again, we note that, in addition to the broken lines pointing upward on the lower right of the illustration, there are similar lines on the lower left, but they are pointing downward. These are to indicate the fact that the powers and qualities, stored within the Self from its many passing experiences, are at all times available to be used for creative activities in the denser worlds and also as the background before which all new experiences may be judged. But all too frequently the new experience brings a reaction from the astral or mental body alone, or the two jointly (Fig. 56B-2 and 3), and there is little or no contact with the Self, from which wiser and deeper counsel would come, for there lie the results of many incarnations rather than of only the one in which the lower bodies have participated. Often the voice of the Self does speak amid the clashes of the material world. We call it "conscience" and it usually remains unheard or ignored. The practice of constant meditation is one of the greatest opportunities which lie before humankind, for it widens the channel between the Self and its lower vehicles, making it possible for the much greater powers of the higher triad to be expressed through the lower, entirely transforming the life of the person in its physical expressions. Only those who have fully accomplished this can say with truth, "I and my Father are one."

An ancient occult commentary states that a person is that being, in any part of the universe, in whom highest spirit and lowest matter are united by mind. In Fig. 45 we can see how well that description agrees with the human constitution to which our studies have led us. In the heavy cross which is the central figure of the drawing, that story is told, and those who follow Christian symbology will see there, too, the symbol of spirit crucified upon the cross of matter. In place of mass consciousness of the group soul, we now see self-consciousness in human beings, for the divine Self is now attached to and working through its vehicles of consciousness.

It is often said that humans have evolved from the prehuman kingdoms, emerging from one of the higher mammals. Such a statement is founded upon a misapprehension as we should now be in a position to see

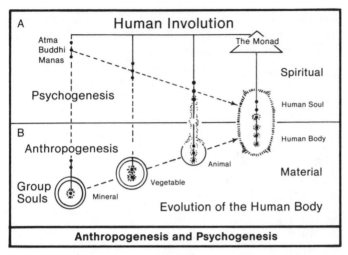

Fig. 58

clearly, for a *person is a spiritual being* who has just emerged
into manifestation (at the time we have been considering)
from the spiritual worlds (Fig. 58). The lower triad, which
we have seen contains three permanent centers for
contact with the three lower worlds, has spent its years
of preparation, for future events, in the group souls,
which fact has no doubt given rise to this idea. But the
monad then *had no conscious link with its lower triad*, as
indicated in Fig. 58 by the vertical broken lines between
the two triads. In that drawing we see portrayed, also,
the gradual awakening of the powers within the three
permanent atomic nuclei as they participate in the
experience of the group souls of the various kingdoms.
Obviously, then, it is wrong to say that *we* have evolved
through those kingdoms. We have not, but our bodies
have. The lower kingdoms were instrumental in helping
to evolve the human body; but even though we now are
living within a human body, we are not that body nor is
it in any way part of us. It is merely an instrument that
we are using for a while, probably not more than seventy
years out of each twelve hundred, as an average. Even
then, we leave it for eight hours out of every twenty-four,

reducing the total time of occupancy to little more than forty-five years of physical existence out of each twelve centuries of our true life.

In Fig. 58A we see the monad coming "downward" or involving into matter through the higher triad, while the events just referred to, the evolution of our bodies, were taking place. When individualization occurs, the two processes are linked into one and the person at last possesses all the vehicles needed to contact all the lower worlds and to awaken, through those experiences, the divine powers sleeping within.

Since the monads emerge into manifestation through the seven planetary chain Logoi, they are of seven fundamental types which, in physical life, may be broadly classified as the ruler, the teacher, the philanthropist, the artist, the scientist, the devotee, and the craftsperson. These divisions are frequently referred to as the seven "rays" (Fig. 33). Similarly, the seven original group souls, observable in the mental world, may be traced to the same source. Though innumerable subtypes follow, they maintain their identity with the primary divisions and are represented at the apex of animal evolution by the higher mammals, such as the dog, the cat, the monkey, the elephant, and the horse. Individualization will bring together the monads of each ray and their lower triads, which will have been conditioned for future service within the group souls of the corresponding type.

Reference to Fig. 59A will elaborate the difference between the Self and its material bodies. The Self is spiritual; the body is material. The Self is life-building; the body is form-building. The Self is subject to spiritual law; the body to material law. The Self grows through successive reincarnations in the denser worlds; the body through the operation of laws of heredity. They are united by mind. Though fundamentally different in nature, these two are mutually helpful, for the Self is evolving through living in forms built by cell life and the matter of which all the food taken into the body is composed is evolving because of that association. This fact applies also to the astral and mental bodies, for the elemental essence which is absorbed and later ejected by those bodies is evolving through its participation in that process.

The monad will now be plunged into the illusions of the material worlds, from which it can escape only by mastering the illusions as their challenges awaken the divine powers within. It will embark upon a long journey into matter, going forth through the gateway of birth to

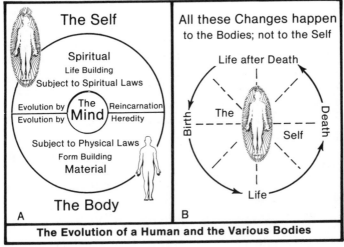

The Evolution of a Human and the Various Bodies

Fig. 59

taste of life (Fig. 59B), and at death will learn of the life which exists beyond death. At first, it will think that *it* is born and lives and dies, but will find out that these things do not happen to *it*; they are changes which occur to the bodies, for it exists changeless whether the bodies live or die, whether they are asleep or awake.

Ages ago, the monad had its beginning within the consciousness of the Solar Deity. Now its divinity in latency is to expand into divinity in potency and perfection.

20

Reincarnation

Probably no single thought can make such a complete revolution in our outlook upon life as that of reincarnation, for from a brief span of three score years and ten spent upon earth there opens up a vision of conscious existence that stretches back into the dim vistas of the past and forward into the distant future to lose itself in a blaze of glory that will crown the final effort of our many achievements.

Scientific research has penetrated into the early history of the human race as it struggled to gain a foothold in the bleak, rugged world of millions of years ago. It has laid bare, in rich detail, fascinating stories of that era. Who has not thrilled to the exploits of those stalwart pioneers as they faced the rigors of nature and prepared the way for us to follow? All the triumphs of these later days have arisen from those early beginnings. Primitive implements of stone and iron were the forerunners of the fine precision steel instruments that we are using now. Our modern methods of transportation, which are rapidly welding the world into one, arose from the simple ox cart of earlier years. From the first simple signals of fire and smoke have come radio and television which speed news to the four corners of the earth almost as it occurs.

But if we have been enthralled by the tales and legends of life in those early days, thinking of them as the deeds of our remote ancestors, how much deeper would our interest become if we could realize that these are not the exploits of our ancestors at all. *They are stories about ourselves and the adventures of our own yesterdays.* Yes, in the dawn of history we fought the mammoth, the mastodon, and the woolly elephant. We roamed the open spaces and lived in caves. We struggled with the elements which we did not understand. In race after race we lived and died. We hunted and fought and raised our families in the manner of those early times. Little by little we increased our knowledge, and our living conditions slowly improved. Century after century has slipped away and gradually we have climbed upward from the lower rungs of the ladder of evolution. Little by little we have become better men and women and we have left our mark upon the world. But *we* have done it, not an endless succession of departed races that have been born and then have slipped into oblivion.

We must now take one step more. If we could realize that we have been intimately associated with the past, it is just one more logical step to see also that we shall have the same intimate relationship with the future, that the world which is to come is not for some new humanity yet to be created, but for us of today, who not only lived in the past but will live in the future too. The world of the future is being built today and we, who are taking part in the building, shall live in the world we are helping to create. Some religions, the Christian religion especially, teach that the human soul is created at birth, and at death goes to some distant place of reward or punishment. Science generally holds the viewpoint that moral and spiritual qualities come through our culture and heredity. It denies any way of knowing whether there is individual continuity, substituting the supposition that all new qualities developed by individuals are carried forward in the future. Neither of these standpoints holds any incentive to individual effort, for the future seems far removed and we will have no part in it anyway. But an understanding of reincarnation gives us a viewpoint which ties past, present, and future together as one. It gives us hope and an incentive to action and a determination to drink deeply from the well of knowledge, since every gain that we can make will be ours forever.

Reincarnation is a teaching that once was accepted universally but lost to the Western world when it was condemned by the Roman Catholic Church in the middle of the sixth century. Referring to its worldwide acceptance and the brilliance of its intellectual ancestry, E. D. Walker, an English psychologist, wrote in his book, *Reincarnation* (Rider and Co., London W.1—pages 3-7):

> Once the whole civilized world embraced reincarnation and found therein a complete answer to that riddle of man's descent and destiny which the inexorable sphinx Life propounds to every traveler along her way. But the western branch of the race, in working out the material conquest of the world, has acquired the compensating discontent of a material philosophy.
>
> Although commonly rejected throughout Europe and America, reincarnation is unreservedly accepted by the majority of mankind at the present day, in all the past centuries. From the dawn of history it has prevailed among the largest part of humanity with an unshaken intensity of conviction. Over all the mightiest eastern nations it has held permanent sway. The ancient civilization of Egypt, whose grandeur cannot be overestimated, was built upon this as a fundamental truth, and taught it as a precious secret to Pythagoras, Empedocles, Plato, Virgil and Ovid, who scattered it through Greece and Italy.
>
> Many philosophers of metaphysical depth, like Scotus, Kant, Schelling, Leibnitz, Schopenhauer and the younger Fichte, have upheld reincarnation. Geniuses of noble symmetry, like Giordano Bruno, Herder, Lessing and Goethe, have fathered it. Scientists like Flammarion, Figuier and Brewster have earnestly advocated it. Theological leaders like Julius, Müller, Dorner, Ernesti, Rückert and Edward Beecher have maintained it. In exalted intuitional natures like Boehme and Swedenborg its hold is apparent. Most of the mystics bathe in it. Of course, the long line of Platonists from Socrates down to Emerson have no doubt of it. Nearly all the poets profess it.

Black Nebula
From such masses of
cosmic dust and gas
new stars are born.
(Horse's Head in Orion)

The Crab Nebula
A star which exploded more than 900 years ago.

The Death and the Birth of Stars

Fig. 60

At this time it reigns without any sign of decrepitude over the Burman, Chinese, Japanese, Tartar, Tibetan and East Indian nations, including at least 750,000,000 of mankind. . . . Throughout the East it is the great central thought. It is no mere superstition of the ignorant masses. It is the chief principle of Hindu metaphysics—the basis of all their inspired books. Such a hoary philosophy, held by the venerable authority of ages, ruling from the beginning of time the bulk of the world's thought, cherished in some form by the disciples of every great religion, is certainly worthy of the profoundest respect and study. There must be some vital reality inspiring so stupendous an existence.

But it must not be thought that reincarnation is something peculiar to the human race. The law of cyclic progression can be seen in operation throughout the whole of nature. We will examine some of its wider manifestations before coming down to its specific application to human beings.

In Plate III two photographs are reproduced. One is of death and the other of the beginnings of a star. Both lie out in the great cosmic spaces. The Crab nebula,

shown on the left, is the aftermath of the explosion of
a star, which suddenly flared up on July 4, 1054, more
than nine hundred years ago. Since that time it has been
expanding at the rate of 680 miles a second. It is now
6,000,000,000,000 miles from border to border. In time it
will become like the huge black mass shown on the right.
This is known as a black nebula and has been named
the Horse's Head. Black clouds such as these are immense
aggregations of cosmic dust, and astronomers have much
evidence to indicate that they are the "raw materials"
from which new stars arise. From the depths of space,
then, there comes evidence of life arising from death, as
in Heliopolis, the Phoenix arose from the ashes of its
own dead self to take on youth and beauty once more.

Referring again to Fig. 28, we see the seven planetary
chains illustrated. It was explained that each of these
chains, of which there are seven in the solar system,
consists of seven globes. Each chain, it should now be
mentioned, passes through seven incarnations, gradually
taking on denser matter and then withdrawing from it.

In Fig. 61 we see illustrated the seven incarnations
through which the globes will pass. The entire period
of these seven incarnations of a chain is called a "scheme
of evolution." Each of the first four incarnations takes
the whole chain one stage lower and toward the densest
matter, so that the densest substance in the first chain
is of lower mental material while in the fourth there are
three physical globes. The last three incarnations repeat
the conditions of the first three, but in reverse order.
In each incarnation of a chain, the life passes seven
times around the globes, after which they are destroyed,
revitalized by the planetary chain Logos and then re-
formed for the next chain one step either lower or higher.
Each world illustrated has, of course, all the matter in it
that is higher than the one shown, but nothing lower.

So we see that in the great open spaces of the cosmos,
among the stars, reincarnation may be seen. And within
the solar system the planetary Logoi follow the same law
of cyclic unfoldment.

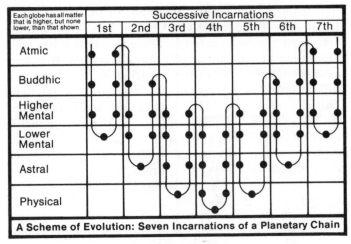

Fig. 61

Natural cycles abound at all levels of manifestation. Our Sun, we have seen, is one among millions of suns which make up the galaxy we call the Milky Way. But that galaxy is not still, for all the stars within it are moving in immense orbits around a common center. It is estimated that our Sun will make one complete revolution within the galaxy in 200 million years (Fig. 62A). The Earth, we know, makes an annual journey around the Sun (Fig. 62B), while the Moon circulates around the Earth in a lunar month of twenty-eight days. The cycle of the seasons (Fig. 62C) is evident every year and brings its succession of changing events. Every twenty-four hours, the Earth turns around on its axis (Fig. 62D), giving us day and night. These cycles, among many others, keep on in unchanging succession, like pulsebeats that mark the progress of the plan at its many levels.

On Earth many natural cycles are to be found. In Fig. 63 the water cycle is illustrated. Here we see that water from a lake is drawn upward into the sky by the Sun, through the process of evaporation. In this manner the clouds are formed. As the clouds become saturated with moisture they precipitate their contents upon the earth,

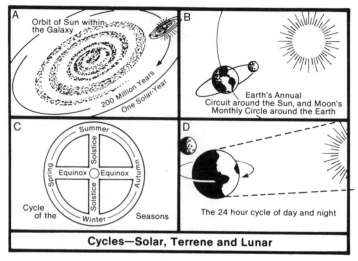

A
Orbit of Sun within the Galaxy
200 Million Years
One Solar-Year

B
Earth's Annual Circuit around the Sun, and Moon's Monthly Circle around the Earth

C
Summer
Solstice
Spring
Equinox   Equinox
Solstice
Winter
Cycle of the   Seasons
Autumn

D
The 24 hour cycle of day and night

Cycles—Solar, Terrene and Lunar

Fig. 62

where it soaks into the soil. Finally, it returns to the lake through the ground to start on the same cycle once more. But while this process is taking place, the vegetation is being provided with the precious fluid needed for its growth and, as time goes on, the life within it unfolds into progressively higher manifestations.

Fig. 63 shows also what is known as the carbon cycle. Here we see illustrated the way in which nature has made the plant and animal kingdoms mutually dependent upon each other. The green plant absorbs sunlight and makes food greatly in excess of its own needs. The animal takes in the green plant as food, producing heat. The plant absorbs energy while the animal uses energy in the form of action. The plant gives off oxygen, a vital need for the animal, and the animal gives off carbon dioxide, a vital need for the plant. So we have this continuous cyclic exchange between the two as they both follow the evolutionary pathway of their respective kingdoms, helping each other.

Carrying the thought of cycles one stage further, we see in Fig. 64 the kingdoms of nature classified from a

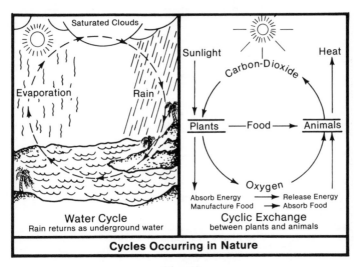

Water Cycle
Rain returns as underground water

Cyclic Exchange
between plants and animals

Cycles Occurring in Nature

Fig. 63

viewpoint a little different from the usual. There are
really three basic kingdoms of nature, each one deriving
from an aspect of the Deity: the mineral, the animal, and
the spiritual, the last mentioned only just emerging into
physical expression. But there are two dual or transitional
kingdoms, the vegetable and the human. These are referred to as transitional because they exist in a transitional
state between two other kingdoms. The vegetable has its
roots in the mineral or inorganic world, buried in the
ground, while its stems and branches shoot upward into
the organic world. It is absorbing minerals from the
earth and sunlight from the sky and, by the process of
photosynthesis, is transforming the material of one
kingdom into another—inorganic into organic. Also, it
is progressing through the seasonal cycles of spring,
summer, autumn, and winter. The human has roots in
the animal world, the physical body, but its higher reaches
penetrate into the spiritual, and the many experiences
gained in the animal form are being transformed into
mental and spiritual powers. This, too, goes on through
a cyclic process: that of reincarnation. In winter the

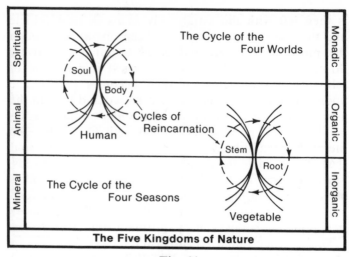

Fig. 64

vegetation seems to have died, but it has only withdrawn
into its invisible roots and, later, it will reappear. When
the physical body is discarded at death, a person seems
to die. But a new incarnation will bring the soul back
again for a new round of activity upon earth. These two
cycles are in continual activity concurrently with that
illustrated in Fig. 63, which operates between them.

So we see that the cyclic growth of human beings, as
evidenced in the law of reincarnation, is not a strange
and unusual procedure, but fits logically into the order
of natural events.

In its essential outline, human reincarnation is a
simple process and easily understood. We have seen
that a person has a spiritual "body," which is carried
from the beginning of the evolutionary journey at individualization, until human perfection is reached.
The Divine Self, functioning through the spiritual body,
in Christian terminology is called the soul (Fig. 65-1).
In the process of reincarnation, which will be dealt with
in more detail shortly, the soul adds a mental body (2),
an astral body (3), and a physical body (4). At the close
of the incarnation the physical body dies. The person

is then left with the astral body as its densest vehicle and the vital forces which have been operating through the physical body are redirected to function directly through the astral body, awakening it into a state of self-conscious existence. It then becomes the vehicle upon which human existence is centered and lives in the astral world for a period of time, under conditions depending upon previous emotional activities. Later, the life of the mental body (2) comes to an end and the soul (1A) is left to live its normal life in the spiritual worlds, unencumbered by the limiting effects of denser bodies of any kind. During this cycle, however, it has unfolded more of its spiritual powers and has taken one more step along the pathway of its spiritual evolution.

Thus, through many incarnations, a person grows in spiritual stature, always unfolding from within the latent powers infolded in the beginning. In Fig. 66 we have one more illustration of the manner in which reincarnation harmonizes with all nature's activities. Climbing the ladder of evolution, beginning in the primitive state, a person advances to the ordinary and on to the civilized, advanced and spiritual states. These outer appearances

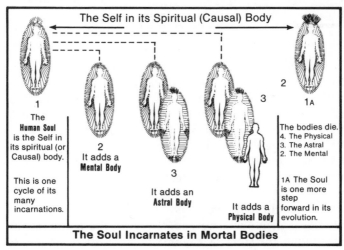

The Self in its Spiritual (Causal) Body

1
The
Human Soul
is the Self in
its spiritual (or
Causal) body.

This is one
cycle of its
many
incarnations.

2
It adds a
Mental Body

3
It adds an
Astral Body

It adds a
Physical Body

2

3

1A

The bodies die.
4. The Physical
3. The Astral
2. The Mental

1A The Soul
is one more
step
forward in its
evolution.

The Soul Incarnates in Mortal Bodies

Fig. 65

are, of course, reflections in the material forms of the growth of the soul. This growth can be compared with the opening of a flower. In Fig. 66 we see each of these human stages placed beneath a similar stage in the flower's development from a small bud to the full bloom in all its beauty. The fully opened blossom bears little resemblance to the bud, but in our illustration we can see how gradually one has arisen from the other. This

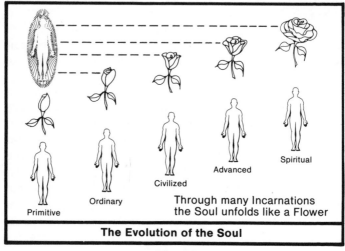

The Evolution of the Soul

Fig. 66

is because the bud is much more than it seems to be, for within it lie all the potentialities of growth which will finally produce the beauty of perfection. So also in a person. In the less advanced we see little of the greatness of saint or genius. Yet greatness lies buried within the enclosing wall of flesh and, by stages, that greatness will be released into active expression and eventually will culminate in the perfection of the spiritual being within.

If we could look over a plant and see on it blooms in all stages of growth, we could read in the many, at the same time, the story of any one flower without having to wait for it to unfold. In the same manner, if we will look around us we can see persons in all stages of spiritual growth. And in the many we can read the story of any one individual from early beginnings to the highest point yet reached by humans. Reincarnation alone can show law and order in the unfolding picture of the human race.

The time we spend in the physical world is often referred to as a "life" and the period during which we function in the subtler regions is thought of as a waiting period of uncertain worth which fills up the time "between lives." If we hold such a concept we should discard it entirely, for it can badly distort our whole outlook upon the subject of reincarnation. Especially in the Western world and largely through the teachings of Christian theologians, the real meanings of the words "life" and "death" have become reversed. *The experience we call "life" is the nearest approach we ever make to "death."* We cannot die. But when we garb ourselves in a physical body we are confined to the greatest restriction of existence. However, physical limitation is for a purpose; this should be clearly understood. Its difficulties and frustrations make our stay in the physical world of the greatest value, for they draw out our sleeping powers of thought and wisdom to overcome them. What we call birth is really death, for the soul is buried in an earthly body. And death, so-called, is the time of release, when the soul once more is liberated from its house of bondage and rises into the greater freedom and beauty of the astral world. It is really birth.

By far the greatest part of our true life is lived in the superphysical worlds.

In the center of Fig. 67 we see a clock face. Each one of its twelve hours represents a hundred years and the total of twelve hundred years constitutes an average lifecycle according to some theosophical writings. Of this total time, we spend only about seventy years in the physical world, about one-seventeenth of the total time. The shaded portion between the two hands gives a graphic idea of the brevity of this earthly visit. Below, ten complete life cycles are shown, stretching across the drawing, with the physical period of each shown in black. The

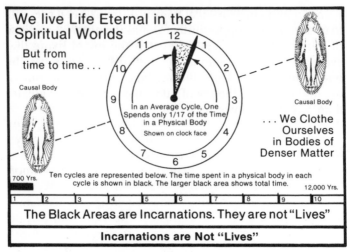

Fig. 67

black rectangle on the left shows, for comparison, the total period spent on earth during those ten cycles. Small though they are, these black markings should really be reduced to two thirds of their size, for eight hours out of every twenty-four we spend in sleep, withdrawn from the physical body and functioning for a while in the astral world. So difficult is physical existence that we cannot spend more than a few continuous hours in that body without withdrawing from it for a while to recuperate from the effects of its severe limitations. It should be clear, then, that our brief visits to the restrictions of earth are not "lives"; they are *incarnations*. They are periods during which we are confined to a carnal body.

Reference to Fig. 61 will show another aspect of this subject, for it will be seen that, during the total period covered by the seven incarnations of a planetary chain, forty-nine globes are created. *Only five of these are of physical matter.* It is of interest to note that the chain to which the Earth belongs is just slightly past the middle point of its career, as shown by the arrow. Therefore we are in the very middle, and at the point of greatest materiality, of physical manifestation.

Incarnation in a physical body is difficult, but it presents to us a wonderful opportunity for making progress because of those difficulties. Yet so great is the joy of living that even amid its restrictions the path of progress can be one of happiness. Only the mistakes bring pain. But in the higher worlds the joy of attainment can be far greater than anything known on earth.

21

The Mystery of Birth

Of all the events that nature holds before us for our wondering contemplation, few exceed in interest and fascination the marvel and mystery of birth. Birth is not only a miracle; it is a series of miracles which become deeper and more significant as we penetrate from our physical nature to our psychic links with the subtler bodies.

Science has gained a great deal of knowledge regarding the processes of birth. The union of two parental cells, one barely visible, the other microscopic in size, begins an ordered succession of cell multiplication, which follows a definite pattern and soon begins to take organized shape, foreshadowing the new human form that eventually will develop.

But no scientist has yet explained how a tiny, helpless, and senseless model in miniature of the human adult can become, in a few short years, an intellectual and spiritually minded man or woman. There is nothing else in all nature's realms which can even approach such a phenomenon. While in its early years the progress of the child in learning is slower than some of the animals, it soon outstrips them all and moves on, with incomprehensible rapidity, to regions into which none of them may enter—for morality and spirituality are unknown in any other creature.

There are facts which science cannot detect by the use of laboratory instruments, and they are of equal importance to a knowledge of cell life and to the laws of chemical reactions. It is true that the human body, in its prenatal growth, passes through many stages similar to those of the lower animals; we have seen that the human *body* has had its antecedents in the lower kingdoms. But there comes a stage in that process when something happens to the human embryo which does not happen to that of any other creature—*the human soul makes contact with the body which is to be its material home.* This cannot be detected by scientific instruments, but it can and has been contacted through occult research. Moreover, it may be known by anyone who will make an unbiased analysis of events.

When the animal is born, it is an animal. When the human is born, it is not an animal. It is a soul taking for its use a body which may be classified as a biped mammal. Only the coming of the human soul into the body can give a satisfactory explanation of the astounding changes in the child as it grows to maturity. And when next you look at a tiny babe, try to realize that *someone else is looking at it too*—someone who may be trying to pierce the same deep mystery that you are pondering over—the spiritual entity who for many years to come will make that living form its physical dwelling place.

In the newly born babe we see not only the miracle of physical birth, but the culmination of a series of events, psychic and physical, which, though often repeated, is one of the greatest wonders of all time: the union of highest spirit with lowest matter in a living, conscious form. As we have seen, two streams of evolution have come into temporary union, to be mutually helpful to each other: the spiritual Self and the human body.

We shall now peer into the inner worlds once more, to see some of the invisible preparations that have been taking place in anticipation of this great event. Were we able to examine the spiritual body we should see it showing a special vital force and a brilliant golden glow would be observed in the region of the physical heart (Fig. 68), where the lower triad, consisting of the three

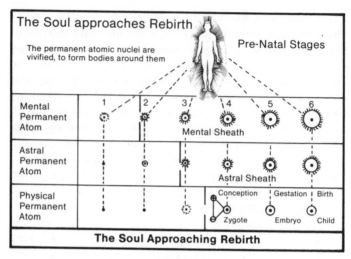

Fig. 68

permanent atoms, has been held in quiescence awaiting the call to a new incarnation. The life web in which they are enclosed, which it is said has the appearance of a "golden cocoon," begins to unfold and the atoms thrill with a new life.

First the mental permanent atom is galvanized into action and draws around itself, by magnetic attraction, a sheath of lower mental matter (Fig. 68-1), which in vibratory development and quality is consistent with the powers within the atom itself. At first this will be a loose, unorganized mass, but after birth it will become organized into a mental body, expanding its capacities as the needs of the lower vehicles stimulate its thinking powers into action.

After the mental sheath has been formed, the astral atom is awakened and sounds out its "note" (Fig. 68-2) and astral matter consistent with its development is drawn to it in the same manner as with the mental atom. This astral sheath will gradually develop into an astral body, as it responds to the calls made upon it by the physical consciousness.

Following these, the physical permanent atom is called

into action (Fig. 68-3) and it attracts etheric matter from which the new vital body will be built but, with the dense physical vehicle, new considerations enter because of its nature. So the method of parentage is used and in Fig. 68-4 the first contact between the spiritual person and its new physical body is depicted. The two parental reproductive cells (+) and (−), known as the gametes, unite at conception to form the zygote, which is the dual cell from which all the other cells will be produced; *but in this union the physical permanent atom has a place* and it will affect the heredity of the new physical vehicle in a manner that will be described. Then follows the period of gestation (Fig. 68-5) and finally birth (Fig. 68-6).

Thus permanent atoms are powerful centers of force in each of the worlds and are instrumental in gathering together the material for new bodies which will be built around them.

In Fig. 69 this thought is carried further to draw attention to a very important fact, one that affects us intimately at all times. It is that *every experience through which we pass produces two effects: one spiritual, the other material.* The Self retains as *character* the essence of all experiences gained through the bodies, while the permanent atoms retain as *vibratory powers* the essence of the same experiences. As we come into a new incarnation, we bring not only the soul qualities and powers that we have developed in the past, but the mental, astral, and physical bodies, too, will be of a quality commensurate with our many past efforts.

We can now examine the means by which the physical permanent atom affects heredity. In Fig. 38 the division of the cell into two cells was shown, in Fig. 38-C the threadlike objects known as the chromosomes were seen and the succeeding drawings depicted the manner in which each chromosome splits lengthwise and its two halves moved to opposite sides of the cell which then divided, forming two new cells. This procedure is followed by the body cells, but in the reproductive cell there is an additional stage known as the "reduction division,"

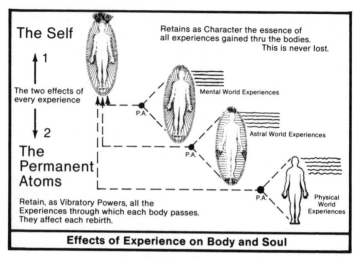

The Self

↑ 1

The two effects of every experience

↓ 2

The Permanent Atoms

Retains as Character the essence of all experiences gained thru the bodies. This is never lost.

Mental World Experiences

Astral World Experiences

Physical World Experiences

P.A.

P.A.

P.A.

Retain, as Vibratory Powers, all the Experiences through which each body passes. They affect each rebirth.

Effects of Experience on Body and Soul

Fig. 69

in which, as the cell divides, each daughter cell receives only half of the original complement of chromosomes. The same process takes place in both male and female cells, except that in the former, half of the new cells carry what is known as an "X" chromosome, while the other half carry a "Y" chromosome. These determine sex: the first mentioned resulting in a female offspring, the latter in a male. When fertilization takes place, each parent contributes one reproductive cell and since each one contains only half the needed number of chromosomes, the union of the two gives the correct number for the species.

Within the chromosomes, science tells us, lie the genes, minute objects almost like beads upon a thread, which are the carriers of heredity. In Fig. 70A, two thread-like chromosomes with their genes are shown. Combinations of these particles of living matter give rise to all the characteristics of the new body, as though they are seeds of various kinds, producing the growth of special features within the total structure of the body.

Explained in simple outline and without unnecessary details, this is the mechanism of heredity. But, after

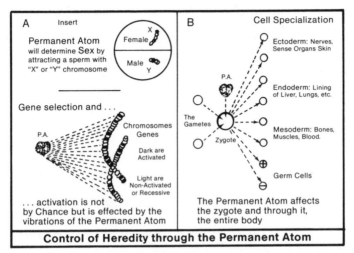

Fig. 70

science discloses to us the wonders of its structure, we are then told that the operation of the machine, that is, the method by which sex is determined and the genes are selected from the parental stock, is *entirely by chance*. Can we possibly believe that human character, God's supreme creation, would be left to no more certain guidance than that which rules the casting of the dice? It should be obvious that Theosophy does not support such a position. We have seen that Theosophy places the origin of the higher human faculties within the astral, mental, and spiritual bodies. The manner in which they form around the permanent atoms which are carried over from previous incarnations and are consistent with human efforts of the past has just been shown and we should now have the key to the manner in which the physical permanent atom can affect heredity. For it is the selecting agency which, while it cannot affect the physical body directly, can affect the genes and select those for activation which will build a body consistent also with earlier human achievements (Fig. 70A). It can also decide the sex of the offspring by selecting the right reproductive cell which will bring the predetermined result. Thus, in place of chance, Theosophy can show a plan that is logical, consistent with known facts, that complies with justice—and rings true.

Since the use of nuclear power, much intensive work has been undertaken to determine the effects of radio-activity upon the genes, especially on those of the human family, and it is now known definitely that changes can be caused in this manner. If the physical atom can liberate forces which will affect the genes and therefore heredity, is it not entirely logical that the atom known in occultism, which is a deeper structure than the atom and therefore even more powerful can also affect the genes, but in this case in a controlled and purposeful way? One of the astounding facts which science has discovered about the atom is its power to emit waves of hitherto unheard-of frequencies, up into magnitudes of billions of times per second. Here, again, we find that known facts agree with the occultist's statements regarding the vibratory development of the permanent atom. These are only a different octave of waves of greater potency which, as yet, scientific instruments have not been able to register.

In Fig. 70B we see illustrated the presence of the three factors needed for normal human conception, the two parental cells and the permanent atom. The result is known as the zygote, as we have seen, in which the acti-vated genes are ready to play their part. The one will divide into two, the two into four, and so on. In one month a tiny heart will begin to beat. In two and a half months the general body structure will be evident. In five months it will have a full complement of 12,000,000,000 nerve cells and, at birth, 200,000,000,000 cells, all specialized in their activities, will have been produced from that one original cell and each will carry the same genetic combination. However, as the bodies—physical and superphysical—grow up together, the higher vehicles will have their impact upon the dense physical, producing modifications that come with advancing years.

While the basic teachings of Theosophy have existed for centuries, the findings of modern science have ampli-fied the ideas that Theosophy presents and have made them more readily acceptable to those who have been schooled within the framework of modern thought. The impressive events of the prenatal and postnatal growth of the structures of the body, as revealed by science, coupled with the wonders of its psychic associations which Theosophy explains, pierce deeply into the human consciousness, for they reveal to us the mysteries of our own being. And who can study such things without an answering echo coming from within and saturating the whole nature with reverence and humility as one contemplates the mighty things that God hath wrought?

There have been many controversies over the relative merits of reincarnation and heredity. We should now be fairly conversant with the value of them both and know that, properly understood, there is no conflict between them. In Fig. 71A we have an illustration showing that heredity is nature's plan for the evolution of a person's body, while in Fig. 71B it is shown that reincarnation is nature's plan for human evolution. The difficulties arise when we try to explain both of these by heredity or reincarnation alone.

Referring to Fig. 71A, we note that two generations are shown and two are inferred. B receives its heredity

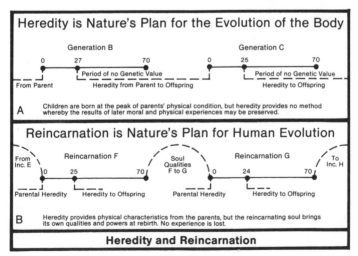

Fig. 71

qualities from A and passes along a selection of those qualities to C, who in turn continues the process to the following generation. But the transference of heredity takes place in the early years before life's greatest experiences have been gained. Therefore it is impossible to conceive that the qualities developed by the parents are intended to be preserved in the growth of a race consciousness. The individual dies and, since it is considered that the person then ceases to exist, the value of most of this life's experiences die as well. Only those gained before progeny are born could possibly be passed along to them by any kind of heredity.

But reference to Fig. 71B reveals an entirely different picture. There it is seen that the incoming soul brings to birth the faculties it has developed in the past and carries on to the future, to its next incarnation, the value of all experiences to the very last day of the physical existence. In material cycles of heredity and spiritual cycles of reincarnation, the human being goes forward toward its goal. There is no loss, no waste, no chance, and every step of the way is under the unfailing operation of natural law.

22

The Days of Our Years

"The days of our years," we read in the Bible, "are three-score years and ten, and if by reason of strength they be fourscore years: yet is their strength labour and sorrow: for it soon is cut off and we fly away" (Ps. 90:10). This statement contains deep occult truths, which we are now in a position to consider. The years we spend incarnate in the flesh are arduous years, but they are our time of greatest opportunity. The very difficulties that we invariably try to avoid are steps which will take us to the top of the ladder of success. The hard knocks of life and the seemingly cruel hand of fate rise before us to challenge the inner Self to further effort; they are angels of blessing in disguise.

Each incarnation brings many changes: childhood changes to adolescence, adolescence to maturity, maturity gradually gives place to the advance of old age. Each age presents its peculiar problems, but it is now becoming generally recognized that there are more divisions than these. According to Theosophy our years of physical existence can be divided into ten divisions, each of which lasts for approximately seven years (Fig. 72). In five of these, the higher links are gradually being made with the physical body, beginning with the vital or etheric body until the highest will (atma) is reached. At this point the soul is at its normally complete state of union with the physical vesture, and the world of mundane affairs is claiming its attention. But from that point onward the soul begins to withdraw from the *domination* of the physical world, and its attention should become increasingly centered upon higher things. The first half of the incarnation is a period of greater learning. It will be recognized as the *Pravritti Marga* (the path of outgoing) of the Hindu religion. The second half is more a period of testing for, as we shall see, during this part of the incarnation, a testing and maturing of the earlier gatherings

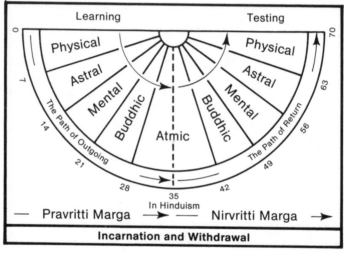

Fig. 72

takes place. It is the Hindu *Nivritti Marga* (the path of return). Fig. 72 gives the essential principles of the plan, which should be understood before we pass along to the next diagram. It must be emphasized that the outline given and the conditions to be described refer to the average, or normal, experience, and all conditions may vary in length or intensity according to the physical, emotional, mental and spiritual development of the individual. Furthermore, there is no sharply defined boundary line between the periods but rather a gradual transition. They may be clearly recognized, however, as the years go by.

We move on now to a more detailed study of the principles which have been enunciated. Let us refer again to Fig. 57. There we see the Self shown within its vehicles of consciousness, through which it expresses the powers of will, love, and reason, and stores the knowledge gained during its many incarnations. Through them it also thinks, feels, and acts. In Fig. 73 the same information is shown but, for convenience in making the diagram, only half-circles are used. The soul does

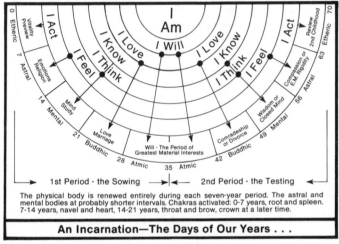

An Incarnation—The Days of Our Years . . .

Fig. 73

not make full contact with the physical body at birth. The higher bodies effect their full union with it gradually. *It is this ordered succession of fuller communication between the bodies* that causes the changing keynotes of the seven-year periods which have been referred to. We will follow each of them in turn, noting the offering that each higher body makes to enrich the physical life through these wider contacts.

From birth to the age of seven, the physical body is developing its vital links with the etheric body, while the root and spleen chakras grow in response to the urges coming from the latter vehicle. Kundalini and prana are absorbed, giving life and energy to the body. *In this period the foundations of physical health and strength for the entire incarnation are being laid down.* It is important that the child should be given every opportunity for healthful exercise in the open air and sunshine, without unnecessary restraint. While the need for simple early educational training may be felt, it should not be allowed to interfere with participation in outdoor activities.

During these early years, the child subconsciously is making a preview of the years to come, anticipating conditions and events of the future by dramatizing them in play. The little girl becomes the mother in her imagination as she plays with her dolls, feeding them with imaginary food and talking to them about imaginary events. The little boy plays with a toy train, carrying imaginary passengers and freight. He rushes a toy fire engine to an imaginary fire and with a toy construction set he builds bridges and great machines to do imaginary work, as some day he may do in reality. The dawning mind looks toward the future, unconsciously urged to participate in the world events. The need for parental guidance cannot be overemphasized, but guidance should never be allowed to deteriorate into compulsion. At birth, the child is entirely dependent upon the parents. As the child grows that dependency becomes progressively less, but the responsibility for wise parental guidance and care continues, though in diminishing degrees and will remain until in the final years of maturity the soul assumes full charge of all its vehicles, accountable for its every thought and deed.

From seven to fourteen years the astral body is strengthening its links with the physical vehicle and the navel and heart chakras are coming into their full normal development. This period marks the growth of the emotional nature. During this time the child can be appealed to primarily through its feelings, though care should be exercised that such appeals do not violate reason. Education should be concentrated on the emotional rather than the mental growth of the child. The almost total lack of such guidance as part of our educational systems has no doubt resulted in many years wasted through lack of emotional control in later life.

The astral body is still in its early stages of growth, though improving in response to the ever-active influences of the permanent atom and the stimuli being received from the dense physical body. It is now contributing its increasing powers to the physical life of the individual. Wise guidance of the emotional nature into desirable channels as its development continues will avoid many mistakes in the future. *This is essentially the period when religion in its most idealistic concepts of love and devotion will be of great value.* Legends and myths of antiquity, stories of the gods and of great people of old, of travel and adventure will touch and inspire. The arts should be encouraged as an avenue of active participation: painting, dancing, music, and drama. And here, to an even greater degree, the love of parents and the example of an ideal home life will help to strengthen and purify the emotional nature of the child.

Somewhere toward the end of this period the widening contacts with the astral body will cause the physiological changes which accompany sexual maturity. If the growing emotional nature has been properly led into higher channels, there will be no difficulties at this time. The child will bring a healthy, strong and radiant emotional nature into the next period when the mind becomes the dominating factor and the emotions will suffuse appreciation of the beautiful and ideal into what otherwise could become a coldly intellectual development. As we follow through these divisions, we shall see how necessary each one is to the proper unfoldment of all that follows.

From fourteen to twenty-one the mind is strengthened in the expanding picture of the incarnation. The throat and brow centers are now especially vitalized into action. *The keynote of this period is essentially that of the rapid growth of the mental faculties.* Concentration should be on the development of the powers of analytical thinking and reasoning even more than on acquiring facts. Again, there is a reciprocal action: the effects of mind upon body, and body upon mind. As mentioned before, the presence of a strong and balanced emotional nature will be of inestimable help during this development.

Reference to Fig. 73 will show that development of both the concrete and abstract divisions of the mind are included in this period, so that before its close there should be observable indications of the growth of the higher mental processes of reason and intuition. An important point to note is that at this time full normal connection at last is made to the soul itself so that, if conditions were ideal, the person would now be in full charge of the lower vehicles. We have seen that this condition is seldom realized, but there is control to the extent of the faculties developed. At the age of twenty-one —or even eighteen—the growing youth is recognized as an adult and is then considered to be socially and legally responsible. We see, from our diagram, that eighteen years is the exact point at which first full contact with the soul begins, whereas at twenty-one it is complete. These few years, it can be observed, make a great deal of difference to the unfolding mental powers, the reason for which should be evident. In this period religion should lead one into paths of reason and enlightenment, yet without loss of any of its quality of true devotion.

We may now assume that the primary necessities for physical health have been taken care of. The emotions have been raised to the highest level of expression attainable, the mind at its practical and conceptual levels has been developed. These should now play an important role as the incarnation unfolds into its next succeeding phase.

From twenty-one to twenty-eight, as Fig. 73 indicates, is the period when buddhi (love) comes into its full material manifestation. So, as we should expect, *this is the natural period for marriage,* a union which in its highest and truest aspects should take place in the spiritual worlds between Self and Self. Marriage should be a great esoteric experience in which the whole nature from spiritual to material takes part. With the limitations of the separated Self transcended, at least temporarily within the family circle, a faint glimpse may be caught of the true joys of living that will be shared by all alike when we can break down the barriers that exist today and recognize the One Life in every being. An ideal union will spiritualize all aspects of marriage, causing them to symbolize in material form the beauties of the higher link. A strong physical body, a balanced emotional nature, as well as intellectual development and the spiritual union itself are necessary for a complete and successful marriage. Even the purely material concomitants of marriage draw the partners away from self-centered activity, for while the home is maintained the needs of the family must be provided for. Love, therefore, is called forth into active expression, though often it may have to compete with the mind and the desires, which would lead the way into less ideal directions.

Following this, comes the period of the will, another aspect of the soul. This takes place between the ages of *twenty-eight and thirty-five.* In this period, *the will must show forth as self-confidence.* To meet the responsibilities of marriage, wealth-producing activities must be undertaken and the driving power of the will must assert itself to bring success. Faced with the economic necessities of married life, the couple may now be almost totally immersed in some business effort while also caring for home and children. Here, it will be seen, the soul is at its point of deepest immersion in matter. Therefore, it is not surprising thirty-five is said to be, statistically, *the age of greatest material accomplishments.*

At the age of thirty-five the turning point of the incarnation is reached, the path of outgoing is finished and the path of return begins. As we follow the further trend of events, we shall see that the accomplishments of the past are now tested and matured, but in the reverse order. Seeds which were planted in earlier years will now be reaped. Raw materials which were prepared before will now be fashioned into the finished product. As each of these periods passes, the real worth of the individual will be revealed, resulting in either failure or success. Success will mean that forces which characterized each period will be consolidated and carried on to enrich the succeeding years. Thus, to the end, the qualities of the soul should shine forth in physical expression, mounting to ever greater heights, until they disappear from view as the incarnation closes only because the physical body ceases to exist and the person has no means of revealing himself or herself in the physical world. Failure brings to old age those things that sadden and repel in place of those that would make it the most beautiful and attractive part of the entire incarnation.

From thirty-five to forty-two the period of the will continues. *Here self-confidence developed in the earlier years should blossom into self-control.* So, as Fig. 73 shows, the full period of most active participation and deepest immersion in material affairs is between the ages of twenty-eight and forty-two. Possibly in the later years a person may face the choice between amassing money for selfish purpose or to be used in wider fields of need for the helping of others.

From forty-two to forty-nine comes the period of buddhi again and, with it, the testing of the marriage ties. At this time there should be a great expansion of the love nature. While still maintaining the sanctity and closeness of the marriage links unchanged, a still greater and more inclusive love should dawn, impartial and impersonal, a reflection of the true buddhi of the spiritual world, pouring out to all, giving with no thought of return. This may be only a feeble glimpse or it may be a vision which can inspire to noble deeds. This should result in a strengthening of the marriage union so that it blossoms forth into a new and wider feeling of true *companionship*. Around this time the physical attractions of marriage are receding, and if the wider states of consciousness are not realized because the union was of the physical world alone, then failure is sure and divorce may be the result. To many this greater urge will follow a lower pattern and they will break the marriage ties to seek gratification.

From forty-nine to fifty-six we observe the maturing and testing of the mind. *This is the period in which knowledge is distilled into wisdom.* There is less study, less activity in gathering facts, but more thinking and pondering over the significance of the facts already collected. In the earlier years, one may have avidly read as many books as possible. Later one still reads books, but ponders over them longer and more deeply. This is the period of the wise guide and counselor. The mind should widen, deepen, and become more tranquil, less disturbed by events and more ready to consider all points of view, and therefore able to come to wise decisions. Failure at this point will result in the mind gradually becoming *closed to all new ideas,* a tragedy which often occurs. Instead of drawing ever nearer to the truth of things, through a wisdom that deepens year by year, we find a stolid conviction within the individual that he or she knows the truth already and, to support this position will not admit any ideas that would challenge the conclusions already reached. Mental progress has ceased, and the "arm chair" period has begun.

From fifty-six to sixty-three the emotions are tested and tried. Within this period emotional strength and balance should be gained. The maturing of the emotional nature should endow the individual with a deep sense of *compassion for all.* It should produce a deep feeling for others. It is the period of the understanding friend who can not only give wise counsel but can feel deeply and understandingly with those who need help. The mellowed emotional nature should be seen and felt in the atmosphere of love and helpfulness which surrounds such a person, even though no words are spoken. Such a one is forever young.

If this period is not met successfully, problems of old age will begin to develop and will be observed in many undesirable emotional expressions: ill temper, lack of consideration for others, unreasonable demands for attention, and a definite emotional rigidity that is distinctly unpleasant. The voice hardens, the skin wrinkles, the face becomes hard and the eyes lose their luster. In extreme cases the elemental will almost entirely force out the owner, causing drastic changes in the personality. A hitherto attractive person may become repulsive, with beauty fading and sweetness gone. Other people, seeing these things, lose their faith in God and humanity, thinking that the character once gained has been lost. It has not been lost, but now it can only partially manifest through its own vehicle of consciousness; the elemental stands in the way. Our friend has not been deprived of the beauty of character that once existed, but there was a weakness that caused a partial obsession with unfortunate results.

*The final period of sixty-three to seventy** ushers in the testing of physical vitality, the foundations of which were laid down at the beginning of the incarnation. At this age the individual may wish to retire from business activities and cultivate the reflective and meditative life. As in the first seven years the vital body was making its links with the physical, now the time is approaching when those links will be broken, and as that early period was one in which the child previewed the coming events in imaginative play, *one should now review the years of physical life as the end is coming near.* The anticipation of former years gives place to recapitulation in the later ones. It should not be a return to dwell in the past, but a bringing of the past into the present and a brooding over the events of the incarnation in order to extract from them all the value that is possible in preparation for the time of transit from physical existence to the astral world. In that way one can prepare to enter the next world, ready to take advantage of the further opportunities for progress that it will provide. The value of a knowledge of Theosophy at this time is beyond measure,

---

*This period may begin later in life now that older people are often healthier and more active.— ED.

for then the evening of one's earthly days can be filled with purposeful action. This action is not dependent upon any outer circumstances because, within the subconscious mind, all the necessities for the review are waiting to be called up into the conscious state. The many old people who constantly tell stories about their early days are doing so in answer to the same inner urge, felt but not understood. Nature is calling them to make the review, but they get lost among the cobwebbed corridors of the long ago. Carried to an extreme, this condition can give rise to the well-recognized state of "second childhood."

A very important point must be mentioned here, one which though entirely unrecognized by the mass of humanity can cause endless trouble and may badly cloud the later years of an incarnation. Reference to Fig. 55 once more will recall to mind the statements made previously regarding the manner in which elementals can cause harmful effects on our astral and mental bodies. They can do this, as explained, only if we lose control of our bodies (Plate II) thereby permitting them to enter. As we have seen, they are always seeking denser and more violent vibrations and in human bodies, which have greater capacities for good or ill than any other, they can find an ideal dwelling place in which they will strive for an increasing measure of domination as time passes. With this knowledge, those who are wise will watch carefully to keep these intruders out, for they can sadly mar the closing years of physical life. Self-control is the key to success in guarding against this possibility.

If the essentials of good health were well laid in the beginning and have been maintained and cultivated during the years that have followed, transition from this world to the next should be as simple as falling asleep, for that is what it really is. *We should not die of disease;* that arises from misuse of the body: too much action or too little, too much food or not enough, lack of sunshine and fresh air, poisons introduced into the system from either physical, astral, or mental sources, fears, hatreds, prejudices, partaking of foods not suitable for the human body. All these contribute to aches, pains, decreased vitality, and unnatural death. For the transition to be normal, the gradual lighting of the vital fires in childhood should now be reversed in action by a progressive decrease in their intensity until, in a "peace that passeth understanding," the soul finally withdraws from the body that has served it so long. The incarnation has reached its close and, in a moment of silent joy, the astral world unfolds its beauties to the soul once more.

A word of warning may be given here. In the later period of the incarnation the soul is intended to gain at least some degree of liberation from the bodies *by becoming their master*. Here again we find a natural urge from within which is often misunderstood because of lack of knowledge of its purpose. Instead of liberation by mastery, some seek liberation by retreat. As this is true of the greater cycle of the entire evolution of the soul, it is also true within the shorter cycle of the individual incarnation. In consequence, as years go by, the will becomes weaker, the powers of love are less in evidence, the mind fails, feelings seem to die out, and the body loses its sensory responses and vital powers. This is not the normal way of life. We should carry all our higher powers with us to our last day upon earth and should gain an increased mastery over them, and they should be used less for our own material advantage and more for the common good, as time goes on.

With this plan before us we can gain a better understanding of past events and be ready for the future, so that we may meet it with open eyes. As the soul unfolds like a flower throughout the entire period of its growth (Fig. 66), so in the minor cycle of three score years and ten a similar story can be seen as the body unfolds to give expression to the higher powers at their appointed time.

23

Transition and the Life Beyond

Death is a mystery before which humankind has raised many altars and erected the statues of many gods. In some countries it has been surrounded by superstitions and made terrible by fear. Science stands before death, uncomprehending—and admits defeat. Yet, in spite of these facts, deeply buried within the heart of every human being there is the hope that life is eternal and that death is one more of those apparent facts which are not true. To earth's greatest minds the fact of immortality has always been known and it is possible that to everyone, in moments of greatness, it is revealed. One thing is certain; though we can create a universe within our mind, we cannot think of annihilation. We cannot conceive of non-being; it is a mental impossibility. But it is not impossible to think of immortality. If we will withdraw in consciousness from the fears and doubts of the lower bodies, from the complexities of the mind and the troubled sea of emotional disturbances, and center our attention deeply within ourselves, we can *know* that we are one with the One Self and therefore can never cease to be. Unaffected by outer circumstances, we shall continue to exist forever.

So we can banish the thought of death from our minds for all time. We do not die. *We cannot die.* The body will drop away, but that will bring liberation to the soul which will enter a larger life in the subtler worlds. It is not death, but a transition from the prison house of the flesh and from the darkness of the physical world into the world of the astral world.

The whole illusion of death has arisen from a lack of knowledge regarding our true nature. If we think of the body as the individual, then death presents an insoluble mystery and every day of our physical existence becomes a mocking mirage, arising each morning with new deceits, while the still small voice that speaks within is only the tantalizing echo of a hope that has ceased to be. However, the evidence presented to the contrary in these pages should have dispelled all possibility of a mistake so great as this.

Some years ago, I stood on the top of one of the tallest buildings in New York and, from a height of seventy stories looked down upon the busy scene below. Standing there, I tried to imagine that I was a visitor from some other planet, unfamiliar with the things of the earth. There below were many small moving forms—we call them automobiles—apparently self-propelled and self-directed. When the traffic control lights showed green, the creatures moved. When the lights went red, they stopped. They showed every sign of being aware of each other's presence, frequently uttering raucous sounds of warning when their right of way was challenged by another. They seemed to possess intelligence. They seemed to live and think. But, as I watched, one of them drew up to the curb and a smaller form got out of it. Now how different its conditions were. At once it was revealed that all its directive power had gone and it was now merely a machine, an aggregation of material parts without power to direct its own movements, unable to make a single decision, nor in any way was it conscious of its surroundings. Can we not apply this thought to our own physical world? The human body is a living machine; its apparent intelligence is not its own, but is drawn from an indwelling Self. Without that Self to guide and control its actions, it is helpless.

As recorded in the *Bhagavad Gita* and so beautifully

translated by Sir Edwin Arnold in his poem *The Song Celestial,* Sri Krishna speaks these words:

> Never the spirit was born; the spirit shall cease to be never;
> Never was time it was not; End and Beginning are dreams!
> Birthless and deathless and changeless remaineth the spirit
>   for ever;
> Death hath not touched it at all, dead though the house
>   of it seems!
> Nay; but as when one layeth
>   His worn-out robes away,
> And, taking new ones, sayeth,
>   "These will I wear to-day!"
> So putteth by the spirit
>   Lightly its garb of flesh
> And passeth to inherit
>   A residence afresh.

The next question that arises in the inquirer's mind is a most reasonable one: "If all this is true, then where are those who have thrown off the physical body?" That question has already been answered: they are here, around us all the while, living in the subtler regions of the astral world which surrounds us in all directions, but which is unseen because of our inadequate sense perceptions (Fig. 21 and 23). Another difficulty which often stands in the way of an intellectual comprehension of the possibility of life after death is an inability to understand how a world, which is composed of matter finer even than the invisible air we breathe, could give real and tangible existence such as we experience in this world. Chapter 2, "The World of Consciousness," in Section I, Figs. 3 and 4, deals with this subject. There we are introduced to the fact that we do not live in this physical world but in a world created within our own consciousness in response to the many waves which reach it from outside and to which the sense organs respond.

The same conditions apply to the astral world. Fig. 74 specifically refers to the question we are discussing. In that illustration we see a television set tuned to Station "A" which is broadcasting on "Channel 1." This produces a certain picture on the screen of the receiving

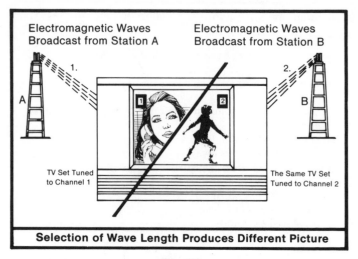

Fig. 74

set. This picture is a "reflection of reality," the quality of which is mainly dependent upon the set itself and its power to give a faithful reproduction of the original scene. Between the original and the reproduction there are only waves in the electromagnetic field, silent and invisible. Other waves, too, are passing through the receiving set, without producing any effect, for it is not "tuned" to receive them. But if the set is switched to "Channel 2" coming from Station "B," an entirely different picture will arise. No movement on the part of the receiving set is involved, only a change in the tuning to catch a different set of waves.

In Fig. 75 we see all this applied to ourselves. The physical body, like a television set though much more wonderful (for its five sense organs make it a combination of five-in-one) is sensitive to a certain area of the physical spectrum. Tuned to "Channel 1" the Self is conscious of a physical world. The astral body is sensitive to waves of the astral world (2) and the same applies to the mental body and the mental world (3). With the key thought that we live in a world created within our own consciousness, we can see that when the Self is using

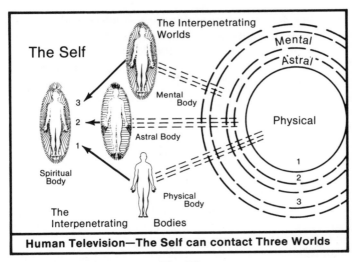

The Self

The Interpenetrating Worlds

Mental

Astral

Physical

Mental Body

Astral Body

Physical Body

Spiritual Body

The Interpenetrating Bodies

3

2

1

1

2

3

Human Television—The Self can contact Three Worlds

Fig. 75

the physical body, then it is tuned to and living in the physical world, and for the time the things of that world seem real. When the physical body is taken away, or before that under abnormal circumstances and during sleep, then it is tuned to, and is living in, the astral world, and during that time the astral world seems to be real. But the astral world, being composed of material subtler than the physical and consequently having a higher energy-release value, is not less but *more real, more tangible and alive* than its dense physical companion. The same fact applies to the mental body, though to a far greater extent, for after the astral body has lived its life of usefulness, it too releases the soul, which is then functioning in the mental world through the mental body. Each subtler world gives the soul a greater freedom of expression, is more vital and vivid, and is a step closer to reality than the one preceding it.

The conditions under which transition from the physical to the astral world takes place will vary with individuals, except that the passing itself is without pain and is an absolutely normal experience. With natural death, the awakening on the other side should be gradual, like from a deep sleep and with a feeling of abundant energy. During physical life, the astral body has been active, contributing the emotional and desire elements to the total activities of the incarnation. According to the qualitative and quantitative measures of that period, the astral body will have been built. Since our astral surroundings will be in accordance with the development of our astral body, we will now live in a world commensurate with our emotional activities of the past. As we sow, so will we reap: high or low, pure or impure.

We now come to consider the actual conditions we may meet as we gradually awaken on the other side. Here we may learn some facts of great interest, for we find ourselves in a remarkable world. We may be fairly sure that old friends will be there awaiting us—those who have passed over before. It is not likely that they will be much changed, though they may look a little older or younger (according to their own thinking regarding age), but they will look more vital than in physical life. The nature of our surroundings will depend largely upon the general level of our emotional life, but it is most likely to be an exact counterpart in astral matter of the physical surroundings we have just left. As time passes we shall discover much more about our surroundings and mingle with many people, taking our place in the astral world and its happenings as we did here. Slowly we shall realize that it is a world of glowing light; that all its objects are self-luminous, seen by their own light rather than by reflected light as we find it in the physical world. Among the most astonishing sights will be the immensity and grandeur of much of the natural scenery and the fact that it does not maintain the enduring contours of the physical world, but is constantly changing its outlines and presenting new enchanting beauties with every passing hour.

So death—as it is so wrongly called—is not the cessation of all that we have held dear in what we—also so wrongly—call life. It is exactly the opposite. If we so order our lives, it can begin a series of experiences more thrilling than anything we can imagine. And nature, wherein we see the mind of God in action, has actually been giving us a foretaste of this world-to-come, for nightly we have visited it in sleep and our dreams are often the fragmentary memories of events that happened there.

In Fig. 73 we saw an illustration of the ten periods into which our physical life is divided and how these divisions provide for our development and that of our bodies in all their aspects. In Fig. 76 we see how the same needs are met in the life which comes to us after death. However, there is a difference between the two because, in the present state of our evolution, the periods spent in the astral world and, following that in the mental world, are principally devoted to the process of absorbing the results of experience gained during physical life. Passage through the astral world may be thought of as having for its central purpose the elimination of the undesirable qualities which the past incarnation disclosed and the purification of the desire nature. Therefore it has been called the purgatorial period. Life in the mental world has as its keynote the assimilation of all the experiences in order to awaken more of the divine qualities and powers latent within the Self.

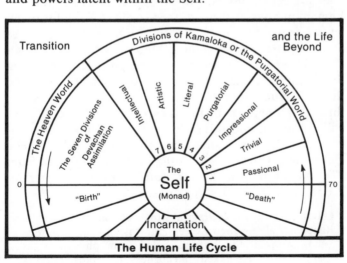

Fig. 76

Fig. 76, it will be noted, compliments Fig. 73, which
covered the incarnation from birth to the period of
transition. Seven periods are shown. These are caused
basically by the preponderence in each of them of one
subdivision of astral matter, from the solid to the atomic
state. In the astral life, these periods are passed through
in succession, analogous in some ways to the periods in
the physical state, one blending subtly into the other;
but contrary to the physical experience, the start is not
always with the first one, but is with the period which
corresponds to the man's general level of emotional
development. For the vast majority of people the astral
life is a wider and freer experience than anything contacted in physical life. There will be periods when past
desires of an unpleasant type and some of the lower
emotions must be burnt away in the fierce cauldron of
astral experience, but the expanding joys of the higher
worlds far exceed those arising during our incarnate
existence.

We shall pass on now to consider these divisions in
turn. As we shall see, some of the denser regions of the
astral world are extremely unpleasant; some are full of
loathsomeness and horror. None but the very worst of
humankind passes through those regions. Even for them,
let us remember, it is not punishment for misdeeds.
Such experiences as come to those who pass through
these lower regions are for the purpose of eliminating
the dense astral material from the body and of cleansing
the individual from such desires, so far as is possible,
through immersion in the fires of its passions. For we
will see all around things that will equal our own most
violent and crassest urges being indulged in by others.
Quotations which follow in the next few pages are from
The Ancient Wisdom by Dr. Annie Besant (chapter on
Kamaloka). Of the first region, she says:

> All the desires and feelings at which we shudder find here
> the materials for their expression; it is, in fact, the lowest
> slum, with all the horrors veiled from physical sight
> parading in their naked hideousness. Its repulsiveness is

much increased by the fact that in the astral world character expresses itself in form, and the man who is full of evil passions *looks* the whole of them; bestial appetites shape the astral body into bestial forms. . . .

Only the very worst would pass through this condition. This region no doubt has given rise to the popular idea of hell. Furthermore the law of gravity operates in some way in each of the worlds. Consequently the heavy astral matter of the lowest subdivision is actually within the crust of the earth. It is, therefore, below us, and that fact has no doubt contributed to the idea that hell is "below." Such facts as these, with many others, lend strong support to the belief held by many people that all the teachings now being disseminated as Theosophy were once taught by the great religions of the world and that their present doctrines are only the outer symbols of an inner truth which has been lost by most of them. Jesus definitely stated that he taught the "mysteries of the kingdom of Heaven" to his disciples, while to the multitude he could only give the symbolic utterances of the parables.

In the second region we find an astral counterpart of the physical earth and all objects associated with it. The majority of very ordinary people start their astral life here: that is, because of the particular quality of their astral bodies this is the level of which they become conscious and in which they will spend much of their time. They are those

> whose interests were bound up in the trivial and petty objects of life, who set their hearts on trifles, as well as those who allowed their lower natures to rule them, and who died with the appetites still active and desirous of physical enjoyment. . . . They are mostly dissatisfied, uneasy, restless, with more or less of suffering according to the vigor of the wishes they cannot gratify.

Often they delay their departure to better regions by trying to communicate with their earthly friends through mediums of little spiritual attainment.

The third of these divisions is a little more refined

than the second. It still presents an astral counterpart
of earthly things but of a somewhat higher nature. Though
not so strongly attracted to earth experiences, still people
here are "susceptible to earthly stimuli and the weakening
interest in terrestrial affairs may be rewakened by cries
from below." Astral life for most people will being here.

The fourth presents a condition in which earthly
attractions are now fading and the call to higher things
is heard. The lower emotional material within the astral
body has almost worn itself out, leaving only the subtler
substances by means of which we have full freedom for
expressing higher and more beautiful feelings.

> Souls of somewhat more progressed types are found there,
> and although they are held by the encasement built by
> the activities of their earthly interests, their attention is
> for the most part directed onwards rather than back-
> wards and, if they are not forcibly recalled to the concerns
> of earth-life, they will pass on without very much delay.

In Fig. 76 this region has been indicated as "purgatorial"
because it seems to be the critical point at which we
have the two choices before us—onward or backward—
and the higher life definitely looms within our consciousness.

In the fifth region many new characteristics are to be
found. The luminosity of astral objects has been developing progressively, and here it becomes strikingly
obvious.

> Here are situated all the materialized heavens which
> play so large a part in popular religions all the world
> over. . . . Men and women who clung desperately to every
> "letter that killeth" have here the literal satisfaction of
> their cravings, unconsciously creating in astral matter
> by their powers of imagination, fed on the mere husks
> of the world's Scriptures, the cloud-built palaces whereof
> they dreamed.

The sixth division is still more refined and is occupied
by souls of a more advanced type, less literal in their
beliefs and creatively artistic in temperament.

> Their surrounds are of the best that are found in Kamaloka,
> as their creative thoughts fashion the luminous materials
> of their temporary home into fair landscapes and rippling
> oceans, snow-clad mountains and fertile plains, scenes
> that are of fairy-like beauty compared with even the most
> exquisite that earth can show. . . . They look forward more
> clearly to passing out of their present sphere, and reaching
> a higher state.

Finally the seventh and highest subdivision is occupied by those who have eliminated much of the lower
nature and particularly by intellectual people who have
gloried in the pure pleasure of mental pursuits.

> Men who have been keenly set on some line of intellectual
> investigation, and have thrown off the physical body
> with their thirst for knowledge unslaked, pursue their
> object still with unwearied persistence, fettered by their
> clinging to the physical modes of study.

Very briefly, this outline has told of the progress of
the soul through the astral world. Though of a more
drastic nature, the changes that confront it are analogous
to those of the physical world as the human being grows
from babyhood to the stature of an adult. Only the worst
of earth's humanity would need the painful purging of
the lowest regions, but in time even they will be released
to work out the better parts of their nature in the higher
realms. The second region will contain few but the most
trivially minded, who would spend time there frittering
away their opportunities until they too would begin to
realize that there is something better beyond. The mass
of humanity no doubt awakens to astral life in the third
division, where they will soon hear the call to go onwards.
No one on earth is wholly good or wholly bad. There is
much of both within us all, though definite evil exists
only in the few. Gradually, as the lower elements in our
bodies lose the capacity for vital action imparted to them
in physical life, the higher powers are released to find
expression.

The value of a knowledge of Theosophy to those who
are facing astral life cannot be overestimated, for they

will know of the greater things that lie ahead and will not become enamored of the lesser attractions which it offers. And here, once more, we find the practical value of even a theoretical knowledge of the elemental life. If we have allowed living forms of the elemental kingdom to enter our astral body, they will endeavor to prolong their stay by drawing all the densest and worst material of the body to its surface, thus creating a hard shell which will lengthen the time spent in that region and prevent any of the higher astral forces from penetrating. Normally, while the lower types of matter will be the first to be activated, the higher will respond to some degree to the calling of its kind, though the finer emotional forces cannot find full expression until the lower have been eliminated. If the will is strongly evoked, the elemental forces can be ejected.

There comes a time when the astral life has run its course, its purposes have been fulfilled and the dross has been separated from the pure metal which is then carried forward to be cast into nobler molds. The permanent atom, which has silently and unerringly registered as added vibratory power the results of all the astral experiences, sinks into quiescence ready for the next call to gather together material for a new and better body. The worn-out body is cast off—an astral corpse—and the person in the mental body, begins to function in the mental world.

Here we find conditions entirely different from any we have met before during our cycle of incarnation. For thought can create, and we must distinguish between contemplative and creative thinking, the abstract and the concrete. Of this transfer, Dr. Besant writes in the same book:

> . . . the Soul sinks into a brief unconsciousness of its surroundings like the unconsciousness that follows the dropping off of the physical body, to be awakened by a sense of bliss, intense, immense, fathomless, undreamed of, the bliss of the heaven world. . . . Softest melodies are breathing round him, tenderest hues greet his opening

eyes, the very air seems music and color, the whole being is suffused with light and harmony. Then through the golden haze dawn sweetly the faces loved on earth, etherialized into the beauty which expresses their noblest, loveliest emotions, unmarred by the troubles and the passions of the lower worlds.

To understand conditions in the heaven world is not an easy task except for those whose intuition is sufficiently awake to comprehend, from a key thought given here and there regarding the principles which apply to it. We know that, in the physical world, all our creations have been developed first in the mind. The artist conceives the idea for a picture first and then tries to depict it upon the canvas with the crude facilities that earth has to offer. The engineer designs a structure, building it first in the imagination before the bridge or machine is built in physical matter. The process is long and arduous, for the matter of this world cannot be made to respond directly to the waves of thought. In the astral world, by using the power of will, we can fashion material to our choosing. But in the mental world that which we think of takes form immediately in mental matter, good or bad, poor or rich, according to the knowledge and power of the thinker.

Therefore, it should be obvious that in *Devachan* (as this region is frequently called) *everything we think becomes clothed in form.* So at once we find ourselves surrounded by the things that in physical life were most attractive to us. We think of friends, and they are with us. Not only are they with us, but we can enjoy their love and companionship. All their finer qualities are there in evidence, only in greater measure than we have ever known before, for all undesirable traits are absent. They are living and vibrant with life.

We, who are immersed in the limitations of physical life, find it difficult to understand how our friends can be present with us—and, of course, with many others too —in the heaven life, while they are "alive" on earth, nor why their good qualities alone should show and not the bad ones. On first thought this may seem to be an impossibility. But there are many "impossibilities" yet to be grasped by our growing minds. Let us go back to the analogy of the television set once more. I was once reminded by an interviewer, as we entered a television studio, that I was shortly going to enter eighty thousand homes all at the same time. My picture and voice would be faithfully reproduced in eighty thousand places at once, and I would be seen and heard in them all. This is a miracle that would have been laughed to scorn had it been suggested a hundred years ago. Yet the mysteries of the subtler worlds go far beyond even the marvels of radio and television, and we have not yet learned more than a fraction of the great things which are implicit in the idea of human beings as gods in the making. If through a humanly constructed television station one person can appear in thousands of places at once and be seen and heard, cannot the same phenomenon occur, though moved to a much higher level, and the soul be able to manifest itself within the thought forms created by one's erstwhile friends of earth who are now in Devachan? For let us remember that we do not see our friends at all on earth, but only their physical bodies through which a portion only of the soul can manifest. Furthermore, since the lower bodies would not be concerned in the devachanic manifestation, the undesirable qualities which are their life and not the life of the soul would not be present.

The kind of heaven that we have believed in, the streets of gold, the pearly gates, the happy hunting grounds, whatever we have clung to in physical life, will all spring into reality before us. Nothing will enter that might bring pain or make us sad; only the best and most beautiful will be there, limited alone by our power of comprehension.

There are two main divisions in Devachan: the so-called lower mental and higher mental. Souls do not proceed through its subdivisions in sequence, as in the astral world, but find their normal level in each division one after the other, expanding their consciousness within first the lower and then the higher as time passes. The keynote of the heaven life is the assimilation of experiences into faculty and power by awakening into life more of the divine qualities sleeping with the Self.

> Devachan, the heaven-world, is a world of bliss, of joy unspeakable. But it is much more than this, much more than a rest for the weary . . . it is the land in which the mind and heart develop, unhindered by gross matter and by trivial cares, where weapons are forged for earth's fierce battle-fields, and where the progress of the future is secured.

In the lower mental world, the soul is using the mental body; but that, too, dies, and we are then left in our spiritual body, unhampered by any vehicles of the lower worlds. The time spent in all the conditions which have been referred to, astral and mental, varies considerably according to the individual. Furthermore, the time which *seems* to have elapsed often bears little relationship to the actual procession of events by which we measure time, for in these regions the illusion of time becomes far more obvious than in the physical world. It is quite possible that a short while spent in the lowest astral region does *seem* to be eternity. And in the higher regions the words of the hymn, "A thousand ages in Thy sight are like an evening gone," can be equally true.

Thus the soul completes the absorption of its physical experiences. It has lived a wonderful life in the higher worlds. This life has been full of great events and, if we follow the pathway of progress with willing footsteps, of happy times of joyful expansions of our conscious existence. If we have endured pains, they have been for our good. In the highest heaven the soul has reviewed its many incarnations, has seen its mistakes and efforts to achieve and has thus been enabled to show forth in greater measure its inherent divinity. One final quotation from Dr. Besant:

> For death is only a change that gives the soul a partial liberation, releasing him from the heaviest of his chains. It is but a birth into a wider life, a return after brief exile on earth to the soul's true home, a passing from a prison

into the freedom of the upper air. Death is the greatest
of earth's illusions; there is no death, but only changes
in life-conditions. Life is continuous, unbroken, un-
breakable; "unborn, eternal, ancient, constant," it
perishes not with the perishing of the bodies that clothe it.

Eventually, the time for another incarnation approaches
and the events illustrated in Fig. 68 take place once more.
The nuclei around which the lower bodies are to be built
will be vitalized in their turn, and soon the limitations
of a physical vehicle will close around the soul. Then,
once more it will grapple with the problems of terrestrial
existence, sowing and reaping, and testing its newly
gained powers in the fierce fires of physical life.

In Fig. 77 we see another interesting adaptation of the
wheel as a symbol of our journey through life and one
more illustration of the manner in which nature's laws
operate equally in the spiritual and the material realms.
In this case the symbol is built upon the wheel in motion.
We may think of the area below the hub as the physical
world and that above the hub as the superphysical worlds.
The hub represents the Self within its vehicles of consciousness. In Fig. 77A, the three essential parts of the

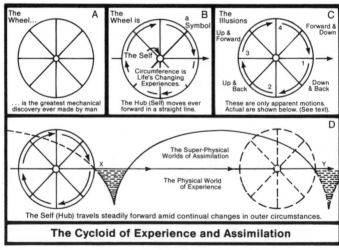

The Cycloid of Experience and Assimilation

Fig. 77

wheel are shown: the hub, the spokes, and the circumference or rim. As the wheel moves forward upon the ground, its outermost parts are in constant motion and any point on the rim is subject to perpetual change in the direction of its travel. But the hub, typifying the Self, moves steadily forward in a straight line toward its destination (Fig. 77B). How often we have felt that we were being forced to move in several directions at once, to our utter confusion, like the wheel we see in Fig. 77C. These motions, however, are only apparent for, as the wheel moves on, strange as it may seem, at no time will any part of the circumference move backward. Surprisingly, its motion will be as shown in Fig. 77D, which is known as a cycloid curve. If we take the point "x" to indicate a certain experience originating in the physical world, it will plunge down into material expression and then will withdraw, absorbed into the higher worlds at the close of the incarnation, where it will be built into added power. This will return for test and trial at the next incarnation. The higher and nobler we can make our physical life expressions, the faster will our wheel move forward toward the goal. Yet so wonderful is the plan that every experience, high or low, will be transmuted into a power, the former through joy, the latter through suffering. Like Fig. 67, the cycloid curve tells the story of our brief contacts with the physical material, and our longer sojourn in the higher worlds.

24

Karma: The Law of Opportunity

Karma is a Sanskrit word which, literally translated, means "action." More specifically, however, it refers to a fundamental law of nature which operates in all known regions, physical and superphysical. It has two major aspects, one of which is immediate and the other, generally, delayed.

The karma which reacts immediately can perhaps be explained most simply and clearly by quoting the words of the great scientific genius Sir Isaac Newton, as enunciated in the third of his famous laws of motion: "To every action there is an equal and opposite reaction." This, we know, applies to all physical manifestations of energy. But it also applies to humans; in fact *it is one of the most important facts that we should keep in mind every day of our lives.* It is illustrated in Fig. 78A, and to explain it we might well paraphrase the third law of motion by stating: "To every human action in the outer, material world, there is an equal and opposite reaction in the inner, spiritual world." Whatever actions we do to others, whether good or ill, kind or unkind, small or large, *there is a synchronous reaction within us,* either in our astral, mental, or spiritual bodies. If we are angry with someone, we may not injure that person at all, but we immediately injure our own astral body. If we practice deception, we may or may not succeed in our deceptive efforts, but we can be quite sure that the act itself will have caused definite injury to our mental body. If we pour out pure

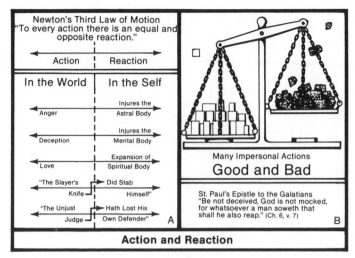

Fig. 78

love to another or to all living beings, that action causes an expansion in the spiritual body and we at once become better because of the deed. As symbolized in Fig. 78B, the many small good and bad actions that we perform every day modify our normal expressions of mind and emotion, and our character is gradually built up as a composite picture of them all.

But we must consider also the effects of these acts upon others. That is where the second aspect of the law of karma is seen. This can be well expressed in the words of St. Paul, in his Epistle to the Galatians (VI:7): "Be not deceived, God is not mocked; for whatsoever a man soweth, that shall he also reap." Yet the reaping, as we know well, is often long delayed, frequently until another incarnation, just as seeds sown in the ground do not spring up the same day as the sowing, but many days afterwards. Gautama Buddha also spoke strongly about this law in words which have been beautifully expressed by Sir Edwin Arnold in his poem *The Light of Asia*:

> The Books say well, my Brothers! each man's life
>   The outcome of his former living is;
> The bygone wrongs bring forth sorrows and woes,

> The bygone right breeds bliss.
> That which ye sow ye reap. See yonder fields!
>   The sesamum was sesamum, the corn
> Was corn. The Silence and the Darkness knew!
>   So is a man's fate born.
> He cometh, reaper of the things he sowed,
>   Sesamum, corn, so much cast in past birth;
> And so much weed and poison-stuff, which mar
>   Him and aching earth.
> If ye shall labour rightly, rooting these,
>   And planting wholesome seedlings where they grew,
> Fruitful and fair and clean the ground shall be,
>   And rich the harvest due.
>
> By this, the slayer's knife did stab himself;
>   The unjust judge hath lost his own defender;
> The false tongue dooms its lie; the creeping thief
>   And spoiler rob, to render.
> Such is the Law which moves to righteousness,
>   Which none at last can turn aside or stay;
> The heart of it is Love, the end of it
>   Is Peace and Consummation sweet. Obey!

This law, then, is simple in outline. We sow, and we reap in accordance with the sowing. We should not expect to plant thistles and grow grapes from them. If we sow tares we shall not reap wheat. If we sow pain to others we shall reap pain in ourselves. How or when this will work out we cannot say, but of one thing we can be sure: "God is not mocked," we shall reap. However, causes seldom remain simple, they become complex. Many new impulses here and there will modify, or even entirely neutralize, the original impulse. But the simple law itself remains and will never fail in its action.

Unfortunately, to some people the existence of law, precise and unchanging, seems to be depressing, even frightening, at first. They feel as though they were in the grip of fate, facing at all times an inescapable punishment, brought upon themselves by past errors. This attitude is only possible when the law is not fully understood. Karma should give us hope and encouragement, for it is essentially the law of *opportunity*. It is precisely *because of this law* that we are *not* in the grip of fate, for under its operation, we reap only the things that we have sown. But here let us clearly realize the difference between humans and nature. Our neighbor may do us harm that we have not deserved, for we are free agents learning the lessons of life, and we make mistakes which we will have to rectify. But nature does not make mistakes and will cast us only into those pathways and visit us with only those joys and sufferings that we ourselves made necessary in the past. They are not rewards and punishments; they are part of the plan whereby wrongs will be righted and weaknesses will be turned into strength. So karma provides for every error the circumstances which will result in its correction and for every right, those which will bring us still greater achievement (Fig. 79).

In the Christian gospels it is recorded that Jesus and his disciples one day passed by a man who had been blind from his birth. The disciples asked the master, "Who did sin, this man or his parents, that he was born blind?" To those who do not realize that reincarnation was known generally and was widely accepted among the Jews of those days, this may be a startling question, for, if the man were suffering because of his past actions they must have been committed in a previous existence, as he was blind at birth. Also, the question itself indicates that the disciples were well aware of the teaching of reincarnation. However, it showed that they still held to the idea of sin and punishment and it was this attitude that the master decried in his reply: "Neither hath this man sinned nor his parents, but that the works of God should be manifest in him" (John IX:1-3). In another translation, the reply is given as "but that the law might be fulfilled." Both of these translations contain the same essential meaning, for the laws of God are works in manifestation. Jesus repudiated the idea of sin and punishment and declared the effect to be a manifestation of the works of God, of the law which we can easily recognize as karma, working within us. For he frequently proclaimed this law by such statements as, "Judge not that ye be not judged, for with what judgment ye judge ye shall be judged; and with what measure ye mete it shall be measured to you again" (Matt VII:2). On another occasion he said, "Therefore all things whatsoever ye would that men should do to you, do ye even so to them: *for this is the law* and the prophets" (Matt VII:12).

In a previous incarnation, a weakness in one's character had caused him or her to do some harm to another. The present condition was the result of that mistake, not a punishment for having sinned. Let us forever rid our minds of the idea that God inflicts punishment upon people because of their mistakes. Anger is a human failing, surely not a divine attribute. Let us banish for all time our difficulties regarding "forgiveness of sins." "To err is human; to forgive, divine." God is divine, and will always forgive, if we wish to think of it in that way, though the very word is founded upon a misunderstanding of the divine nature. Would it not be much better to become so fully conscious of divine love that we could know that God would lavish nothing less than divine love upon us, who are God's own creations? Because of that love, God allows us to reap the fruits of our own actions, whether they be pleasures or pains, for they will help us onward under the beneficent law of karma. That is not punishment.

Let us refer to Fig. 79A. Starting at (1), we see that an act of cruelty is committed. This is a cause set going in the physical world, the immediate effect of which, as we have seen, is an injury to the astral body of the originator. Some suffering is caused to the victim. All these effects must be balanced by the law. After we have made our transit from the physical to the astral world, the injury in our astral body will cause us to suffer. Later, in the spiritual body, we will review the situation without emotional reactions and will see, in vivid retrospection, the error of our ways. We will learn the need for kindness, and it will awaken within the Self (3) an added measure of the divine quality of love. Then, the new power must be tested in action. So, in a new incarnation we will meet those who suffer, as we caused suffering (4), and if we meet it with kindness and action to alleviate their condition, our debt will have been repaid, the wrong will have been righted, and the balance of nature restored. Out of that which we call evil, good will have arisen, though at the cost of suffering.

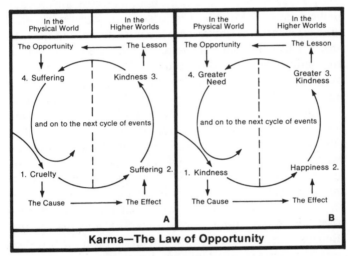

Fig. 79

Fig. 79B shows a different condition. This time a good deed is followed to its time of reaping. The cause is a deed of kindness (1). This, as we have seen, will result in an immediate expansion of the astral body. After transition to the astral world, that expansion will add to our happiness there (2). In the spiritual world (3) the event will be reviewed, and the result will be the acquisition of a greater measure of the spirit of kindness, a further unfolding of the divine power of love. This, too, must be tested, and so in another incarnation we will be met by a need greater than before (4), to test whether our newly acquired spiritual strength can rise to the new heights which the circumstances will demand. In this case, out of "good" has come that which is "better," but the way has been that of happiness.

It may be wondered how, in the complex pattern of

events of human life throughout the world, the individual can possibly be directed to the circumstances which would be commensurate with, and of the nature required for, the balancing of one's particular karmic needs. Modern radio controlled equipment can do as much as this even now in physical affairs, for minute differences in the length of radio waves can cause an astonishingly large variety of selective responses in a wide variety of fields of use. The human being is not an entity separate from other humans, as one may seem to be. Each one has a "wave length," a composite of all the many wave lengths contained within the bodies. We are conscious of this fact in the "likes" and "dislikes" we feel for other people. So, karmically, the individual is attracted to the circumstances needed according to specific auric emanations. An illustration may help. The waves of the ocean ceaselessly beating upon land have caused an inlet here and a point jutting out into the water somewhere else. The contours of the shore line are of many shapes and sizes. The waves dash on day after day, and the outline changes, but the changes do not arise because the successive waves are gifted so that they will act in one place and refrain from action in another. They do not consciously carve out the bays and caves and favor the highlands by leaving them untouched. They roll on, only carrying out the natural urges that lie within them as they answer to the forces of nature. The strength or the weakness of the land controls the results. So forces beat upon us from the inner worlds and we respond to them according to our strengths and weaknesses, and the karmic law is carried out.

Note especially in Fig. 79 that the law of karma brings us the opportunities, but the urge is always to *action,* and until action takes place the karma is not balanced. It is of little value if, faced with suffering, we rejoice because we feel a kindly disposition toward the sufferer. We must act to relieve that suffering. If our own karma is to reap suffering, we shall never repay the debt by merely "bearing" it. We should analyze our situation to the best of our ability to try to determine its cause. It might be that our suffering is meant to draw us nearer to those who suffer even more than we. Perhaps, because of it, only we can help them with the sympathy and understanding they need. Or possibly, because we have been too immersed in mundane affairs, we must now be brought face to face with the silence of the inner worlds and, whether we wish it or not, must have time to meditate upon higher things, thus strengthening the links of soul to body. There are many reasons that could lie behind our suffering. Only as we search within and, learning the cause, "take arms against a sea of troubles, and by opposing end them" can we balance the karmic debt. Thus, the whole of nature, seen and unseen, yesterday, today, and forever, is linked into one vast scheme of evolving life, every part joined to every other part by this fundamental law of cause and effect. There is no fate, no chance and no punishment. We reap precisely as we sow. The plan is simple, the way is clear, and in our hand we hold the pen by means of which we shall inscribe upon the indelible records of time the story of our future attainments.

V

The Mastery of Illusion

Before the soul can see, the Harmony within must be attained, and fleshly eyes be rendered blind to all illusion. . . . Before the soul can comprehend and may remember, she must unto the Silent Speaker be united just as the form to which the clay is modelled, is first united with the potter's mind.

The Voice of the Silence
H. B. Blavatsky

25

Toward Liberation

The first, and the most important, step that we can take toward the solution of any problem is to state the problem clearly and accurately, so that our efforts can be applied in the right direction. Every generation has had its own unique difficulties to face and probably will have for many ages yet to come; but in the latter half of the twentieth century the peace and security of the entire world seems to be threatened by more baffling enigmas than ever plagued the struggling human race before, and to the point that the very survival of humanity is threatened. Further, as each problem is solved, two more seem to follow in its wake, arising with still greater and more insistent demands upon human ingenuity for their solution. The urgency of each problem, too, increases with growing numbers. Furthermore, these questions are no longer superficial and local; they are fundamental and worldwide. Also, they exist not only on the international stage of political and social relationships but within us too, in our mental and physical constitutions. Everywhere in the world we find hospitals filled with those who are physically sick, prisons filled with the morally sick, and substance-abuse centers and mental hospitals overflowing with those who suffer from mental and emotional disorders. Contagious diseases now sweep from country to country and here, too, it seems as though the conquest of one of them brings others which are worse than the first.

The plain and unvarnished fact is that palliatives have failed to correct both human and international disorders. Partial answers are unsatisfactory. Remedies have not gone deep enough into basic causes. All these may ease the pains, but they do not cure. The creation of millionaires in any country does not indicate that it is prosperous if the common people are made poorer thereby. Faced with these facts, it is imperative that the world's thinkers should set themselves, without delay, to a search for the real causes which underlie the woes of humankind, for further deterioration of the situation could cause a tragedy the like of which has never been known before. Now, only fundamental concepts are of any value; wrong must be eradicated at its roots.

A fundamental concept, inspired by the teachings of Theosophy, has been put forward in these pages. It has been suggested that all life's problems arise from three illusions which were drawn over mankind at the beginning of history, when the Solar Deity, who is omnipotent, omniscient, and omnipresent within the solar system, drew three limitations which gave rise to the three primary illusions: of (1) *space*, or objects existing in space (as dimensions); (2) of *time* (as a succession of events); and (3) of *self*, the illusion of separated existence. We are overcoming the first of these by the development of scientific knowledge, so that we are learning to know the physical world and the nature of our bodies. The second we are overcoming by developing our powers of reason, intuition and wisdom and so endeavoring to formulate a satisfactory philosophy which will promote successful living. The third, the most difficult of all, will be mastered when we can expand the idea of the self as separate from other selves to embrace a knowledge of the unity of all life within the One Life. If we can grasp the significance of, and all the corollaries that stem from, these simple facts, we shall see that they lie at the root of all our troubles and that, as we gradually master them, all the minor difficulties will disappear in succession along the way. To quote the words of Jesus, "Seek ye first the kingdom of God and his righteousness; and all these things shall be added unto you" (Matt. VI:33).

We must get down to fundamentals. It is useless to do otherwise, for illusion can be overcome only by knowledge. To deny pain by a process of self-hypnosis and so prevent its manifestations will not cure a diseased condition of the body. To cover poverty with a cloak of charity will not cure the economic ills of a nation. To imprison violators of the law will not elevate the morals of the people. To win our battles by blasting our opponent nations from the face of the earth with hydrogen bombs will not move the world even one small step nearer to justice for all, without which there can be no assurance of lasting peace. Nor will an examination of petty details, a little patch here and there on the crumbling walls of society, cure the ills of humankind. Nothing less than a careful examination of the blueprints, a full inspection of the building, both the basements and superstructure, and a complete overhaul in accordance with the needs disclosed can save the building from an otherwise inevitable collapse.

To state that we have released ourselves from the illusion that the sun rises in the east and, passing over our heads, sets in the west, because we have come to a belief that it is not true, is only adding one more illusion to the many we face already. Release can come only when we learn the facts and the illusion becomes obvious in the light of the knowledge we have gained. Refusing to gain experience of life and withdrawing into a forest, there to arrive at a theoretical belief that life is not real, do not dispel the illusion; only a new and more subtle illusion has taken its place. We must learn about life by meeting it face to face, by immersing ourselves in its illusory spells and its false shows and, seeing them for what they are, repudiating their mocking imitations of reality. Then we can stand conqueror of illusion and can taste the sweetness of true liberation.

In the previous sections of this book we have examined some facts which we can now use in approaching our present subject—overcoming illusion. Science agrees that space and time are not two separate phenomena; they are jointly involved in all physical events. However, scientists as yet have not given full recognition to the fact that, in human experience, a third factor is always involved. That is the Self.

But a general recognition of this fact cannot be long delayed, for many individual scientists are realizing that all our knowledge is nothing more than a product of various manifestations insofar as they affect the human consciousness and that since sense perceptions are known to be far from perfect, our knowledge of physical happenings must be equally incomplete. Being incomplete, it is illusory. That is, it is something that appears to be that which it is not. Our aim must be to overcome the illusions of space, time and self by acquiring knowledge and interpreting it through the use of reason and intuition.

Let us refer to Fig. 80. On the left lower part of the drawing we see the Earth represented in two positions, in order to keep the illustration clear. In the upper right we see the Sun. Now let us imagine that in the year 1990 a jet plane left the Earth at a steady speed of 600 miles

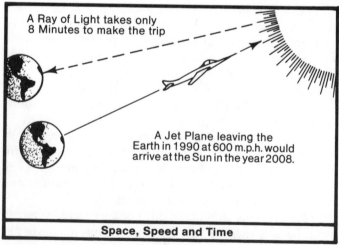

A Ray of Light takes only 8 Minutes to make the trip

A Jet Plane leaving the Earth in 1990 at 600 m.p.h. would arrive at the Sun in the year 2008.

Space, Speed and Time

Fig. 80

per hour. Its destination is the Sun, 93,000,000 miles away. The pilot would have to fly on and on for eighteen years before he arrived there. It would then be the year 2008. So, in terms of travel, we could say that the Sun is an eighteen year journey "by air" from the Earth. There is something that travels faster than a jet plane, much faster. Light rushes through space at the amazing speed of 186,000 miles every second. A ray of light, therefore, will cover the distance between Earth and Sun in eight minutes. That is, in terms of light rays, the Sun is only eight minutes distance from us. As the time consumed during the trip is shortened, the Sun seems to get nearer to us. Since our concepts of space and time are inextricably interwoven, as travel has increased in speed, our world has become smaller and now a journey which a few generations ago would have been considered to be the outstanding event of a lifetime is a commonplace.

Space and time can cast their mantle of illusion over the human consciousness in many ways. Light, it has been mentioned, travels at the rate of 186,000 miles a second, thus taking eight minutes to reach us from the Sun. This means that we never see the Sun where it really is, but where it was eight minutes ago. This illusion, however, becomes more pronounced when we come to consider the stars. Let us now imagine that we are looking up into the heavens, and there we see those thousands of scintillating points of light, each of which is a sun. We will pick out Sirius, the "dog star," the brightest star in the sky. Though a long distance from us, it is one of our nearest celestial neighbors, being only a little over 50,000,000,000,000 miles away, a distance of no great magnitude to an astronomer. It takes light nine years to travel over that space. The very rays of light that strike our eyes left Sirius nine years ago and have been rushing through space ever since. This means, of course, that Sirius is not where we see it; it is millions of miles away. In Fig. 81A the black line shows the point in the sky where Sirius appears to be; the broken line points to the place where it really is.

Now we can apply these facts to every object we see

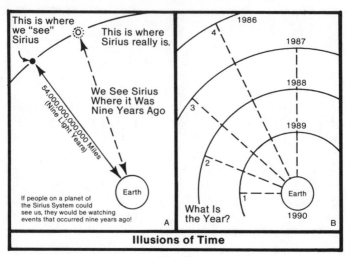

Illusions of Time

Fig. 81

above us. *Not one of the stars we are looking at is there.* Each one has moved to a new position, far away, and *where they are now we cannot see them.* So, the whole celestial picture is an illusion. Once more we see that the visible is not true; truth lies in the invisible. Furthermore, there are stars and nebulae that are so far away and their light takes so long to reach us that they may have been blotted out of existence long before the first primitive people walked the Earth, and it would be thousands of years more before people on earth would know of their demise. Conversely, it is possible that stars or even universes may have come into being and are out there in space, but their light will not announce the news of the fact for many years yet to come.

In Fig. 81B we see another application of the same facts. If we could create a great bubble, which had its surface 6,000,000,000,000 miles from the Earth, and we could look down with perfect vision, we should see events taking place on Earth, but they would be those of one year before, for the light by which we viewed them would have taken one year to traverse the space between us. If on Earth it was the year 1990, up there, to us, it would be

1989. At a distance of 12,000,000,000,000 miles the year would be 1988, for its events would be parading before our eyes, and so on. For each additional light year that we traveled away from the Earth, the date would move back a year. Theoretically, then, if by means of some magical process not yet known, we could transport ourselves a thousand light years into space and we had a telescope of sufficient power, we should see the Earth as it was ten centuries ago—a whirling, boiling, maze of intrigue, with battles and struggles for wealth and power, re-enacted before our eyes. Extending the same thoughts still further, at some distance in the vastness of space, there must exist a record of every event that ever happened at any time upon the Earth. And then, to make our confusion still more nearly complete, according to accepted theories, if we could travel outward at a rate of speed which exceeded that of light, all the events we should see on Earth would be moving in reverse, that is, effects would take place before their causes, people would be walking backward, the Sun would rise in the west and set in the east, rain would fall upward and the evening would gradually give place to afternoon, then morning, and then would come the preceding night.

So the more we penetrate into the mysteries of space and time, the more do we see their obvious illusions and the need for interpreting their phenomena in the light of reason. We shall now try to analyze these two things separately. Space, it is said, has three dimensions. The falsity of this statement should be obvious. Space can have no dimensions, we can only apply the term to things which exist in space. For dimension is only a mathematical concept developed to assist us in our computations of size.

In Fig. 82 we see some illustrations of the mathematical concept of dimensions. In Fig. 82A, we see that a point extended becomes a line—one dimension. A line extended in a direction not contained within itself becomes a plane (Fig. 82B)—two dimensions. A plane extended in a direction not contained within itself becomes a cube (Fig. 82C)—three dimensions. Theoretically, a cube

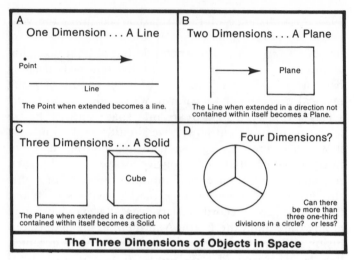

Fig. 82

could be extended in a direction not contained within itself, and it would produce a four-dimensional solid which would have many remarkable properties. However the original conditions laid down for computing dimensions preclude more than a threefold division, as a similar limitation would be produced if we divided a circle into three equal segments (Fig. 82D). There could not be more than three-thirds in the circle since we placed that limitation there in the beginning. Nor can there be more than three dimensions, since the method of computing them laid down that limitation by its very nature. We shall return to this subject a little later to discuss the illusory nature of dimensions.

In Fig. 83 we see some illustrations which draw our attention to the illusion of size, of things that exist in space. We think of a marble as a small object; but compared with the almost infinite smallness of the atom, it is very large. Compared with a balloon it becomes small and the balloon large. But the large balloon becomes very small compared with the Earth, which is an immense object floating in space. But once again we must modify our conception of size, for, compared with Jupiter, Earth

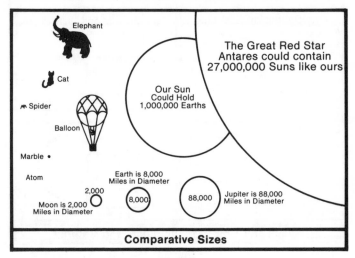

Comparative Sizes

Fig. 83

is quite small. In turn, Jupiter becomes small compared with the Sun, which could contain a million planets the size of ours. Once more, however, we must modify our conception of size, for our great Sun, immense and magnificent as it is, shrinks into almost entire insignificance when we look at the great red star Antares, which is no less than 27,000,000 times the volume of the great center of our solar system, which placed beside Antares would seem so minute that it might be overlooked altogether. So we can see that nothing is "small" or "large" in itself, but only within a perceiving consciousness which is comparing it with another object, consciously or unconsciously. To the consciousness of an elephant a cat must be small, yet to a spider the same cat is huge. We shall now draw together some of the illusions of space and time, and bring them to light more clearly.

Objects that exist in space can be considered both psychologically and mathematically. Psychologically, we think of them as large or small. But we have just seen that these appellations merely signify different states produced within the consciousness for purposes of comparison. They have no reality, for the same object can be

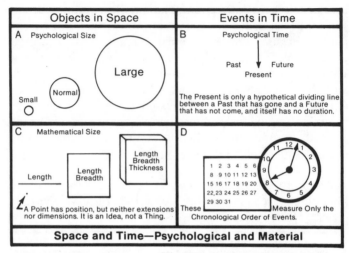

Fig. 84

both large and small at the same time. The mathematical measurements of an object are computed in terms of length, breadth and thickness. Mathematical size does not deal with "small" or "large." We have seen also that the basis of dimensions is the point which when extended makes a line. The line produces a plane and the plane a three dimensional solid such as the cube. But let us note carefully: all this began with the point which, we may recall, has only position. It has neither extensions nor dimensions. This means that the point is only an idea; it is not a thing, it is *no-thing*. Therefore, all these conceptions of dimension are invalid for, if we multiply nothing by the largest number we can think of, our answer will still be nothing. To extend a mathematical point in any direction is an impossibility, for it is only an idea of location, without size or dimension, and therefore it does not exist as an object which can be extended. Length, breadth, and thickness are three qualities or characteristics of matter which came into existence at the dawn of creation, as a reflection of the basic trinity of nature. Therefore, there can be no more than three dimensions; but within them there may be an infinite number of combinations in extension and direction. The smallest point that we can make, in order to exist as an object that can be extended in any direction, must already exist in three dimensions. The period, or full stop, at the end of this sentence, exists in three dimensions: it has length, breadth and the thickness of the ink with which it is printed. A line is merely an idea unless it is created physically in three dimensions, though one of them is greatly exaggerated. A plane, too, remains in the conceptual world until it is given three dimensional manifestation, though, in this case, two of them are greater than the third. Three dimensions, *neither more nor less,* are necessary for all phenomenal existence. In *The Secret Doctrine* (Vol. I, page 271), H. P. Blavatsky writes:

> The process of natural development which we are now considering will at once elucidate and discredit the fashion of speculating on the attributes of two, three and four dimensional space. . . . To begin with, the superficial absurdity of assuming that space itself is measurable in any direction is of little consequence. The familiar phrase can only be an abbreviation of the fuller form of the *fourth dimension of matter in space.* But even thus expanded it is an unhappy phrase, because, while it is true that the progress of evolution may be destined to introduce us to new characteristics of matter, those with which we are familiar are really more numerous than the three dimensions. . . . Thus when some bold thinkers have been thirsting for a fourth dimension to explain the passage of matter through matter and the production of knots on an endless cord, they have been in want of a *sixth characteristic* of matter. The three dimensions belong really to only one attribute or characteristic of matter—extension; and popular common sense rebels against the idea that, under any condition of things there can be more than three such dimensions as length, breadth and thickness. . . . Meanwhile, the expression is far more incorrect than even the familiar phrase of the sun's "rising" and "setting."

Referring to Fig. 84D we see what Einstein has called "chronological" or physical time. These are based on methods by means of which months, days, hours, and minutes may be measured. Chronological time, like mathematical size, is measured by human-made devices. In the words of Einstein, as reported in the daily press, "Physical time knows only the chronological order of situations, but no present, no past, and no future." Psychological time (Fig. 84B) is divided into the three divisions of past, present, and future which, like the divisions of psychological size, exist only in the human mind.

We have already seen some of the many ways in which space—considered as dimensions—is an illusion. We shall now see that this is equally true with time when it is considered as succession. The past we know has gone. The future we know, with equal certainty, has not yet come. So we are left, apparently, with the present as the only reality, in fact we know that all our experiences happen in the "present," for as we progress through all our changing circumstances, the present is always with us. But what is the measure of the present in terms of time? By no process of reasoning can we assign to it any measured period of time. It is, in fact, only a hypothetical dividing line between a past that has gone and a future that has not come, and in itself it has no duration whatsoever. So, like the point, it does not exist. Yet, paradoxically, it can never leave us, and it is the only direct contact that we can have with time, for we can know the past only by recalling it into the present and we can know the future only by anticipating it now. Quoting once more from *The Secret Doctrine*, H. P. Blavatsky writes (Vol. I, pages 68-69):

> Time is only an illusion produced by the succession of our states of consciousness as we travel through Eternal Duration and it does not exist where no consciousness exists in which the illusion can be produced. . . . The present is only a mathematical line which divides that part of Eternal Duration which we call the future from that part which we call the past.

So the conception of space as having dimensions is built upon a "point" which does not exist in space, and the conception of time as a succession of events is built upon a "present" which does not exist in time. Thus, from an analysis of known facts and by the exercise of reason, we must see that both of these concepts are illusions. As we gain more knowledge of the universe in which we live, we shall realize space, not as having the limitations of dimensions, but as Infinity. As we expand our philosophy of life and the great plan becomes revealed to us in greater measures of its beauty and wonder, we shall realize time, not as a succession of events, but as eternity. Then we must face the third, and greatest, illusion of them all—the illusion of the separated Self.

The illusion of space as dimensions can be mastered by knowledge. The illusion of time as succession can be understood by the exercise of reason. But mastery of the illusion of the self as being separated from other selves can be gained only in quiet meditation in which the affairs of mundane existence are excluded from the mind and the intuition is given free play to contact the inner things of the spirit. Science can tell us nothing of value regarding the Self. A view widely held among psychologists is that what we call the self is merely a bundle of faculties and attributes which have arisen from the peculiar combination of cells that comprise the human body, plus conditioning from experiences in the environment. In other words, it declares that the whole can be greater than the sum of its parts. But, as we have seen, Theosophy has much to say, and the essential features of its teachings so far as the present subject is concerned are contained in symbolic form in Fig. 85. There we see physical humans represented by the black triangles at the outermost parts of the drawing. Here we have complete separation, as we limit ourselves to physical body manifestations; but as our consciousness is raised to higher levels, we approach nearer to others until, at the buddhic level, we can function at the level of the Christ consciousness, a harmonious contact with all others is gained and, finally, there is a merging of all in the consciousness of the Solar Deity, where Self is realized as unity and separation is seen to be an illusion. The

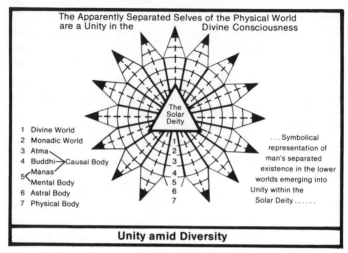

The Apparently Separated Selves of the Physical World
are a Unity in the   Divine Consciousness

The Solar Deity

1 Divine World
2 Monadic World
3 Atma
4 Buddhi → Causal Body
5 Manas
   Mental Body
6 Astral Body
7 Physical Body

1
2
3
4
5
6
7

... Symbolical
representation of
man's separated
existence in the lower
worlds emerging into
Unity within the
Solar Deity . . . . . .

Unity amid Diversity

Fig. 85

three illusions have been transcended and in their place comes a vision of infinity, eternity, and unity. The pilgrim can now say with truth, "I and my Father are one." That sublime accomplishment, however, lies far away for most of us. There are many steps yet to be taken.

Many people may accept these facts but think that they are far removed from the actual demands of life and the baffling problems that we must face from day to day. Nothing could be further from the truth, for they are the very basic knowledge that we must gain before we can be released from the self-made chains that hold us in slavery.

We still will struggle for power and land, for money and possessions, until we realize the fundamental fact that such things are illusions, that the material world as we know it is only a phantasmagoria, a great show of things that only seem to be, and that we can never really possess any material object. The only possessions that we can possibly gain are the character and power that lie within us ready to unfold into active expression when called upon. We will still try to subjugate others, individually as master and servant, employer and employee, intellectual and dullard, or collectively as between nation and nation, until we know that time is not of the essence of reality, that the succession of events is not what it seems to be, for in the eternal all are equal. And we will still try to glorify the individual self and to set it above all other selves, to think of ourselves as proudly superior to others because of our own good works, until we know of the illusion of the self and that, spiritually, all are one within the consciousness of God.

26

The Three Paths to Perfection

Mention has been made of the great advances which were recorded by science in the later decades of the nineteenth century. At that time, the physical world as it had been known for centuries suddenly disappeared and a new world, far greater and more wonderful, took its place. This world did more than reveal itself, for unknown to those who were instrumental in its unveiling, it paved the way for still greater revelations which some can see taking place even now: the advent of a practical knowledge of the higher reaches of the mind and of the conditions under which we shall live beyond the change we call "death."

Psychology is now cautiously watching the growth of parapsychology, a scientific study of so-called "psychic experiences." As psychology observes and analyzes the operations of sensory perceptions, parapsychology similarly is studying "extrasensory perceptions," that is, knowledge that comes to the mind through other than the normal channels of perception. Abnormal phenomena, which the psychologist as yet refuses to notice seriously, are being studied with infinite patience and meticulous care by the parapsychologist. They include psychokinesis, the direct influence of mind upon matter, telekinesis, research into the validity of claims that material objects can be moved through the spiritualistic manifestations of mediums, thought transference, precognition, retro-cognition, psychometry, and other related phenomena.

From such work is arising a new outlook upon human life, which can be demonstrated by experimental and mathematical methods and which undoubtedly will contribute largely to the newer world of the future.

Theosophy has carried its researches much further into the unknown than has the parapsychologist, but by their very nature results cannot be demonstrated by statistical or visual demonstrations, yet they can be known by each individual as a personal experience, as many have testified. Here we begin to scale the rugged steeps, and new methods of transportation must be used. New heights of mind must be attained and spiritual vision must be awakened to bring the inspiration to go forward. Reason must develop into intuition, knowledge must expand into wisdom and mere feeling must give place to love. We must listen less to the voices around us and more to the still small voice that speaks within.

An endeavor has been made in these pages to put forward the thought that the whole purpose of life is the conquest of illusion so that, rising above illusion, we may come to a full and complete understanding of reality. We, who are spirits, must therefore be plunged into the illusions of matter so that, by overcoming the fascinations of its false pageantry, we may know ourselves to be what we really are. We, who are immortal, must face the illusions of death, that by unmasking its deceptions we may know that we cannot die. We, who are sinless, are plunged into sin and shame and wrong doing, that we may rise above them all and know that we are spiritual. We, who are timeless, must bow to the dictates of time, that we may come to a knowledge of eternity. We, who are one with God, must experience the illusion of separation, so that by our own attainments we may regain the unspeakable joy of conscious union with God. We must learn the facts of the mystery of incarnation and must realize for ourselves what we are, God incarnate in the flesh, and we must rise above the forces which, on earth, have been making us slaves. We must realize that the things we thought were true are false. They were illusions and we became bound by them, and the purpose of our sojourn here is that we shall become free.

All these illusions, it has been stated previously, can be classified under three main groupings. So it is not surprising to find that in our endeavors to understand the world and ourselves, there have developed quite naturally three primary avenues of study which, while those who follow them may not know, will eventually bring liberation from the bonds which the illusions have produced. They are: (1) *science*, by means of which we develop knowledge and gain freedom from the illusions of matter; (2) *philosophy*, by means of which we develop reasoning powers, which will ultimately lead to freedom from the illusions of time and bondage to participation in the passing events of life; and (3) *religion*, by means of which we develop a devotional nature, eventually gain mastery over the illusion of separation, and will know that all life is one.

In her book *The Three Paths*, Dr. Annie Besant writes (pages 1-2):

> Three Paths have been traced by the Sages, along any one of which a man may tread and, by following, may attain liberation. Three are the paths and yet, in a sense, they are one. Differing in their methods, their end is one and the same. Differing in their external conditions they all lead to the One Self. . . . They all seek the same goal. These three paths—the three Mārgas, as they are called in Indian philosophy—that of Karma, or Action, Jñāna or Wisdom and Bhakti, or Devotion . . . finally blend into one, each of them acquiring the qualities of the others, each of them passing, as it were, into the other two, blending into one the characteristics of the three. . . . Let men travel along one or the other, they seek the One Self, whether by Action, or by Wisdom or by Devotion, and those who seek shall surely and inevitably find Him, for the Self of all is One and the goal of all the three Paths is the same.

It should not be difficult to see in these statements the link between the ancient and the modern, for science, which gains the knowledge that is necessary for action,

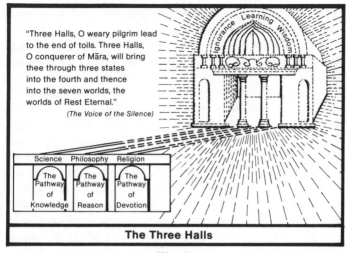

"Three Halls, O weary pilgrim lead to the end of toils. Three Halls, O conquerer of Māra, will bring thee through three states into the fourth and thence into the seven worlds, the worlds of Rest Eternal."
(The Voice of the Silence)

Ignorance   Learning   Wisdom

Science	Philosophy	Religion
The Pathway of Knowledge	The Pathway of Reason	The Pathway of Devotion

The Three Halls

Fig. 86

will lead to the karma marga, philosophy which develops the powers of reason and intuition will lead to the jnana marga, and religion, when it develops into the realms of inner experience, will lead to the bhakti marga.

The mere outward study of these things will never lead to liberation; they must all become inner experiences within the individual. They must pass far beyond the concepts of the ordinary student, but inevitably we are being led toward the higher stages wherein we will see the light.

Attention is now drawn to Fig. 86, a drawing which is but a poor attempt to present a tremendous subject. Words, too, fail to do more than convey a thought here and there which may stimulate toward a deeper understanding. Yet it will be profitable to study both with care, with the mind stilled and the intuition given full play. When the seeker for truth begins to rid the mind of preconceived mental pictures and to open it up to higher things, the consciousness, released from incessant dwelling upon material things, will expand and, though only a little, each expansion will bring a growth that does not permit the consciousness to fall back entirely to its previous limitations. Furthermore, when given a quiet place, the intuition will speak.

The subject now to be introduced belongs to those higher reaches of the mind. It will pass the bar of reason; but to understand it fully the intuition must speak. It belongs to the material worlds and to the conceptual levels of consciousness also, but beyond the areas of general experience. Mention has been made of the fact that there is no such thing as empty space in the solar system, that it is one mass of evolving life and form. There is a similar unity between the various material levels of our planet. Its physical, astral and mental worlds act together in one ascending order of comparable manifestations. Since persons of all grades are active in each of the worlds, it should be obvious that human creative genius will carry on after the period of transition into the higher worlds, and in each of them will leave the marks of its activities. In the astral world especially, there may be found great centers of learning where those whose lives on earth were given to the education and upliftment of their fellow beings continue their activities. Conditions are different in detail, though in general outline they are similar. The lessons are different, but although there are some who still need elementary instructions, most of the teachings relate to things which lie more to the forefront of human evolution.

For those who, while they were on earth, had reached a stage where the realities of life had become of paramount interest, there are seats of higher learning. Here instructions in deeper matters are available to those who have passed over to the astral world; also to those who are sufficiently advanced and whose astral bodies are of the needed development, who are still in the physical world, but can participate in the instructions while that body is asleep. A beautifully worded description of such a mystic center of learning is given by H. P. Blavatsky in her small book *The Voice of the Silence*, which has been mentioned previously and which is a translation from one of the most ancient eastern manuscripts (pages 124-127):

> Three Halls, O weary pilgrim, lead to the end of toils. Three Halls, O conquerer of Mara, will bring thee through three states into the fourth and thence into the seven worlds, the worlds of Rest Eternal. If thou would'st learn their names, then harken and remember. The name of the first Hall is Ignorance—*Avidya*. It is the Hall in which thou saw'st the light, in which thou livest and shalt die. The name of Hall the second is the Hall of Learning. In it thy Soul will find the blossoms of life, but under every flower a serpent coiled. The name of the third Hall is Wisdom, beyond which stretch the shoreless waters of AKSHARA, the indestructible Fount of Omniscience.

These are mystical utterances of great importance, the meanings of which are not easy to understand and which, it is suggested, cannot be properly interpreted unless they are considered in their proper setting, for they form a part—the climactic part—of a greater picture which takes in the whole story of human evolution. So we shall quickly review, by word and diagram, the story of evolution as presented in these pages, placing the teaching of the "three halls" as the capstone of our edifice. In this way, it should be possible to penetrate into some of the mysteries that are held out to the seeker who will persevere and that offer help along the way. That will form the basis for the next chapter.

VI

Glimpses of the Real

Thou canst not travel on the Path until thou hast become that Path itself. Let thy Soul lend its ear to every cry of pain like as the lotus bares its heart to drink the morning sun. Let not the fierce sun dry one tear of pain before thyself hast wiped it from the sufferer's eye. But let each burning human tear drop on thy heart and there remain, nor ever brush it off, until the pain that caused it is removed.

The Voice of the Silence
H. P. Blavatsky

27

The Three Halls

As stated in the preceding chapter, *The Voice of the Silence* was translated by Madame Blavatsky from a very ancient manuscript. It consists of a selection of verses from a book used for many centuries by mystic students of the East, known as *The Book of the Golden Precepts*. However, regardless of its origin or antiquity, the thoughts presented in it stand on their own merits and the seriously minded student of today will find echoing chords of intuitive response if they are pondered over in quiet meditation. In fact, it is useless to read the book in any other manner.

Also, as stated before, the verses which tell of the "three halls" indicate one of its profoundest utterances, giving a key to human evolution from the beginning of our pilgrimage on Earth, up to the time when it will be finished and our evolution as "superhuman" will begin.

Some years ago, a Swiss physicist, Charles-Eugène Guye, pointed out that we invariably consider any phenomenon in the light of our own level of observation, but that the same phenomenon would appear to be different if observed from any other level. For example: if we describe a movement as being in a straight line, that statement is true only insofar as our own immediate experience is concerned, that is, in relation to the Earth. But the same movement, observed from the point of view of the solar system, would not be in a straight line, as it would then be modified both by the Earth's rotation on its axis and its motion around the Sun.

A chair is thought of as a solid object, made and used for a particular purpose. But, at the level of observation obtained with a microscope of sufficient power, the chair would disappear entirely and its place would be taken by millions of molecules and great regions of apparently empty space. Reducing the level of observation again to a sufficient degree, we should find ourselves surrounded by a veritable universe of sparkling atoms, darting hither and thither with inconceivable rapidity. Which of these descriptions is correct? We cannot say that any one of them is nearer to the truth than another. They are all parts of one whole, which is greater than any one of its more limited aspects.

The three halls, similarly, can be observed from several levels, which differ in appearance only because of the level from which they are seen. Humankind, in general, does not recognize the existence of a plan in life. That, however, does not in any way change the fact of divine nature and that the God within is ever seeking for union with the source. Our constant activity and insatiable desire to accomplish are urges from that unseen source and we must obey them even though we do not understand them. Our footsteps may be halting and often turned aside, yet we must carry on. Evidence of this inner urge can be seen in the fact that from all our strivings there have emerged three outstanding channels of study which, though we do not comprehend their significance, are leading us to take definite steps toward the conquest of the three great illusions and are preparing us to tread the three pathways to perfection. These are science, philosophy, and religion.

Attention is now drawn to Fig. 87 which shows, in retrospect, an outline of the plan of life which we have considered in previous chapters. In the lower part of Fig. 87 the three halls are referred to: the halls of (1) ignorance, (2) learning, and (3) wisdom. *Symbolically*, these three halls represent the total plan. Certain phases of the plan also are shown. At the top of the diagram, the three aspects of the Deity in manifestation are indicated, which, it will

The Three—	1	2	3
Divine Limitations	Matter	Consciousness	Spirit
Great Illusions	Space As Dimensions	Time As Succession	Self As Separation
Methods of Conquest	Science The World	Philosophy The Plan	Religion God
Pathways to Union	Knowledge Karma Marga	Reason Jnana Marga	Devotion Bhakti Marga
The Three Halls	Ignorance From Ignorance to Knowledge The Self identifies itself with the Not-Self	Learning From Knowledge to Wisdom The Self realizes itself as Self	Wisdom From Wisdom to Illumination The Self withdraws itself from the Not-Self
The Three Halls and the Plan of Life			

Fig. 87

be realized are limitations of that greater being. They are: (1) matter, (2) consciousness, and (3) spirit. These, in turn, give rise to the three great illusions: (1) space (as dimensions), 2) time (as succession), and (3) self (as separation). The whole of life, it has been suggested, revolves around the necessity to overcome these illusions.

The first step in the conquest of illusion is the development of consciousness, and Dr. Besant has said that consciousness has three phases. These are, as shown in Fig. 87: (1) the Self identifies itself with the not-self; (2) the Self realizes itself as self; and (3) the Self withdraws itself from the not-self. These three stages constitute a primary act of consciousness, and they should easily be identified with the three halls at that level of observation. Spirit gives rise to self; matter, to the world, the not-self. For consciousness to arise, the Self must first identify itself with the not-self, but it must not remain identified there. It must, while in that state of illusion, realize that it is the Self, and then withdraw from the not-self.

As this is the story of every act of consciousness, it is also the story of the whole of human evolution, which is the record of innumerable acts of consciousness. At first, a person identifies with the not-self, the physical world. One is in the hall of ignorance, thinks it is the physical body, and pursues the world's many transitory pleasures. Gradually one acquires knowledge and learns to exercise powers of reason. Then, symbolically, one passes into the hall of learning and begins to realize oneself as Self. Finally, understanding leads to the hall of wisdom. Here the Self withdraws itself from the not-self and wisdom leads to the great illumination, which is the realization that God and humankind are one.

Jesus gave this same outline of our evolutionary journey in his parable of the prodigal son who left the father's home and went into a far-off country. Here we see the Self identifying itself with the not-self, spirit losing itself in the illusions of matter. In that far-off country the son became a menial and even partook of the food that the animals are, but finally he realized that the paternal home would still be open to him. Similarly the spirit takes to itself bodies of the flesh, which are of the animal kingdom, and gains experience through them, but gradually realizes itself as the Self, the divine being. Then the prodigal son returns home, the Self withdraws itself from the not-self and is once more united with the father.

In science, philosophy, and religion, we find ourselves in the outer world, unconsciously seeking those avenues of knowledge by means of which we will reveal the illusions of (1) space, (2) time and (3) self (Fig. 87). In acquiring scientific knowledge of the material world, we constantly identify ourselves with the not-self and reveal the illusion of material things. At this level of observation we can see scientific research as an expression of the hall of ignorance, for it must be realized that this is the hall in which we *overcome* ignorance and gain knowledge. By establishing a philosophy of life, by endeavoring to gain some knowledge of the causes which underlie facts and events and thus using reasoning powers, we gradually acquire wisdom, the self realizes itself as Self and slowly pierces to some degree the illusions that time is unrolling before us. Here we can see, at this level, our activities in the hall of learning. Through religion we are introduced to the thought that we are children of the one Father, and we begin to see the illusion of the separated self, and so in thought, though not in actual realization, the Self withdraws from the not-self. In the outer forms of religion we can see an expression, at this level, of the hall of wisdom, for when from an outer creed, religion becomes an inner realization and a true spiritual vision, it will lead to greater vistas which the future will unveil.

Referring again to Fig. 87, we see that the three "methods of conquest" lead to the three "pathways to union," and the principles of the former are repeated in the latter, though at a higher level. This stage is distinguished by the outstanding fact that *purpose* has now entered into all activities. The student has become the true seeker. Knowledge is no longer sought merely for the pleasure of obtaining knowledge but for the liberation of the Self. The student has become dissatisfied with the things of earth and no longer craves possessions, having found that they bring no lasting satisfaction. So the mind looks to higher things and perceives something of the greater horizons which urge us ever onward. In the three pathways, science, philosophy, and religion have been stepped up to higher-plane activity, which expresses itself in the growth of an inner consciousness, leading into wider conceptual regions rather than to material accomplishments.

We now come to the three halls themselves, not in symbol this time, but in actuality. For they exist. As we have progressed in these studies we must have seen that there is a guiding hand at every step of the road that we must tread, as indeed there is throughout the whole of nature. As this has been so in the past, we may be sure it will be equally true in the future and, furthermore, for the few who are qualified, such teachings and teachers are, even now, ready to guide the aspiring souls who have glimpsed the light. While physical words can never fully express the subtler conditions of the higher worlds and must of necessity limit great concepts to a likeness of known material things, it can be said with truth that in the higher worlds *the three halls actually exist* as an institution for imparting the deeper knowledge to those who are ready. However, while they are actual and real, in the sense that we ordinarily use these words, let us not be too physically literal, but rather intuitively imaginative, in our conception of their structure.

Here it would be well to quote some comments that follow the descriptions of the halls, which have been given previously:

> THE FIRST HALL. If thou would'st cross the first Hall safely, let not thy mind mistake the fires of lust that burn therein for the sunlight of thy life.
> THE SECOND HALL. If thou would'st cross the second safely, stop not the fragrance of its stupifying blossoms to inhale. . . . The Wise Ones tarry not in the pleasure-grounds of the senses. The Wise Ones heed not the sweet-tongued voices of illusion. . . . This Hall is dangerous in its perfidious beauty, is needed only for thy probation.
> THE THIRD HALL. Seek for him who is to give thee birth, in the Hall of Wisdom . . . wherein all shadows are unknown, and where the light of truth shines with unfading glory. . . . If through the Hall of Wisdom thou would'st reach the Vale of Bliss, Disciple, close fast thy senses against the great dire heresy of separateness that weans thee from the rest.

From these comments, it should be clear that the subjects which are studied in the hall of ignorance pertain to the physical world, with all its allurements and temptations which would turn the seeker away from the path. Those who would attain must not let the fires of lust deceive them into a belief that they are the sunlight of life. While those who are to be instructed in this hall approach it in ignorance, it is not the ignorance which marked the beginnings of our physical existence, but rather ignorance of the higher teachings which are available only to those who qualify. Aspirants must realize that all their knowledge, so far, has merely been preparation for the greater knowledge which will be revealed now that they are ready. Jesus expressed this same thought when he said that to enter the kingdom of heaven the seekers must "become as little children."

In the hall of learning, that which has been called "kama-manas" is the main theme of the higher instruction. Kama-manas refers to the close association which in actual life prevails between the desires and feelings and the "lower" or analytical mind. Most physical life activities of the average person revolve around the expressions of kama-manas. Of this hall it is said that we shall find the blossoms of life, but under each blossom we shall find a serpent. The possession of mind is our distinguishing feature, but we are cautioned that we should not lose ourselves in the satisfaction of intellectual attainments. Many of the world's most brilliant thinkers are lost in the hall of learning at one of its levels of manifestation, for the acquisition of knowledge has become to them a goal in itself. When this happens, with knowledge there comes a serpent, poisonous and deadly, preventing further progress. We should assimilate every piece of knowledge. Then, as it comes into flower, it will mature into wisdom— of which the snake has always been a symbol.

In the hall of wisdom the highest mental and spiritual worlds are contacted. Here all previous experiences are transcended, the seeker becomes the disciple and a guru or master may be found. Glories unknown on earth now open before us, and all previous light becomes as darkness when compared with the effulgence of those regions into which we are now ushered.

In the first hall the aspirant must overcome the illusions presented by material things. In the second, we will conquer, one by one, the illusions which the procession of events in time place before us. In the hall of wisdom we must rise above the illusion of the "great dire heresy of separateness" and learn to know the Self as one with all Selves.

In this brief outline of a tremendous subject, we may see how the whole of life which, without any inner knowledge, seems to be a hopeless confusion of unpredictable events is really one integrated plan that is moving forward with the same exactness and precision as the Earth is moving in space. We can see in the past the promise of the future. Though we are living in space and time, which present many illusions, from which as yet we cannot escape, we can gain an intuitive realization of their many deceptions and, gradually piercing their secrets, can approach nearer to Reality.

28

Toward Infinity

In imagination, we have seen the Earth with its Sun and sister planets emerge from the black mists of space. We have seen life begin as a scum on the surface of the waters and human life appear, primitive and uncouth, countless aeons ago. We have seen life unfold over the ages in a record of struggle and growth, defeat and victory, that leaves us almost overcome with the might and majesty of it all. Such a story never was invented by the human mind. The lamp of fiction pales into utter obscurity when the sunlight of truth throws its rays upon the stage of world events.

Now we must look into the future. Because we have been able to penetrate some of the mysteries of ages long gone by, we can have hope for those which are yet to come and, since we have learned some of the teachings that the Ancient Wisdom has to offer, we can look forward to the future with unshakeable confidence. However, we must be prepared to follow the human race into attainments which would be as completely incredible to the average person of today as the miracles of modern science would have been to the caveman. But how could it be otherwise? For time does not stand still and progress must go on. We must advance to actual participation in the vastnesses that surround us. There are no vistas of greatness into which we have pierced that some day we will not attain ourselves, however remote they may seem to be from our field of action now.

As Gods in the making, our future has no limit, and the expanding knowledge of today has opened up to our understanding some of the magnificence that some day will be ours. Such glimpses, however, impress upon us the needs of our times and the magnitude of the task that lies before us. In the three great illusions we found the fundamental facts that focus our problems in clear and understandable outline and also show the way in which they can be solved.

Because Theosophy penetrates to the very foundations of life, it can offer help in every department of human activity. The nations of the world could live together in peaceful cooperation if they realized the unity of all life, the kinship of all, and the future toward which the whole human race is moving. Employer and employee could work together in mutual harmony and helpfulness if they knew that the karmic law will restore balance whenever injustice is done. The great religions of the world could work side by side for the upliftment of humankind, in every country, if they knew that they all have a common source and that their followers worship the selfsame God, though under different names.

Theosophy offers to all religions a rational concept of God, inspiring to the soul and yet acceptable to the mind. It can show to the physicist that the laws of nature are the will of God in manifestation, so that we may know the wonder of the work that God is doing. It can clear away the most difficult problems of the psychologist by offering an explanation of consciousness itself and telling of the existence of the subtler bodies. It can enlighten the studies of the astronomer by telling of gods and greater gods, rulers of solar systems, galaxies, and beyond to the near infinities of immeasurable space, to inspire and uplift us as we penetrate ever further into the unknown. It can tell the geologist that the recurring eras of growth and quiescence are the "rounds" of life as it evolves in cycles through the planetary chains, revealing God unfolding creation before our eyes. It can tell the statesperson of the One Life that exists in all, so that we may be moved to work for the upliftment of the people of all nations. It can tell the nature student of the instincts of the group soul and of the purpose of the prehuman kingdoms and reveal the ladder of life that connects all living things into one unfolding plan. It can tell the educator about the reincarnating soul which brings at birth the abilities and character that were developed in previous visits to earth, and can point out that education should prepare the new bodies to serve the old soul, so that it can successfully make its links with the changed conditions of life that it is now entering.

Theosophy can tell the father and the mother about the wonderful opportunity that lies before them and how they can give counsel and guidance until the soul itself can assume full control of its bodies as they mature. To everyone, Theosophy opens up the possibility of an entirely new existence and a future upon which no limit can be placed. In its light, ordinary things become extraordinary and simple things become full of greatness. We find that we are not automatons; we are not pawns in a great game of chess; nor are we poor miserable creatures whose only value in life is to worship and to hope. We are integral parts of one mighty plan and there is nothing in heaven or on earth that we cannot achieve, for we are divine.

Theosophy has many more valuable contributions to make to the numerous branches of learning. One very important question which insistently demands attention is that of preserving bodily vigor and good health, for here we have an anomalous situation. In spite of the brilliant work which has been done along medical and surgical lines, our health, such as we possess, is being maintained almost entirely through continuous and intensive efforts on the part of countless surgeons and physicians and hospital staffs the world over. This situation is not satisfactory, especially as we look forward to the needs of the future. However, it cannot be entirely remedied until the existence of our inner bodies and the

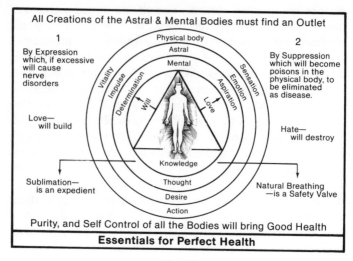

Fig. 88

effects of thought and feeling on the physical body are recognized and studied in as practical and assiduous a manner as are the viruses, bacteria, and the curative properties of drugs. There are many methods by which ills are treated, but our greatest need is to prevent disease by natural living. To reach this goal we must realize how closely the mental, astral, and physical bodies work together and that a disorder in any one of them will affect the others.

Attention is now drawn to Fig. 88. In the center of the drawing we see a representation of the spiritual body, with the three lower bodies—mental, astral, and physical —around it. The Self, in the spiritual body, as previously mentioned, expresses itself as will, love, and knowledge. In the mental body, will shows itself as determination. In the astral body it is seen as impulse, and in the physical body as vitality. Love expresses itself in these bodies as aspiration, emotion, and sensation. Knowledge shows as thought, desire and action. We are constantly creating in the mental and astral bodies by exercising our powers of thought and feeling, *love emotions which build and hate emotions which destroy.* The effects of these creations will be felt in all the three bodies. Thoughts of pride, exclusiveness, intent to do harm, prejudice—any thoughts or feelings that would cause injury and suffering to another—are creations within the bodies, and *they must come out.* If they are expressed, they will cause deterioration in the body in which they originated and also have a deleterious effect upon its physical counterpart. If they are suppressed, they will remain within the body, slowly disintegrating, and finally will release their energy within the physical vehicle as toxins. These must be eliminated and thereby will give rise to what we call disease, which is one of nature's methods of cleansing the body.

It is interesting to note that, to a limited degree, nature has provided us with a "safety valve" for our excess emotions. This is through the breath, which we know is a means by which poisons are expelled by the rhythmic action of the lungs. All emotional excesses, such as fear, anger, or even pleasurable excitement, tend to induce deeper breathing, unless they are too strong, in which case tension may cause a complete, though temporary stoppage. Deep breathing relieves the body of the gathering toxins. A harmless, though excellent, illustration of this fact may be seen—or heard—when a goal is scored at a football match or a home run is hit at a baseball game. A deep roar goes up from the watching multitude. Emotional excitement rises to a high pitch, but relief from that tension is gained to some degree by the increased volume of breath used to produce the sound. *Natural* deep breathing is helpful at all times in building a healthy body and maintaining an emotional stability. Unnatural breathing of any kind can do as much harm. The gradual improvement of emotional expressions by sublimation is helpful; but the final answer can only be found in self-control. These are factors which contribute in a large measure to the health or sickness of the physical body and the condition of the higher bodies too. Unfortunately, the existence of the subtler bodies is not yet generally recognized, so they can be given no practical study, except by the few who have some knowledge of them and who also possess the requisite medical training and practice to provide opportunities for careful and continued observation of both psychic and pathological conditions. It is now widely recognized that emotions affect the physical vehicle. Anger is known to constrict the blood vessels, and fear can produce toxins. No doubt in time it will be realized that our whole physical frame and all its workings are but an outer representation of our innermost thoughts, desires, and feelings. The saying of Jesus, "But seek ye first the kingdom of God and his righteousness; and all these things shall be added unto you" (Matt VI:33), applies to health as well as to spiritual welfare.

Of equal importance, of course, are the foods we eat, the liquids we drink, the air we breathe, and the bodily exercise we take. Too little food, or too much, or the wrong kind of food, will cause trouble, for the correct chemical balance of the body must be maintained. Many people—and the number is growing—have demonstrated that physical well-being can be preserved without recourse to the slaughter of sentient creatures, with all the horrors that it entails.

The intricacies of the chemistry of food and nutrition are beyond the capacities of this writer to discuss; but I once made a visit to the great stockyards of one of our large cities where animals by the tens of thousands are slaughtered every day. Cruelty and suffering is inflicted upon animals which poisons the very flesh that is to be used for human consumption. Later, I visited a famous medical museum where there were many rooms, each with many shelves all filled with glass bottles containing specimens of actual diseased parts of the human body. a vivid record of the many maladies that the flesh is heir to. The connection between these two should be clear. From Theosophy we learn of the law of karma, by which we reap whatsoever we sow. In the slaughterhouse we sow pain, so much pain that it must be seen to be believed, and these seeds are being sown every day. So we who sow pain, *or we for whom it is sown,* will reap pain within our own body. That is the law. As we make progress mentally and spiritually, we shall need better bodies to give expression to the greater powers that develop within us. Those bodies can only be built from vital foods. Products of the slaughterhouse can have no part in the physical vehicles of the humanity of the future.

Many more of life's mysteries are explained by Theosophy. Only a little has been mentioned here regarding the elemental life and also the angel or deva kingdom. The astral and mental worlds are thickly populated with these forms of life, as well as with those of the human kingdom. Angels, under various names, are mentioned in nearly all the world's religious writings. They deal with nature's forces in a multitude of ways and are of many different orders and grades. Quite mistakenly, it has been thought by some that we become angels after death, if our earth lives have been of sufficient merit to warrant this reward. This is not true. The two streams of evolution—human and angels—are quite distinct and have different functions to perform in the plan. Through angelic cooperation the human permanent atom is placed within the mother's body, so that the appropriate paternal reproductive cell will be attracted to the ovum at conception. This is not left to chance, as thought by science. Lesser members of the angelic kingdom work with the plants and flowers, in fact, in some measure with all living things. Greater angels perform highly important tasks in wider fields of action.

At a high level of the mental world are the archetypes of all material forms. These may be described as the original idea or "thought form," in the mind of the Deity, of living forms to be worked out in physical matter. The existence of the archetype explains the difference between the scientific and the theosophical ideas of evolution.

Fig. 89 gives a simple illustration of the principle behind the theosophical concept of evolution. The

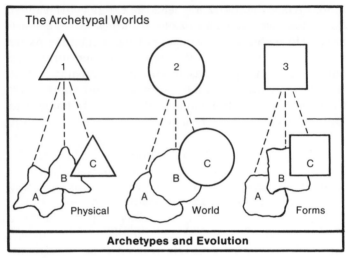

Fig. 89

triangle (1), the circle (2), and the square (3) represent
archetypes existing in the Divine Mind. These are to be
worked out into physical forms by the help of the building
angels. As they gradually reproduce these forms in
successively denser kinds of matter, the first attempts
in the physical world may be far from the requirements
of the archetypal form, as for example (1-A). Making
use of all the physical laws that can affect the growth
of the form by guiding "mutations," selecting environments or other means appropriate to the plan, improve-
ments in the direction of the archetype are gradually
brought about (1-B) until, finally, the perfect form, so
far as physical matter can respond, is produced (1-C).
Similar processes are illustrated in 2-A, B, C, and 3-A,
B, C. The form does not change because of chance mutations, nor merely by the survival of the fittest, but is
guided in this manner toward the closest possible reproduction of the archetypal form. Then it is left to test its
ability to survive. Even at the level of a Solar Deity there
are mighty problems that must be solved and the course
of evolution tells of continuous efforts toward greater
things.

So, we face the future: we, who are called by Alexander Pope "the glory, jest and riddle of the world." We stand looking forward, not knowing our own power and thinking that we are weak while all strength is concentrated in our being, a god who has forgotten our divinity, a Self who has identified with the not-self, who thinks that we are of the earth but whose true home is in the glories of the heavenly places. As Carlyle wrote:

> He is of the earth, but his thoughts are with the stars. Mean and petty his wants and desires; yet they serve a soul exalted with grand, glorious aims—with immortal longings —with thoughts which sweep the heavens, and wander through eternity. A pigmy standing on the outward crest of this small planet, his far-reaching spirit stretches outward to the infinite, and there alone finds rest.

In *Pilgrim's Progress,* that immortal classic from the seventeenth century, John Bunyan has drawn a highly symbolical word-picture of a man who, with body bent down, is raking up the dirt and straws from the earth. So intent is he upon his menial task that he fails to see an angel hovering above his head and offering him a golden crown. This picture is typical of humanity today. So intent are we upon securing material possessions, so immersed in the allurements of earthly life that the golden opportunities of spiritual attainment are unseen and the constant call to higher things is unheard.

Sooner or later, however, this picture will change and we will at last see the light. This does not mean that the scientist must renounce science as worldly, that the philosopher must forsake the exercise of reason as though it were an invention of the Prince of Darkness to bring confusion to humanity, and that all must embrace religion and worship or offer sacrifices to the gods. It means that followers of these branches of learning must purge themselves of all desire to gain knowledge for the sake of possessing it, to gain wisdom for the pride they feel in being thought wise or to gain salvation or liberation for one's self alone.

The scientist can follow scientific research; it is necessary for the progress of humankind. At the present time it is probable that science, though unknowingly, is making a greater contribution to the establishment of a world community than any other branch of study. Railway trains, automobiles, steamships, airplanes and other means of rapid transit for long distances have made interstate and international travel a commonplace thing and people of all nationalities are freely mingling with each other. Radio, television, telegraphs, and international news agencies are distributing news and pictures around the world through transmission by satellite, with such speed that events that take place in our own country are known in the antipodes within a few brief minutes. Motion pictures are shown in every civilized country around the globe so that the people there can learn about those who live in other lands. Their appearance, their habits, and their cultures are now portrayed in glorious colors. Even their voices are heard. In this way, science is helping people of all nations to know each other without even leaving their own city or village. And when people know each other they will like each other, for there is something unique and fascinating in every country and in all the people of the world. These things are breaking down the barriers that once existed between nations and are helping to unify the world into one great family.

It is true that science has given humankind its greatest terror: nuclear weapons. But only because of the exigencies of war were the scientists compelled to adapt nuclear power to warlike purposes, and many of them rebelled against making further developments in its destructive power. Furthermore, nuclear power is filling peacetime needs, though this too has problems and dangers. As the research of the scientist gradually becomes the pathway of knowledge, because we have gained a glimpse of purpose in all things, we can follow our chosen way to union with the Supreme and, as we do so, we will realize the need for philosophy and religion, for reason and devotion, and all these pathways will finally merge into one.

The philosopher can continue efforts to arrive at an understanding of life through the pursuit of logic, by analysis and synthesis, in all walks of human society. Philosophy has, or should have, its foundations outwardly in science and inwardly in religion. So the philosopher should have little difficulty in combining the three paths into one, stepping out of the realm of speculation, perceiving the facts of material law, and analyzing the varieties of religious experience. By this pathway, too, as it blends with the others, union with the One Self may be achieved.

Those who follow the prescribed rituals of a church, who offer worship at any altar or shrine, who bow in adoration before the image of any God or symbol of Truth or who see in any great religious teacher an outstanding ideal which they choose to follow, can discover the pathway of devotion when they come to know that religion is not an outer form but the realization and practice of an inner truth, and they perceive that the purpose of life is the attainment of individual spiritual growth rather than the acceptance of any plan whereby liberation or salvation may be gained through the virtue of another, in any form whatsoever. As they follow the pathway of devotion, they will find that their inner illuminations are of little use for helping others until they can translate them into a practical philosophy of life and can match with spiritual values the advancing knowledge of science. Then they, too, will find the One Source of all Being.

Thus we see the fundamental value of these three basic studies by means of which, at first unknowingly but later with open eyes, we are marching onward to the goal of life.

But what of art?

Surely art belongs to all these pathways and is the outer indication of the inner level of truth which has been attained. The true artist must have the inspiration of the devotee, the wisdom of the philosopher, and the knowledge of the scientist. Art is the way we *do* things. There is an art in sweeping a floor, in arranging the furniture of a room, in sharpening a pencil, in walking and in talking. Dancing, music, sculpture, architecture, and painting are specialized forms of art, which have science, philosophy, and religion as the background from which the material production springs. True art, therefore, is good, is beautiful and is true in its relation to life.

As the things of earth lose their attraction for the seeker and the pursuit of truth becomes the dominating factor in life, one becomes increasingly aware of deeper layers of consciousness opening within, which herald a new era in the long history of the soul's unfolding powers. We will begin to realize that, along the entire journey, through calm and storm, through times that were difficult and those which were easy, we have been guided every step of the way. Now this realization is to blossom into a new and wonderful experience. For in the hall of wisdom, if we continue to press onward with firm determination and with the love of God and humanity within our hearts, we may meet our Master.

Here it should be explained that perfect human beings exist. They are great souls who, by intensive effort and

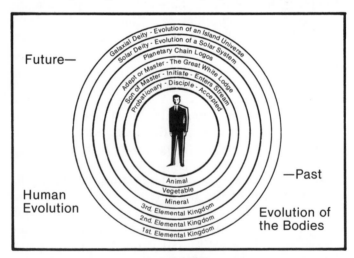

Fig. 90

one-pointed seeking, have passed far beyond all others and already have attained to that union which a few, who follow afar, are seeking. These great ones have reached a state of human perfection, but instead of going on into superhuman pathways of evolution which would lead them to regions of activity far removed from the struggles and pains of earth, they have chosen to remain with the human race so that they may help those who are ready, by imparting to them the higher teachings needed for their further steps along the path. They are known as "Master of the Wisdom," or "Adepts." To understand the nature and work of the Masters we must not restrict ourselves to thinking in terms of the limitations of normal earth life, for, while most of them have physical bodies, they are not imprisoned within them as we are in ours. They use their bodies freely when they are needed and leave them, just as freely, when they are no longer required. Though the Masters tower above us, far above us, in spiritual growth, to be in their presence is to realize that they are great "elder brothers" many times nearer, dearer, and more truly understanding than our nearest, closest friend. Their strength and wisdom seem to irradiate our whole being. We are inspired, exalted, and filled with an intense determination to accomplish.

The Master will be ready to take the pupil, when the pupil is ready for the Master. To find the Master, one of them said, "You must come out of your world into ours"; and in the description of the three halls, we may recall the words, "Seek for him who is to give thee birth in the hall of wisdom." This is the only real place to meet the Masters. Some expect to find them in the physical world, to see them physically. Yet to contact them in the physical world means that three veils—the three lower bodies—would exist between us and them. That is why we must find the Masters in their world, not ours.

Let us now refer to Fig. 90. Here we find in the lower part of the drawing the stages of the growth of the body, as recorded in the past. In the upper part are shown stages that the spiritual being will pass through.

There are several steps on the path of discipleship. First is the stage of "probation," followed by "acceptance" when the disciple is ready. Then comes a closer stage in which one becomes a "son of the Master." Here it is said that the disciple "enters the stream," and from that time on success is assured. About this same time comes the "first great initiation," followed by others in their turn. At each one there is an expansion of consciousness and, at the fifth, the initiate becomes an Adept, or Master.

Many volumes have been written about the higher pathways of the soul, gathered from a wealth of ancient records in the various religions of the world. These show how we, step by step, must liberate ourselves from those fetters which bind us to the earth. The qualifications for initiation have been given in *At the Feet of the Master,* as follows:

    I. Discrimination.
   II. Desirelessness.
  III. Six Points of Conduct:
        (1) Self-control, as to the mind
        (2) Self-control, as to action
        (3) Tolerance
        (4) Cheerfulness
        (5) One-pointedness
        (6) Confidence
  IV. Love.

There is a great brotherhood of adepts, which is known as the "Great White Lodge," in whose hands lies the inner government of the world. They work unseen and unknown, but exercise a powerful influence upon the nations. The Masters are adepts who take pupils and are many fewer in number than the total body of the Brotherhood. The life of these great ones, it should be realized, is vastly different from ours, since they are not limited as we are in methods of communication and so forth. Physically they reside in a number of different countries, using the physical body only when necessary for a particular piece of work. Most of their work is done in the higher worlds.

The glories of the material universe are only an infinitesimal fraction of the glories which unfold before the inner vision of one who is treading the higher pathways of progress. We began in ignorance. We have climbed a long, hard way, but must keep on going forward. As material things recede, the things of the spirit gain in strength and beauty. Some day we shall become Adepts. There is, however, more beyond that. From the human we pass to the superhuman and, finally, in a blaze of glory ineffable, we shall once more be united to the Source from which we came, our humanity merged into divinity. The great work finished, we will become a god.

Such is the divine plan. Yet, although this is an end, it is also a beginning, for still mightier conquests lie ahead in the vaster fields of space. Here, once more, science has led the way, unconscious of the significance of its discoveries. The Ancient Wisdom tells of union with God, the Solar Deity. It also tells of greater Gods existing beyond the veil of human conception. The astronomer has bared the secrets of the galaxies and supergalaxies, thus revealing material evidence of this deeper spiritual fact (Fig. 12). Fig. 13 introduces the thought that each of these great structures has at its head a Deity at the solar, galaxial, or supergalaxial level. When the millions of our humanity attain to union with divinity, having acquired all power, all knowledge and all wisdom at the solar level, this ending becomes a beginning, as they now will go forth from the bosom of the Father once more and use their powers to create solar systems. This will bring a new galaxy into existence that will be ruled over by our Deity, who will become a Galaxial Deity and guide the evolution of the total group. So the great plan will unfold, moving on to ever higher levels, until that which we call the infinite is reached.

We have ventured far into the future and perhaps we have caught a fleeting glimpse of great happenings which are to come. Now we are in the midst of the battle in more lowly regions, but knowing the goal and the

powers that lie within us we can take heart and move
steadily forward.

We have found that the house of civilization, which
was built through ages of effort, has its foundations in
sand. The rains are descending and the floods are coming.
We fear that the house may be destroyed. Gods of gold
and silver, which used to seem so wonderful, have been
found to have feet of clay and are crashing to the ground.
For in a world that was fashioned for spiritual growth
we have set up material standards, and they are inadequate and will not endure. Yet we need not fear, for
only those things will be destroyed which are not worthy
to survive. The old will break down only to give place
to the new, which will be better, stronger and more
beautiful. Sometimes the thunder rolls, the lightning
flashes and rains make progress almost impossible.
Sometimes the sun shines and gentle breezes waft to
us the scent of beautiful flowers, and we may pause to
enjoy their alluring beauty. But we must press on. For
earth's dark night is passing, and those who have made
their way in front of us and scaled the heights tell of
great things that lie beyond. Already the first faint streaks
of dawn are to be seen flickering above the horizon.

In aeons to come, great sages tell us, when we have
gained a realization of infinity, eternity and unity and
have merged them in the One Reality, when we have
returned to the Father's home whence we came, the
supreme mystery will be revealed and we shall understand. We shall perceive that, in some mysterious way,
we never left that home at all. We only thought we did.
We thought that we were separate from each other and
from God. That was false: we have always been children
of the One Father. We thought that we were going on a
long journey. That was not true. But at the final triumph,
when our conditioned consciousness becomes blended
with Absolute Consciousness and the last illusion has
been overcome, we shall know that, at all times and
on every step of the way, we have lived and moved and
had our being in the Divine.